CW01091548

The Reign of the Customer

Claes Fornell • Forrest V. Morgeson III
G. Tomas M. Hult • David VanAmburg

The Reign of the Customer

Customer-Centric Approaches to Improving Satisfaction

palgrave
macmillan

Claes Fornell
American Customer Satisfaction Index
Ann Arbor, MI, USA

G. Tomas M. Hult
Michigan State University
East Lansing, MI, USA

American Customer Satisfaction Index
Ann Arbor, MI, USA

Forrest V. Morgeson III
Michigan State University
East Lansing, MI, USA

American Customer Satisfaction Index
Ann Arbor, MI, USA

David VanAmburg
American Customer Satisfaction Index
Ann Arbor, MI, USA

ISBN 978-3-030-13561-4   ISBN 978-3-030-13562-1   (eBook)
https://doi.org/10.1007/978-3-030-13562-1

This Palgrave Macmillan imprint is published by the registered company Springer Nature Switzerland AG.
The registered company address is: Gewerbestrasse 11, 6330 Cham, Switzerland

Dedicated to all the customer-centric researchers, managers, and executives we have engaged with during our collective century of being immersed in understanding levels, changes, and impacts of customer satisfaction relevant to people, companies, industries, economic sectors, and countries.

Preface

The authors of this book have spent several decades working on the collection and analysis of the American Customer Satisfaction Index (ACSI) data discussed in the book. Per Google Scholar, Claes Fornell is the top-ranked professor worldwide in customer satisfaction (in citations), G. Tomas M. Hult is ranked second, and Forrest V. Morgeson III is among the top 15, while David VanAmburg has been the person in charge of ACSI's management and day-to-day operations since its early beginnings. Our co-author team is committed to customer satisfaction, have the knowledge about what it takes to manage and achieve the appropriate levels and changes in customer satisfaction, and are immensely proud of this book that tells our unique customer satisfaction story. Our more-than-century of collective dedication to customer satisfaction is captured in *The Reign of the Customer: Customer-Centric Approaches to Improving Satisfaction*.

At the same time, a commitment of this depth and breadth to understand and continually push the boundaries on what it takes for companies to achieve satisfied customers profitably unavoidably has effects on those involved. Each of us, it is fair to say, has become immersed in the concept of customer satisfaction in a way alien to most others. We have authored—collectively and separately—hundreds of articles on customer experience, customer satisfaction, customer loyalty, the link of these to companies' financial performance, and so forth. Our goal in this book is to present the fruits of all of these labors to the reader in an accessible manner. Only through such a presentation can these ideas truly help consumers, researchers, marketing managers, businesspeople, CEOs, companies, and the global economy as a whole.

In the pages that follow, we will discuss the ACSI project and the findings and lessons derived from it over the past 25 years. There are multiple dimensions to these discussions, just as there are multiple dimensions to most consumer experiences. The one thread that connects all of the findings is the concept of customer centricity. When first designed in the late 1980s and refined in the early 1990s, the ACSI model was focused on better understanding what makes customers happy, keeps them coming back to a company, and keeps the economy expanding. To achieve these goals, companies must adopt a customer-centric approach that emphasizes the importance of customer relationship management, customer satisfaction, and customer loyalty. We often talk about "customer asset management" to capture the collective nature of these customer-centric issues from the viewpoint of a company.

Yet, customer centricity is neither homogenous across industries nor an "at all costs" proposition. Customers demand different things from different types of goods and services. Companies must provide these uniquely satisfying experiences from within the context of their own industry and relative to their competitors. They also must always do so in a way that is profitable for the business, or at least where revenue equals cost over the long term. The ideas presented in the pages that follow will, we hope, simplify these complexities in a useful way.

A project the size of the ACSI—with tens of millions of customer surveys over the years—and the findings from it can only be produced by a team. Beyond the authors whose words collectively make up this book, several researchers deserve thanks for their efforts in creating the data central to this book. Udit Sharma of the ACSI and Michigan State University provided immeasurable assistance in data aggregation and visualization for this project and deserves special mention. Tanya Pahwa and Yuyuan Pan, both researchers at ACSI over the last several years, have helped in many ways. Tina Detloff and Christina Stage, also of ACSI, have supported the efforts of the researchers in many ways, and are key to keeping the ACSIproject moving forward. Finally, Google Scholar tells us that more than 12,000 articles have been written using the ACSI data or ACSI results in some way. We are tremendously grateful to these authors for helping us push the customer satisfaction boundaries and linking work by the ACSI team to myriad positive individual, company, and country behaviors and performance metrics in the international marketplace.

Ann Arbor, MI   Claes Fornell
June 11, 2020   Forrest V. Morgeson III
                                                          G. Tomas M. Hult
                                                          David VanAmburg

Contents

List of Figures

List of Tables

1

Defining Customer Satisfaction: A Strategic Company Asset?

Chapter Overview

In this chapter, we provide an overview of customer satisfaction as a strategic company asset, as seen from the lens of the American Customer Satisfaction Index (ACSI). Included is a brief review of the ACSI project's history and the economic forces that originally inspired it, the methodology and model that guide its research, and the structure of the index vis-à-vis the sectors, industries, and companies included therein. The primary goal of this chapter is to explain the source of the ACSI data—which centers on customer satisfaction—that informs many of the insights that come in the chapters to follow, to provide a methodological primer to the data, and to reiterate the importance of customer satisfaction measurement today and in the future. The chapter closes with an overview of the chapters that follow.

Key Conclusions

- The ACSI project was launched in response to the emerging "customer-centric" economy and the need to measure the quality as well as the quantity of national economic output.
- In addition to customer satisfaction, the ACSI model includes measures of customer expectations, perceptions of quality, value, complaint behavior, and customer loyalty (retention) at the company, industry, sector, and national levels.
- Measurement is conducted for companies, then weighted and aggregated to the industry, sector, and national economy levels.

© The Author(s) 2020
C. Fornell et al., *The Reign of the Customer*, https://doi.org/10.1007/978-3-030-13562-1_1

- While the ACSI was launched before the most profound changes brought by the Information Age, its mission and purpose—to measure the quality of economic output for a more competitive and customer-centric economy—is more relevant than ever.

1.1   A Brief History of the American Customer Satisfaction Index

To understand more fully the modern economy, and the firms that compete in it, we must measure the quality of economic output, as well as its quantity. *Claes Fornell, Chair of the Board and Founder, American Customer Satisfaction Index, 1995*

As in all good journeys, let us begin this book with a bit of history and foundation-setting. Given the primary subject of the book—to understand changes in the perceptions of American consumers over the last quarter-century and how to manage customer satisfaction given these changes—it is important to start with a brief overview and history of the American Customer Satisfaction Index (ACSI). How and why was the ACSI project created? How does it measure consumer satisfaction with individual companies, industries, and economic sectors? How has it evolved over the course of a quarter of a century? The fact that a large portion of the material contained in this book draws on ACSI data and findings, such an introduction is wise and necessary before proceeding. But beyond this straightforward goal, a clearer notion of how and why the ACSI was created and how it measures satisfaction across the U.S. economy and around the world will provide the foundation for a deeper understanding of the most important and enduring purposes of consumer insights and customer satisfaction measurement. In turn, this information will enhance the insights and lessons derived from 25 years of ACSI data and research offered in the chapters that follow, with personal insights from the founder of ACSI himself. So how and why did this project emerge?

In the early 1990s, researchers at the American Society for Quality (ASQ)—a prominent professional association founded shortly after World War II with the goal of advancing quality improvement principles and practices within economies around the world—recognized the need for a comprehensive national measure of quality for the U.S. economy. Only with such a measure, so it was thought, could a clear understanding of how well the U.S. economy was performing be achieved. ASQ began by investigating whether a national, cross-company, cross-industry measure of quality already existed, and if not, whether its development was feasible. With the help of a team of experts on the topic, ASQ examined myriad approaches to quality measurement and determined that no standardized measure of quality existed that could be applied to the multitude of diverse products and services offered within a modern economy. While many different quality measures existed, none was designed to effectively compare and benchmark these measures across distinct industries and categories (e.g., goods vs. services, cars vs. consumer-packaged goods (CPG)), or to *aggregate them into a national index of quality* (i.e., an economy-wide, macroeconomic view of quality). However, one potentially useful model that was being implemented outside the U.S. at the time was brought to the attention of ASQ: the Swedish Customer Satisfaction Barometer (SCSB).

A few years before ASQ began its search, in 1989, a Swedish economist and professor at the University of Michigan in the U.S. named Claes Fornell had designed and launched a national index of customer satisfaction for the Swedish economy, a project called the Swedish Customer Satisfaction Barometer (SCSB). Fornell had spent the first decade of his academic career writing extensively on the topics of customer satisfaction, consumer complaint behavior, the economic impacts of customer relationship management, and advanced statistical analysis of consumer survey data. It was this expertise that had led him to conceive and create the SCSB.

With support from the Swedish government, which had seen its economy struggle with increased competition and slower growth throughout much of the 1970s and 1980s as the effects of the European Common Market became fully apparent, the SCSB was the first project to apply a single, standardized statistical model for measuring both quality and customer satisfaction across the diverse sectors of a large national economy. In its first year, the SCSB successfully measured satisfaction with nearly 100 Swedish companies across 28 distinct consumer industries, interviewing approximately 25,000 customers of these companies in the process. Ultimately, it was this model that would attract the attention of ASQ, be chosen as the best alternative for measuring quality and satisfaction in the U.S., and be transported across the Atlantic to be applied to the larger U.S. economy as the American Customer Satisfaction Index.

It was on the basis of the SCSB project that the ACSI was founded in Ann Arbor, Michigan, by a group of professors at the University of Michigan's Business School (now the Stephen M. Ross School of Business), under the direction of Fornell. With funding from ASQ, the University of Michigan, and several other organizations, an extensive "first wave" pretest of the ACSI was conducted in 1993.[1] Analysis of these results confirmed what had previously been discovered in Sweden: that a cross-industry, cross-sector measure of the quality and satisfaction of a nation's economic output was indeed possible, providing highly informative results about the conditions of the economy. One year later, in 1994, the baseline American Customer Satisfaction Index study was produced. This first wave of the ACSI study measured satisfaction with seven sectors of the U.S. economy, 30 industries, and approximately 180 large business-to-consumer (B2C) companies. The study has been replicated each year since, with fresh results collected and released throughout each calendar year. And as we will show below when reviewing the methods and models of the ACSI, the study has grown significantly in the intervening 25 years.

The central purpose motivating Fornell and his collaborators to create the ACSI was simple and relates to the mission that originally sent the American Society for Quality (ASQ) on its search for a national index of quality. This objective remains important in both understanding the material to follow in this text and in understanding the modern economy better. While nations had for many years (since at least the 1940s, and in some cases earlier) measured the quantity of output produced within their economies through a variety of different metrics (and continue to do so today), they had up until the 1990s predominantly ignored a more elusive but arguably more important feature of sustainable economic growth—the *quality* of output. In Sweden, for example, the SCSB was created with the explicit goal of increasing the quantity of economic output in that country, and thus its gross domestic product (GDP) growth, but doing so by measuring, monitoring, and improving the quality of that output *as perceived by consumers*. This would, it was hoped, increase consumer demand. The quality improvements were thus intended to make struggling Swedish firms more competitive both domestically and internationally by better pleasing consumers and inspiring them to spend more with domestic firms.

By the 1980s and 1990s many companies had begun to measure customer satisfaction internally (along with related "consumer insights" and the "voice of the customer" (VOC)). However, lack of access to this data and the disparate research methods (e.g., different survey items, samples, timeframes, statistical methods) used to conduct measurement across these companies, coupled with divergent quality of the resulting output, made comparison and aggregation of the data to the macro level impossible. In short, new economic realities were increasing competition dramatically and making quality and innovation more important than ever, but standardized data permitting a clear understanding of the quality of goods and services being produced were largely unavailable.

It was from within this context that Fornell and his collaborators on the ACSI project recognized that growing domestic and global competition demanded a clearer idea of the factors that satisfied increasingly powerful consumers. What motivated these consumers to open their wallets to spend money on certain brands of goods and services more so than others? Measuring satisfaction (alongside its drivers and outcomes) in a systematic, standardized fashion across the entirety of a national economy would provide vital information for fully understanding the health of companies, industries, and entire economies from the perspective of the ultimate and most important judge, the individual consumer. Clearly this perspective is more relevant than ever today, and will likely become even more so in the future as ongoing changes in the global marketplace appear to be dictating.

As the Information Age has evolved from science fiction to a fully developed reality over the last few decades, consumers now have more choice and greater power than ever before. The internet revolution has profoundly changed how buyers and sellers relate to one another, and in the amount of leverage and power held by consumers. The changes ushered in as part of the Information Age have given consumers many new advantages. These include greater access to information about specific products and services prior to purchase and consumption, greater access to information about alternative suppliers (sellers) of goods and services, an increased ability to punish sellers through more impactful complaint behavior and word-of-mouth, and an increased ability to more directly influence new product/service offerings (i.e., co-production of goods and services). As such, these changes have forced companies of all kinds to reconsider how they measure and manage their performance, and to focus more on the voice of the customer. In all of the chapters that follow, some mention will be made of this changed global marketplace spawned by the Information Age and how it has impacted consumer expectations, perceptions of quality, perceptions of value, satisfaction, complaint behavior, and customer loyalty.

Nevertheless, whereas companies—and national economies in their entirety—once relied almost exclusively on measures like labor productivity, market share, revenue growth, profitability, stock market valuation, and gross domestic product as performance indicators, now external, customer-facing measures and the linkages between these measures and financial performance are at the forefront. Indeed, practices like customer relationship management and concepts like "customer-centricity" now occupy a central place in the discourse of corporate performance precisely because of this changed landscape. More and more, measuring consumer satisfaction and related consumer perceptions and insights is viewed as a vital, necessary activity for the firm hoping to adequately compete for buyers in increasingly competitive free markets. The same imperative holds for the national economy looking to compete in an environment with fewer boundaries and obstacles to free trade. It is our hope that the findings and lessons in this book will reinforce the continued and growing importance of customer satisfaction and its measurement under these circumstances.

1.2   An Interview with Professor Claes Fornell, Founder and CEO of the ACSI (Image 1.1)

Question When you founded the ACSI more than 25 years ago, what was your primary goal? What did you hope the project would provide that didn't already exist (to researchers, companies, policymakers, etc.)?

Claes Fornell It was about that time 25 years ago when three big trends were beginning to become evident. The first was global competition, the second was the growth of services in most advanced economies, and the third was that consumers were beginning to be better armed with information (about purchase alternatives, prices, quality, etc.). These trends led to more buyer

Image 1.1   Source: American Customer Satisfaction Index LLC

power and fewer monopolies in the overall economy. In other words, there was a major shift in power away from producers to consumers. It also meant that the conventional measures about the performance of firms and economies needed updating and change. At the company level, it was clear that the more we knew about how satisfied customers were, the better we could predict future revenue from repeat buyers. At the macro level, we could also infer what an increase (or decrease) in aggregate customer satisfaction meant for aggregate consumer spending. This was very important since consumers account for about 70% of gross domestic product in the U.S. It is not possible to have strong economic growth without robust growth in consumer spending.

Question Have changes in the economy over the past 25 years impacted how customer satisfaction is measured?

Fornell Yes. Just about every company now measures customer satisfaction in one way or another. That's an important first step. The problem is that most companies still do not have enough quality in their measurements. Very little attention is paid to the integrity and properties of the measures. The concepts of reliability and validity seem foreign to many companies, which have led to measures that don't reflect what they purport to measure and contain more random noise than authentic variation. Over the long run, this is, of course, untenable.

Question Can you give us some idea of the economic and financial importance of customer satisfaction, both to companies and to national economies?

Fornell Most companies depend heavily on repeat business. There are only a few things we consume only once. In a competitive market, where consumers have a great deal of choice, it is therefore necessary to make sure one has satisfied customers. Otherwise, they will go elsewhere. We can see the financial impact not only in revenue and profitability, but also in stock returns. For more than 15 years now, we have had a stock fund that invests in companies with superior customer satisfaction (as measured by the ACSI), with very good results. The stock portfolio of these companies had a return of 518% between March 2000 and March 2014. This is much better than the market. The S&P 500 went up only by 31% over the same period of time.

Question Given that the ACSI has existed for 25 years, and that satisfaction measurement in general is more popular than ever, why do some companies (and even entire industries) continue to treat their customers so poorly (cable TV companies perhaps being an example here)?

Fornell The major reason for this is some form of monopoly power. Despite what I said about the increase of competition in general, there are exceptions. There are markets where purchase alternatives are few and/or where the cost of leaving a company can be substantial. I would put cable companies in that category. In industries with few product and service options, customers have limited powers to punish offending companies.

Question Finally, if you had one lesson or piece of advice from all of your research and all of your experience that you think would help companies most, what would that advice be?

Fornell Let me answer by first saying what advice I would *not* give. For example, it is a folly to believe that the customer is always right. Economically speaking, the customer is only "right" if there is an economic gain for the company in keeping that customer. Some customers are very costly and not worth keeping. It is also not helpful to believe that customer loyalty is priceless and customer satisfaction worthless. Unless the company has a monopoly, loyalty can be very costly unless it is produced by customer satisfaction. If loyalty is gained by price discounts instead of having satisfied customers, for example, it is usually a path to failure rather than to healthy profits.

Now, let me turn to some more constructive advice. The first is to realize that measurement equals information. Companies with the best measurements have the best information. Companies with the best information often win. However, the data gathered from surveys, focus groups, social media, and so on are not information. They are raw data. Data can become information, but that needs to be processed first. Think of crude oil and gasoline. There is a refinery between the two. We don't put crude oil in our gas tank. Without knowing how much noise there is in the data, what is causing what, and what the effect of a specific action will be on customer satisfaction, likelihood of repurchase, earnings, and ultimately stock price, the raw data points do not have much value. Data must be analyzed and processed. Many companies today act on raw data and, to the extent they do any statistical analysis at all, it is too primitive—with techniques that are often more than 100 years old. These techniques are not sufficient for customer satisfaction data, which are not normally distributed—no bell curve here—and have extreme multicollinearity (everything is correlated to everything else).

The second piece of advice I would give is that the most important thing to do in order to improve customer satisfaction is not what most managers think it is. It is not better service. It is not better quality. It is not better price. Consumers are individuals. They differ from one another, at least in most markets. Accordingly, the most important aspect of customer satisfaction is "fit." Pick the right customers (targeting) and customize the products to the extent necessary—there is a cost constraint here of course. It is the "fit" between the buyer's needs and wants and the company offering that determines the customer's satisfaction. Sell to the wrong customer and that customer will not come back. Treat everybody the same, and unless they actually are, nobody is going to be happy.

1.3   The ACSI Model and Methodology

Having discussed the background and history of the ACSI, along the nuggets provided in the interview with its founder Claes Fornell, we can turn now to a discussion of the structure, methods, and models underlying the ACSI system and measurement. We begin with a brief, non-technical review of the data collection and statistical methods used by ACSI to analyze the hundreds of thousands of consumer interviews collected annually for the study. We turn then to a macro view of ACSI, looking specifically at the structure of ACSI as it pertains to the economic sectors, the industries and companies included for measurement, and how satisfaction scores are produced and interpreted at these different levels of data aggregation. Again, the primary goal of this review will be to prepare the reader for the related analyses of ACSI model variables in the chapters that follow.

To measure customer satisfaction, ACSI relies on the perceptions of actual customers of companies, or what is sometimes called the voice of the customer. The ACSI study begins with survey data collected through interviews, and all ACSI satisfaction results (and those of all the other measured variables) are produced using information collected from actual customers of the companies being measured. To collect this information, ACSI uses a standardized survey instrument (questionnaire) designed to collect information about a set of consumer perceptions as quantitative (numeric) variables to be included for analysis within the ACSI statistical model.[2] The survey instrument, which has remained largely unchanged since it was first created in 1994, was specifically designed to apply to consumer experiences across diverse economic industries and sectors. It seeks to tap into multi-item variables (sometimes called "latent variables") for measuring the six focal constructs contained in the model: customer expectations, perceived quality, perceived value, customer satisfaction, customer complaints, and customer loyalty. The construct of customer satisfaction is often labeled simply as ACSI since customer satisfaction is the "ACSI score" or "ACSI index" as reported in media and updated publicly on the ACSI website.

Survey interviewing to collect the data for all ACSI constructs is conducted using standard market research approaches, including internet panel online interviewing (currently) and computer-assisted telephone interviewing (CATI) methods (in ACSI's first years, but no longer).[3] Multiple checks are employed to ensure a random sample of consumers as representative as is possible of each individual company's actual customer base (this is often called stratified sampling). "Representativeness" in the context of the ACSI study indicates that potential respondents are screened before interviewing to determine eligibility to participate, with eligibility meaning that the potential respondent has personally purchased and consumed the good/service for which interviewing is being conducted within a narrowly defined time period consistent with the repurchase cycle. The time periods range from a current subscription in certain services (such as an active bank account or current subscription to subscription TV service) to purchase and consumption within the last three years (for durable goods products purchased less frequently, like automobiles or household appliances).

The statistical model used to analyze the data and to measure satisfaction with companies and industries across the U.S. consumer economy—the "ACSI Model"—is represented graphically in Fig. 1.1. Appendix 1 includes a generic version of the ACSI survey instrument and discusses some of the technical science of the multi-equation econometric cause-and-effect system.

The ACSI model functions as a tool for accurately and reliably measuring not only the central construct in the model (customer satisfaction), but also the most important determinants or "drivers" of satisfaction (e.g., consumer

Fig. 1.1 The ACSI model. (Source: Authors' creation from American Customer Satisfaction Index data and methods)

perceptions of product/service quality and value) and the most vital outcomes of satisfaction. The latter, viewed as future consumer behaviors driven by satisfaction, includes customer complaints and customer loyalty. Because the model measures perceptions common to virtually every consumer experience, results produced through it can be compared and benchmarked across companies, industries, sectors, and national economies. The model produces various output, but two pieces of information are most essential: (1) *Scores* or ratings for the variables—produced on a 0–100 scale—which are most useful for determining levels of performance and benchmarking performance across companies, industries, economic sectors, over time, and so forth; and (2) *Impacts*, which dynamically relate the variables to one another (represented by the arrows in the model), and which are useful for identifying the most impactful drivers/outcomes of satisfaction.

Expanding on this general description of the ACSI model and providing some insight into the composition of the latent variables[4] and the relationships between them, customer satisfaction (ACSI) is the central variable in the model and it is measured with questions asking about the consumer's overall cumulative satisfaction with their experience (overall satisfaction), the confirmation or disconfirmation (either positive or negative) of prior expectations produced by the experience (confirm/disconfirm), and a comparison of the experience to an imagined ideal experience (comparison with ideal). Satisfaction has three primary antecedents (or drivers/influencing factors) in the ACSI model—perceived quality, perceived value, and customer expectations. All three latent variables are anticipated to have direct, positive effects on satisfaction, with satisfaction predicted to increase at higher levels of these drivers. Yet both empirically and theoretically, the relationship between quality and satisfaction is expected to be the largest, as consumer satisfaction has almost universally been found to be predominantly a function of a consumer's quality experience with a good or service with few exceptions (this anticipated result is further discussed and confirmed in Chap. 3). As conceptualized in the ACSI survey, there are three primary elements of the quality experience included in the perceived quality latent variable: perceptions of overall quality (overall quality), the degree to which a product or service fulfills subjective individual consumer requirements (customization), and how consistently and reliably the product or service performs (reliability).

The second variable anticipated to have a direct and positive effect on customer satisfaction is perceived value, which is measured in the ACSI survey as the level of perceived quality relative to the price paid, and the price paid relative to the perceived quality of the good or service. Adding perceived value to the model incorporates price information, yet still allows for comparison of results across disparate companies, industries, and sectors where pricing can vary substantially. In other words, perceived value does not ask solely about price, where perceptions can differ significantly across different industries and categories with widely different pricing structures. Because the perceived value variable is measured as the ratio of price paid relative to the quality received (and vice versa), perceived quality is also predicted to have a positive and direct effect on perceived value.

Finally, the third determinant of customer satisfaction in the model is the level of quality or performance the respondent expected to receive with the product/service prior to their experience, or the customer's expectations. Because expectations are generally rational and serve as a primary reference point in a consumer's product/service evaluation, they are predicted, like both quality and value, to directly and positively impact satisfaction. Expectations capture all of a customer's prior knowledge (through recommendation, earlier experiences, advertising, news and information, etc.) and consumption experiences with a firm's products or services. Similar to quality, expectations in the ACSI model are measured as the consumer's anticipated perceptions of overall quality, customization, and reliability. Furthermore, customer expectations are also positively and directly related to both perceived quality and perceived value. These relationships recognize the consumer's ability to learn from experience and to anticipate, based on this prior knowledge, the quality and value of a product or service.

The two most essential outcomes of customer satisfaction—that is, the most important future consumer behaviors predicted to be driven by changing levels of satisfaction—included in the model are customer complaints and customer loyalty. When dissatisfied, customers have the option of leaving the company and defecting to an alternative supplier (if one exists), of silently stewing in their dissatisfaction, or of voicing their dissatisfaction to their supplier in an attempt to receive some kind of recovery. Thus, an increase in satisfaction is negatively related to complaint rate, with the implication that a firm will get a decreased number of complaints as satisfaction increases. While predicted to positively lead to a lower complaint rate, increased satisfaction is predicted to improve and lead to higher customer loyalty. Customer loyalty is the ultimate customer-related dependent variable in the model—as well as being an essential business objective—and it is modeled by questions asking how likely the customer is to remain a customer of the company, and how tolerant the customer is (based on past experiences) of price increases. The importance of customer loyalty lies in its relationship to business outcomes like customer retention and price tolerance, and in forecasting market share, revenue growth, and profitability.

The final outcome relationship in the model is the effect of customer complaint behavior on customer loyalty. The direction and size of this relationship reveals, by and large, the efficiency and quality of a company's complaint recovery and complaint handling system. That is, when the relationship between complaint behavior and loyalty is positive, this shows that a company is successfully converting complaining customers into loyal customers; when the relationship is negative, complaining customers are more likely to defect due to their complaint, and that an increase in complaints will cost the firm a larger number of customers over time. In the latter scenario, the company was not able to handle or rectify the complaint to such a level that the customer remained loyal to the company.

While we need not elaborate on segmented, or unique, scenarios of the ACSI model because they overwhelmingly mimic the model just described, other variants of the ACSI model—for instance, a version that measures product and service quality separately when both are central to a consumption experience, and one designed specifically for government services and their relatively unique nature—are also utilized for measurement by ACSI. The core ACSI model has been used for 25 years to measure satisfaction with a vast majority of the companies, industries, and sectors included in ACSI, and the alternative models are nearly identical to it. Importantly, these alternative ACSI models perform at the same high level, in terms of reliability and validity, as the original. However, these alternative models are important in the portfolio of ACSI to ensure data equivalence across unique industry and economic sector scenarios (i.e., construct, measurement, and sample equivalence).

What is the structure of ACSI as it relates to the sectors, industries, and companies included for measurement? Because the ACSI project was designed to serve as a macroeconomic indicator of the quality of economic output, it measures consumer-facing companies, industries, and economic sectors, and defines these following the structure of the North American Industrial Classification System (NAICS), with comparable and matching structures within the Standard Industrial Classification (SIC) and the worldwide Harmonized Commodity Description and Coding System (HS). Table 1.1 outlines the NACIS sectors and industries measured each year by ACSI.

As shown in Table 1.1, ACSI conducts annual satisfaction measurement for 48 industries in ten economic sectors as defined by the NAICS. Each of the sectors and industries measured is included because the companies included make products and services sold directly to and consumed by a large number of household consumers, and are a central part of the national economy. The ten included sectors are as follows: Manufacturing—Nondurable Goods, Manufacturing—Durable Goods, Retail Trade, Transportation,

Table 1.1 Sectors and industries in ACSI

NAICS economic sector	Consumer industry
Manufacturing—nondurable goods	Apparel
	Athletic shoes
	Breweries
	Food manufacturing
	Personal care & cleaning products
	Soft drinks
Manufacturing—durable goods	Automobiles & light vehicles
	Cellular telephones
	Household appliances
	Personal computers
	Televisions & video players
Retail trade	Department & discount stores
	Gasoline stations
	Health & personal care stores
	Internet retail
	Specialty retail stores
	Supermarkets
Transportation	Airlines
	Consumer shipping
	U.S. postal service
Telecommunications & information	Fixed-line telephone
	Internet service providers
	Subscription television
	Video on demand
	Video streaming
	Wireless telephone
	Computer software
	Internet news & opinion
	Internet search engines & information
	Internet social media
Finance and insurance	Banks
	Credit unions
	Financial advisors
	Internet investment services
	Health insurance
	Life insurance
	Property & casualty insurance
Health care and social assistance	Ambulatory care
	Hospitals
Accommodation and food services	Hotels
	Internet travel services
	Full service restaurants
	Limited service restaurants
Public administration/government	Federal government
	Local government
Energy utilities	Cooperative energy utilities
	Investor-owned energy utilities
	Municipal energy utilities

Source: Authors' creation from American Customer Satisfaction Index data and methods

Telecommunications & Information, Finance and Insurance, Health Care and Social Assistance, Accommodation and Food Services, Public Administration/ Government, and Energy Utilities. All told, the economic sectors that are included in the ACSI contain the major business-to-consumer industries across the U.S. economy. These sectors collectively represent about 70% of the total U.S. economic activity as measured by GDP.

Currently, within these diverse sectors and industries, satisfaction with about 400 companies is measured each year. This number fluctuates slightly as companies are added or removed, due to changes in industries, rising or falling market shares, mergers and acquisitions, and so forth. Companies are measured within industries based on market share, with the largest, most economically important companies in each industry included, regardless of whether the company is a local/domestic or an international firm. Yet because some industries have a smaller number of economically large companies and/ or companies with substantial market share that could be included for measurement—due to government regulation, lesser competition, and so forth—not all industries include the same number of measured firms. At one extreme, only a single company may be available for inclusion due to monopoly conditions, as in the case of the United States Postal Service for regular (non-express) mail delivery. But for most measured industries, several large, national-scale companies are included, as in the example of the department and discount stores industry shown in Table 1.2.

Table 1.2 An example ACSI industry with companies

Economic industry	Company
Department & discount stores	Costco
	Sam's Club (Walmart)
	Nordstrom
	Kohl's
	BJ's Wholesale Club
	Dillard's
	Belk
	Dollar Tree
	Ross Stores
	Target
	Macy's
	JCPenney
	Meijer
	Fred Meyer (Kroger)
	Big Lots
	Dollar General
	Walmart
	Sears

Source: Authors' creation from American Customer Satisfaction Index data and methods

Using the ACSI model, satisfaction scores (along with customer expectations, perceived quality, customer loyalty, customer complaints, and customer loyalty) are produced for each company within an industry, based on unique samples of responses to surveys by people who have purchased and consumed from each particular company. Generally, between 800 and 1000 cases/survey interview responses are collected for each company throughout each year, with total industry-level samples ranging up to several thousand cases. Across all companies, industries, and sectors, a total sample of nearly 3,500,000 interviews is now collected annually.[5]

Once variable scores are produced for each company in an industry, those scores are multiplied by a weighting factor—reflecting the market share of each company—and aggregated to produce industry scores reflective of a market-share-weighted average for each industry. In other words, the scores for larger companies (in terms of revenue/market share) are given more weight in producing industry-level index scores than are the scores for smaller firms. Similarly, sector-level scores are created for each sector based on weighted averages of each industry in the sector, again weighting the industries based on their economic size relative to the total sector. Finally, national scores are produced from the weighted sector scores, with the national-level scores reflective of the weighted contribution to GDP of each measured sector. These national level scores—and particularly the variables produced that reflect aggregate, national customer satisfaction (such as the economy-wide "National ACSI score")—can and have been used for a variety of purposes toward better understanding the health of the national economy, something we review in Chaps. 5 and 9.

1.4 Customer-Centricity, Customer Satisfaction, and the Information Age

With the historical, foundational, and methodological review of the ACSI complete, the last theme that we will introduce in this chapter will inform much of the material that follows in the book: the Information Age, the internet, and their profound impact on the perceptions and experiences of individual consumers and, by extension, the economy as a whole.

In the discussions of changes in consumer perceptions of industry and overall macroeconomic-level performance over the last 25 years, the Information Age and the transformations that have followed in its wake often play a prominent role in explaining and understanding these changes.

Dramatic improvements in customer perceptions of value, for example, are explained in Chap. 4 in large part through the efficiencies, cost-savings, and price competition between firms that have been made possible by new information technologies. Similarly, the impact of online social media on both customer complaint behavior and firm complaint recovery will be highlighted in Chap. 6. These particular explanations are offered because they are the most convincing, of course, but also because any understanding of how consumer perceptions have changed since the mid-1990s absolutely requires consideration of the most important development in the economy over this time, and the development comes in the form of new information technologies.

Today, consumers are more powerful than ever before. Few would deny either this claim or the source of this new power—the Information Age and the emergence of the internet. As we will also discuss at various points throughout the chapters that follow, because of these technological innovations, consumers now have far easier access to information about specific goods and services, far easier access to information about alternative suppliers (companies) of goods and services, an increased ability to punish sellers through drastically amplified complaint behavior and word-of-mouth, and an increased ability to influence the goods and services offered by companies through co-production. In these ways, among an innumerable array of other fundamental changes, the Information Age has created a paradigm-shift in how buyers and sellers relate to one another, and in the amount of power held by consumers (e.g., power that stems from, for example, the amount, type, and flow of information consumers are able to generate and share about products, services, companies, and marketplace dynamics).

Likewise, as consumers have grown more powerful this newfound strength has been recognized by both marketers and business leaders. As a consequence, this has changed both how businesses operate and how they measure the performance of those operations. Whereas companies once relied almost exclusively on measures like market share, revenue growth, quarterly profitability, stock market growth, and so forth as indicators of their performance and their future strength and potential, now measures like customer satisfaction, customer loyalty, recommendation and word-of-mouth, and the linkages between these customer-centric measures and financial performance have become far more prominent. Indeed, practices like customer relationship management and customer asset management, and concepts like "customer equity value," "customer-centricity," and "intangible assets" now occupy a central place in the discourse of corporate performance because of this changed landscape.

Understanding these interrelated factors—the Information Age and new information technologies, changing consumer perceptions of the economy, increased consumer power, and the evolution of how firms measure performance—reinforces the importance of the ACSI project, as well as the objectives of this book. That is, the original purpose of the ACSI at its inception was to provide a consumer-centric measure of the quality of economic output to augment the many measures of economic quantity. This purpose has taken on even greater importance now than in 1994 when ACSI started. In the fast-paced and hyper-competitive economy made possible by modern communications technologies, with more powerful and more demanding consumers, understanding the wants and needs of these consumers is critical, at least for any company hoping to stay in business. Most importantly, in these conditions, understanding consumers' satisfaction is absolutely vital, or so we will argue, and should be a focus of every firm that hopes to remain competitive.

1.5   Book Overview

The remaining chapters in the book investigate the ACSI model's variables that have been described briefly in this chapter, with a focus on the timeline from inception of the project and, for the most part, through the last quarter of a century of data and analysis. We also add a variety of other important and related findings from the research as well as in select places forecast into future years. The book is focused on ACSI, but integrates customer satisfaction research from a broad and deep variety of sources (e.g., see Appendix 2, which ranks the top-100 all-time research publications on customer satisfaction). The chapters are organized as follows.

In Chap. 2, we review changes in the expectations of American consumers over the last 25 years, with a focus on what many professionals and marketing "experts" claim to be the "sky-rocketing" expectations of consumers in the modern economy. Next, the chapter investigates industries with high and low expectations, and industry-level changes in expectations over the last decade (2008–2017). While we investigate national-level changes in expectations and all of the other ACSI model variables to start each chapter, we focus on ten-year changes at the industry level, with the goal of giving the reader a more recent and relevant understanding of what has happened within these industries. The chapter closes with a look at the wisdom of the popular imperative for businesses to aim to "always exceed customer expectations," and what future trends in expectations might look like.

In Chap. 3, we examine changes in consumer perceptions of the quality of goods and services provided by the U.S. economy since 1994. Included in the chapter is a comparison of industries that perform well and poorly on quality, sector- and industry-level explanations for this varying performance, and the changes in industries over the prior decade. We next examine the predominant role of quality in driving customer satisfaction, over and above pricing and consumer perceptions of value, and proceed to an examination of two perspectives on what constitutes "quality" itself—reliability and customizability—and why the latter dominates the former as a predictor of customer satisfaction in the modern, "mass customization" economy. The chapter closes by examining the prospects for continued gains in customer satisfaction absent improved quality.

In Chap. 4, we examine variation in consumer perceptions of the value of the goods and services provided by the U.S. economy over the last 25 years. During that period, perceptions of value have improved enormously, more so than for any other driver of customer satisfaction measured in the ACSI model. This leads to the conclusion that national-level satisfaction improvements over the last 25 years appear to have been driven mostly by a stronger value proposition in the minds of consumers. Following a discussion of industry and company leaders and laggards, we close with a discussion of the probabilities—for both individual companies and the economy as a whole—of a continued focus on the value proposition as the primary driver of customer satisfaction.

In Chap. 5, we focus on the central, most critical metric for understanding any customer experience offered by a company and the health of the customer-firm relationship—customer satisfaction—and examine the evolution of the satisfaction of American consumers since 1994. We then identify the most and least satisfying industries across the entire U.S. consumer economy, and the changes in those industries over the previous decade. We next discuss customer satisfaction as an important predictor of macroeconomic growth and related changes in the economy, one that can help us both forecast and generally better understand macroeconomic dynamics. We then turn to a discussion of those rare cases in which satisfaction itself can provide a misleading indicator of a firm's health, and the potential effects of merger and acquisition (M&A) activity on the consumer experience and customer satisfaction. Finally, we discuss the future of customer satisfaction, focusing on how artificial intelligence and related technological advances promise to have a revolutionary impact on customer service.

In Chap. 6, we begin with a discussion of changes in customer complaint behavior and the aggregate national customer complaint rate, testing the hypothesis that the internet, social media, and related channels have made complaining easier and more impactful, and thus possibly complaint rates far higher. We next turn to a detailed discussion of cross-industry differences in customer complaint rates and highlight how the nature of distinct economic sectors and the products and services consumed therein helps explain variations in quantities of complaint. This is followed by a review of why many (or even most) dissatisfied customers choose not to complain at all, and the negative consequences of this fact for companies. Finally, we discuss the importance of complaint management for firms, a practice critical to converting dissatisfied customers into enduringly loyal ones and examine whether companies have improved their complaint management practices over the past decade. The chapter concludes with a brief discussion of the benefits for companies of maximizing customer complaint rates.

In Chap. 7, we consider changes in the loyalty of consumers over the last 25 years. We find that loyalty measured as an estimate of customer retention has increased substantially over this period. Furthermore, and contrary to the many warnings of marketers, we find that Millennials are among the most loyal customers across the generational cohorts, behind only the rapidly dwindling Silent Generation. After considering the industries with the strongest and weakest customer loyalty, we more fully examine the "service recovery paradox (SRP)" introduced in Chap. 6, the finding that customers who experience a problem with a good or service and complain about it, but receive highly effective complaint management from the firm, end up with stronger-than-average loyalty. The loyalty of these customers is even stronger than those with a problem-free experience. The chapter closes with a discussion of the future of loyalty measurement—and in some sense, measurement of the entire consumer experience—with an examination of recently popularized but highly flawed methods.

In Chap. 8, we examine the linkages between customer satisfaction as measured by ACSI and actual firm financial performance, or what is sometimes called the marketing-finance interface. While not included in the formal ACSI model, the financial performance of the firm is of paramount importance to ACSI, its clients, and to customer asset management. Financial performance, if included, appears on the right-most side of the ACSI model, being affected by customer loyalty but also customer satisfaction and customer complaints. In Chap. 5, we will see that customer satisfaction as measured by ACSI is related to essential macroeconomic trends, like GDP growth. But in Chap. 8 we ask the question: Does customer satisfaction really matter, or is it just a marketing and public relations tool? The link between customer satisfaction, customer loyalty, actual future loyalty behaviors, and firm financial performance, so it turns out, is real and very important for companies. This is even more accurate today than it was 25 years ago, as both consumer options and access to information about these alternatives have skyrocketed. To bring clarity and highlight these findings, we review studies using ACSI data that have found that more satisfying companies outperform less satisfying companies in stock performance, and by a wide margin. Evidence of this above-market performance is so striking that it sometimes strains belief. Given this, most companies (and CEOs) cannot afford to ignore customer satisfaction.

Finally, in Chap. 9, we examine the future of customer satisfaction and satisfaction measurement in a globalized world. Here, we argue that as the world economy continues to globalize and become more competitive, customer satisfaction will become even more important for both individual firms and national economies as a whole. This is particularly true for national economies that face outside pressure from multinational companies and want, for example, to insulate and protect key domestic industries, identify internal satisfaction performance leaders for other firms to emulate, and track the performance of domestic multinational firms operating in several markets. In an increasingly globalized world, it is incumbent on companies to deliver, via their global supply chains, the products and services that customers want and need worldwide. If a product exists anywhere in the world, customers will know about it and expect to be able to buy it. Tracking customer satisfaction in such a globalized world presents challenges and opportunities for firms, and we address those prospects and areas in Chap. 9.

Notes

1. In the chapters to come, our analysis will often talk of "25 years of ACSI data." In reality, though, most of the comparisons and analyses of over-time changes will involve data between 1994 and 2017, or only 24 full calendar years. The difference is mostly semantics, however, as including the pre-test phase, the ACSI project entered its 25th year as a measurement project in 2017.

2. Importantly, almost all of the ACSI survey questions are asked on a 1–10, low to high scale from, for example, "very poor quality" to "very good quality," "very dissatisfied" to "very satisfied," and so forth. For ease of interpretation, the resulting 1–10 scaled variables are converted to a 0–100 index score, primarily for ease of interpretation among non-statisticians. Two exceptions that will be relevant for understanding later chapters are customer complaints— measured as a 0–1, no-yes variable—and customer retention, which is the product of a non-linear transformation of a 1–10 repurchase likelihood variable transformed to a percentage estimate of retained customers.

3. Multiple quality control checks were performed before ACSI transitioned from CATI data collection using random-digit dial to online panel interviewing in the early 2010s. Results from these pre-tests consistently provided evidence of little to no survey mode effect in the resulting data.

4. While we will avoid going into too much esoteric statistical detail throughout the book, a simplified definition of a latent variable is any variable that cannot be directly observed, but is rather observed indirectly by combining multiple pieces of observed information together—in this case, multiple related but separate survey questions. In short, for our purposes latent variables are multiple survey questions statistically weighted and modeled together, and that produce the key scores and impacts analyzed in the ACSI model.

5. Due to fluctuations in the number of companies measured and in the quantity of individual survey interviews per company collected, the total annual sample collected by ACSI has varied over time. In 1994, the first year of regular measurement, approximately 50,000 survey interviews were collected. By 2017, and for the aforementioned reasons, that annual sample had increased to more than 200,000. As of publication of this text, that number has increased to nearly 300,000.

References and Further Reading

Aksoy, L., Cooil, B., Groening, C., Keiningham, T. L., & Yalçin, A. (2008). The Long-Term Stock Market Valuation of Customer Satisfaction. *Journal of Marketing, 72*(4), 105–122.

Anderson, E. W. (1996). Customer Satisfaction and Price Tolerance. *Marketing Letters, 7*(3), 19–30.

Anderson, E. W. (1998). Customer Satisfaction and Word of Mouth. *Journal of Service Research, 1*(1), 5–17.

Anderson, E. W., & Fornell, C. (2000a). The Customer Satisfaction Index as a Leading Indicator. In *Handbook of Service Marketing and Management* (pp. 255–267). London: Sage Publications.

Anderson, E. W., & Fornell, C. (2000b). Foundations of the American Customer Satisfaction Index. *Total Quality Management, 11*(7), 869–882.

Anderson, E. W., Fornell, C., & Lehmann, D. R. (1994). Customer Satisfaction, Market Share, and Profitability: Findings from Sweden. *Journal of Marketing, 58*(3), 53–66.

Anderson, E. W., Fornell, C., & Mazvanchery, S. K. (2004). Customer Satisfaction and Shareholder Value. *Journal of Marketing, 68*(4), 172–185.

Anderson, E. W., Fornell, C., & Rust, R. T. (1997). Customer Satisfaction, Productivity and Profitability: Differences between Goods and Services. *Marketing Science, 16*(2), 129–145.

Anderson, E. W., & Mansi, S. A. (2009). Does Customer Satisfaction Matter to Investors? Findings from the Bond Market. *Journal of Marketing Research, 46*(5), 703–714.

Edvardsson, B., Johnson, M. D., Gustafsson, A., & Strandvik, T. (2000). The Effects of Satisfaction and Loyalty on Profits and Growth: Products versus Services. *Total Quality Management, 11*(7), S917–S927.

Fornell, C. (1992). A National Customer Satisfaction Barometer: The Swedish Experience. *The Journal of Marketing, 56*(1), 6–21.

Fornell, C. (1995). The Quality of Economic Output: Empirical Generalizations about its Distribution and Relationship to Market Share. *Marketing Science, 14*(3_Suppl), G203–G211.

Fornell, C. (2001). The Science of Satisfaction. *Harvard Business Review, 79*(3), 120–121.

Fornell, C. (2007). *The Satisfied Customer: Winners and Losers in the Battle for Buyer Preference*. New York, NY: Palgrave Macmillan.

Fornell, C., Johnson, M. D., Anderson, E. W., Cha, J., & Bryant, B. E. (1996). The American Customer Satisfaction Index: Nature, Purpose, and Findings. *The Journal of Marketing, 60*(4), 7–18.

Fornell, C., Mithas, S., & Krishnan, M. S. (2005). Why Do Customer Relationship Management Applications Affect Customer Satisfaction? *Journal of Marketing, 69*(4), 201–209.

Fornell, C., Mithas, S., & Morgeson, F. V., III. (2009a). The Economic and Statistical Significance of Stock Returns on Customer Satisfaction. *Marketing Science, 28*(5), 820–825.

Fornell, C., Mithas, S., & Morgeson, F. V., III. (2009b). The Statistical Significance of Portfolio Returns. *International Journal of Research in Marketing, 26*(2), 162–163.

Fornell, C., Mithas, S., Morgeson, F. V., III, & Krishnan, M. S. (2006). Customer Satisfaction and Stock Prices: High Returns, Low Risk. *Journal of Marketing, 70*(1), 3–14.

Fornell, C., Rust, R. T., & Dekimpe, M. G. (2010). The Effect of Customer Satisfaction on Consumer Spending Growth. *Journal of Marketing Research, 47*(1), 28–35.

Johnson, M. D., Anderson, E. W., & Fornell, C. (1995). Rational and Adaptive Performance Expectations in a Customer Satisfaction Framework. *Journal of Consumer Research, 21*(4), 695–707.

Keiningham, T. L., Cooil, B., Andreassen, T. W., & Aksoy, L. (2007). A Longitudinal Examination of Net Promoter and Firm Revenue Growth. *Journal of Marketing, 71*(3), 39–51.

Morgan, N. A., & Rego, L. L. (2006). The Value of Different Customer Satisfaction and Loyalty Metrics in Predicting Business Performance. *Marketing Science, 25*(5), 426–439.

Morgeson, F. V., III. (2013). Expectations, Disconfirmation, and Citizen Satisfaction with the US Federal Government: Testing and Expanding the Model. *Journal of Public Administration Research and Theory, 23*(2), 289–305.

Morgeson, F. V., III, & Mithas, S. (2009). Does E-Government Measure up to E-Business? Comparing End-User Perceptions of U.S. Federal Government and E-Business Website. *Public Administration Review, 69*(4), 740–752.

Morgeson, F. V., III, Mithas, S., Keiningham, T. L., & Aksoy, L. (2011a). An Investigation of the Cross-National Determinants of Customer Satisfaction. *Journal of the Academy of Marketing Science, 29*(2), 198–215.

Morgeson, F. V., III, & Petrescu, C. (2011). Do They All Perform Alike? An Examination of Perceived Performance, Citizen Satisfaction and Trust with U.S. Federal Agencies. *International Review of Administrative Sciences, 77*(3), 451–479.

Morgeson, F. V., III, Sharma, P. N., & Hult, G. T. M. (2015). Cross-National Differences in Consumer Satisfaction: Mobile Services in Emerging and Developed Markets. *Journal of International Marketing, 23*(2), 1–24.

Morgeson, F. V., III, VanAmburg, D., & Mithas, S. (2011b). Misplaced Trust? Exploring the Structure of the E-Government-Citizen Trust Relationship. *Journal of Public Administration Research and Theory, 21*(2), 257–283.

Rego, L. L., Morgan, N. A., & Fornell, C. (2013). Reexamining the Market Share-Customer Satisfaction Relationship. *Journal of Marketing, 77*(5), 1–20.

Tuli, K. R., & Bharadwaj, S. G. (2009). Customer Satisfaction and Stock Returns Risk. *Journal of Marketing, 73*(6), 184–197.

2

Customer Expectations: What Do Your Customers Demand?

Chapter Overview

In this chapter, we begin by reviewing changes in the expectations of American consumers over the last 25 years. What do consumers hope (and demand) they will receive in their experiences with companies? We particularly focus on what many have claimed to be the "sky-rocketing" expectations of consumers in the modern economy. Next, we turn to an investigation of industries with high and low expectations, and industry-level changes in expectations over the last decade. The chapter closes with a look at the wisdom of the popular imperative for businesses to aim to "always exceed customer expectations," and what future trends in customer expectations could look like.

Key Conclusions

- While customer expectations have increased over the last 25 years, the change is not nearly as dramatic as many have depicted.
- In the aggregate, over this period customer satisfaction has kept pace (roughly) with rising expectations.
- Levels of customer expectations vary widely among industries, and changes in expectations vary widely as well, dispelling the notion that rising expectations are a universal phenomenon.
- Firms should avoid either attempting or promising to "always exceed expectations," as such a strategy is virtually impossible to achieve and may ultimately be self-defeating.

© The Author(s) 2020
C. Fornell et al., *The Reign of the Customer*, https://doi.org/10.1007/978-3-030-13562-1_2

- While companies must continue to set, manage, and meet expectations, it is unlikely that expectations will spiral out of control in the years ahead, even as innovations progress at a more rapid pace.

2.1   Are Customer Expectations Really Sky-Rocketing?

A near-consensus among business and marketing professionals seems to have emerged: the expectations of consumers are rising rapidly, dramatically, and across the board. The specter of "sky-rocketing customer expectations" is often referenced as a warning to marketing professionals and companies as a whole: fail to meet these lofty and ever-increasing consumer demands, and it could mean financial doom.[1] In particular, the paradigm-shifting technological innovations of the last 25 years have made consumers spoiled and their expectations unrealistic, so the argument goes. In the age of Amazon and Apple—firms that have revolutionized, respectively, the variety of offerings delivered fast and efficiently via a single channel and new consumer electronic product innovation—any company that fails to keep pace with these trillion-dollar behemoths is headed for failure.

But have expectations really been spiraling out of control, constantly racing upward and forcing firms to strive for new, perhaps unachievable heights? Are customer expectations really "higher than ever before?" Proclamations suggesting this dramatic increase in expectations are ubiquitous, but reliable data confirming their existence are much harder to come by. The ACSI model outlined in Chap. 1 includes a measure of customer expectations, a multidimensional variable that has captured the dynamics of national-level customer expectations, along with expectations of product/service reliability and customization, each quarter since 1994. As with all ACSI constructs in Fig. 1.1 from Chap. 1, the expectation metric is based on consumer data from all industries and economic sectors which is then aggregated to the national level to better understand trends. And the timing of the ACSI expectations metric is, in many ways, ideal; it spans from a time when the internet and related information technologies were still very young and had relatively little impact on the economy (1994, coincidentally, the year Amazon was founded) to the present time when the internet, e-commerce, and other Information Age innovations that radically altered customer service delivery had already "changed everything" for consumers.

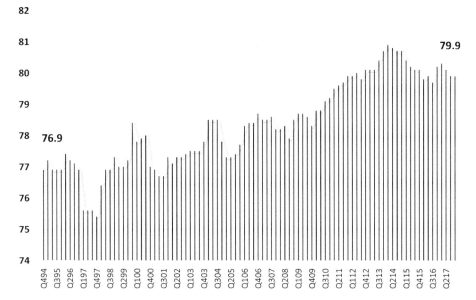

Fig. 2.1 National customer expectations, 1994–2017. (Source: Authors' creation from American Customer Satisfaction Index data and methods)

ACSI data provide some evidence of rising consumer expectations among American consumers over this period. Figure 2.1 shows data for aggregate national customer expectations across all major consumer sectors and industries in the U.S. economy between 1994 and 2017, measured on a 0–100 scale (see Chap. 1 for a review of both the industries and sectors included, and the nature of the 0–100 scaled variables). As this figure shows, national customer expectations scored 76.9 on the 0–100 scale when first measured in 1994. In the intervening years, expectations have generally trended upward, with a few periods of significant decline mixed in. All told, expectations have increased 3.0 points on a 0–100 scale to 79.9, a substantial and statistically significant 3.9% increase over the period.[2] Moreover, if we focus on a slightly shorter timeframe, customer expectations can be argued to have increased even more. Expectations declined to a low of 75.4 in 1997, a few years after the ACSI project began, and from that point forward have increased to the current score of 79.9, an even bigger gain of 4.5 points (6.0%). Thus, consumer expectations appear to have indeed increased significantly over the last 25 years.

However, several finite trends within this data stand out, and these should perhaps temper our confirmation of the prevailing wisdom vis-à-vis runaway consumer expectations. First, if we focus on only the most recent five years of data—which includes the period when the most dramatic quotes about runaway expectations were offered—expectations have actually *declined* slightly, down almost a full point over that period from 80.7 to 79.9. In other words, for those CEOs and CMOs fretting about exploding and unmanageable consumer expectations, the trend seems to have stalled over the last few years, and has even reversed slightly. While this dip could portend either a prolonged decline in expectations or just a temporary adjustment followed by renewed growth moving forward, as of now consumers' expectations have flattened out, and are at about the same level they were in 2011.

Second, while relying to some extent on a broader understanding of the changes in the other ACSI model variables covered later, which we review sequentially over the next several chapters, it is important that we do not overemphasize a three-point improvement in the customer expectations variable, as it must be viewed *relative to changes in other consumer perceptions*. That is, while customer expectations are significantly higher over the last 25 years, over the same time period customer satisfaction is up nearly as much (+2.5 points), and consumer perceptions of value are up much more (+6.7 points). This indicates that companies are, by and large, keeping pace with advancing customer expectations by offering both a stronger value proposition and more satisfying experiences. Figure 2.2 compares the changes in customer expectations, perceived quality, perceived value, and customer satisfaction (ACSI) since 1994. While we will discuss the underlying dynamics of the changes to

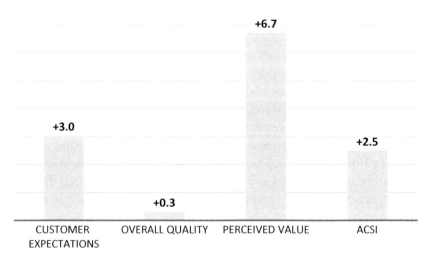

Fig. 2.2 Twenty-five-year changes in expectations, quality, value, and ACSI. (Source: Authors' creation from American Customer Satisfaction Index data and methods)

each of these variables individually in the chapters that follow, the most important take-away vis-à-vis the "theory of skyrocketing expectations" is that while they have in fact grown, they have not done so to such an extent that companies cannot keep pace and provide satisfying experiences. Indeed, as customer expectations have increased, companies have managed to meet these rising demands with (roughly) equally stronger customer satisfaction.

Third, while to this point we have been discussing expectations at the economy-wide, national aggregate level, it is important to remember that they are always formed by consumers within a particular context and tend to vary significantly—both in their levels and in their movement over time—across diverse economic sectors, industries, and companies. Yet much of the worry about rising consumer expectations seems to imply the outright claim that the phenomenon is all-encompassing and economy-wide, impacting industries of all shapes and sizes more or less equally. An investigation of the varying levels of expectations across diverse industries and the largest gainers and losers over the past decade reveals that consumers are not anticipating more from every industry, nor do consumers expect as much more from some industries as they do from others.

In sum, while ACSI data confirms that customer expectations have increased over the past 25 years, and that consumers do indeed appear to demand more from the companies from which they purchase, when viewed in context it is difficult to characterize this growth as out-of-control, unprecedented, equally distributed across economic contexts, or beyond the capacity of firms to manage adequately.[3] As has happened since the dawn of the market economy, consumers have come to expect new innovations introduced by some particularly creative companies to become part of the regular product and service offerings of all companies competing in that industry, even innovations that were once (in some cases, quite recently) almost unimaginable. But while the scope and pace of these innovations may seem different, and thus give rise to a misperception that consumers have developed unrealistic, "higher-than-ever" expectations from the firms with which they do business, the reality is somewhat less dramatic. Most importantly, companies seem to be responding well in general to the climb in customer expectations.

2.2 Who Expects the Most, and Why?

Are customer expectations at all-time-high levels and rising equally across all of the many distinct economic industries in the U.S. economy, or are these phenomena distributed unequally? In other words, do customers really expect much more from each different industry and company they purchase goods and services from? The widespread unease among business leaders and pundits alike about rising customer expectations often suggests that expectations are, in fact, high and increasing everywhere and for everyone, regardless of the industry within which companies operate. At least implicitly, these claims appear to rely on a *normative* (what level of quality *should* I receive?) rather than an *empirical-rational* (based on my experiences and other sources of information, what do I think I will actually receive?) conceptualization of consumer expectations. Yet, if we rely on what consumers think they will actually receive and thus should actually expect from companies, as the framing of the expectations questions are by ACSI, we find that expectations have not increased dramatically and equally for all industries. Beginning with an examination of ACSI data from 2017, the most recent year of the study, and including more than 350 companies in 44 industries, Table 2.1 illustrates that expectations vary substantially across the industries included for measurement in the ACSI, and that recent changes (over the last ten years, 2008–2017),[4] a time when aggregate expectations were up 1.8%, have varied widely as well:

At the high end, customers expect the most from companies in a handful of industries: soft drinks, computer software, household appliances, and automobiles and light vehicles, which all score 84 (on the same 0–100 scale discussed earlier).[5] Another handful of industries—food processing, breweries (beer), banks, property and casualty insurance, credit unions, personal computers, televisions and video players, and wireless telephones—come in just a point lower at 83. Eight of these twelve highest-expectations-scoring industries fall within the manufacturing sectors (durable and nondurable goods manufacturing). We will see this theme repeated when we examine high scorers in other categories and for other variables in the chapters that follow. That is, manufacturing companies tend to focus more narrowly on the production of physical goods (rather than the generally more complex and variable domain of human service provision), are "old economy" industries that have mastered these production processes over decades (or more) in business, and as a result provide higher aggregate quality and satisfaction. Basically, these old economy industries are better able to consistently deliver on quality and satisfaction within a more consistent range—not too high and not too low— in the metrics used. In turn, this comparatively, on average, stronger quality and satisfaction performance that consumers have long experienced results in higher expectations among consumers regarding their (future) consumption experiences.

The other high expectations industries outside the manufacturing sector might be considered more surprising, as they include three financial services

Table 2.1 Industry customer expectations, ten-year changes, and growth rank

Sector	Industry	Customer expectations, 2017 (0–100)	Ten-year change (%)	Ten-year growth rank
Telecommunications & information	Computer software	84	5.0	9
Manufacturing-nondurables	Soft drinks	84	−3.4	35
Manufacturing-durables	Household appliances	84	−3.4	36
Manufacturing-durables	Automobiles & light vehicles	84	−3.4	37
Finance & insurance	Banks	83	7.8	2
Finance & insurance	Credit unions	83	5.1	7
Manufacturing-durables	Wireless telephones	83	5.1	8
Finance & insurance	Property & casualty insurance	83	2.5	15
Manufacturing-durables	Personal computers	83	0.0	24
Manufacturing-nondurables	Breweries	83	−1.2	30
Manufacturing-durables	Televisions & video players	83	−1.2	31
Manufacturing-nondurables	Food processing	83	−2.4	33
Accommodation & food services	Limited-service restaurants	82	6.5	4
Retail trade	Internet retail	82	0.0	25
Manufacturing-nondurables	Athletic shoes	82	−1.2	32
Transportation & warehousing	Consumer shipping	82	−3.5	38
Retail trade	Specialty retail stores	81	5.2	6
Finance & insurance	Internet investment services	81	2.5	14
Retail trade	Health & personal care stores	81	0.0	26
Accommodation & food services	Full service restaurants	81	0.0	27
Manufacturing-nondurables	Apparel	81	−3.6	39
Manufacturing-nondurables	Personal care products	81	−3.6	40
Retail trade	Supermarkets	80	3.9	12
Finance & insurance	Life insurance	80	−3.6	41
Telecommunications & information	Wireless telephone service	79	5.3	5
Retail trade	Gasoline stations	79	1.3	21
Health care & social assistance	Hospitals	79	1.3	22
Accommodation & food services	Internet travel services	79	1.3	23

(continued)

Table 2.1 (continued)

Sector	Industry	Customer expectations, 2017 (0–100)	Ten-year change (%)	Ten-year growth rank
Accommodation & food services	Hotels	79	0.0	28
Health care & social assistance	Ambulatory care	79	−2.5	34
Energy utilities	Cooperative utilities	79	−6.0	44
Transportation & warehousing	Airlines	78	18.2	1
Retail trade	Department & discount stores	78	4.0	11
Transportation & warehousing	U.S. postal service	78	1.3	18
Energy utilities	Municipal utilities	78	1.3	19
Telecommunications & information	Fixed-line telephone	78	1.3	20
Energy utilities	Investor-owned utilities	78	0.0	29
Telecommunications & information	Subscription TV	77	4.1	10
Finance & insurance	Health insurance	77	1.3	16
Telecommunications & information	Internet news & opinion	77	1.3	17
Telecommunications & information	Internet search engines & information	77	−4.9	43
Telecommunications & information	Internet service providers (ISPs)	76	−3.8	42
Public administration	Public administration	75	3.7	13
Telecommunications & information	Internet social media	73	7.4	3

Source: Authors' creation from American Customer Satisfaction Index data and methods

industries: banks, credit unions, and property and casualty insurance. In these cases, high and increasing customer expectations may be directly attributable to broader trends playing out across the economy. In other words, while these industries have not always been high performers in terms of quality or customer satisfaction, financial services providers like banks have been expected (more so than many other industries) to not only rapidly change their business model from brick-and-mortar to digital service provision, but also to stay at the forefront of new digital service innovation. The result has been high and increasing expectations among consumers of these companies.

However, only half of the twelve high-expectations industries have seen expectations grow over the last decade; the other six have customers whose expectations have actually declined in the aggregate. As mentioned above, financial service providers like banks (+7.8%) and credit unions (+5.1%) are among the industries where customers' expectations have grown the most; banking customers in particular have registered significantly higher expectations over this period. Only one industry has seen its customers' expectations grow more than banks over the past decade: airlines. For airlines, expectations have risen more than 18.0%. Once again, it would be wrong to assume that the dramatically growing expectations of airline passengers in general apply to each and every company, or even to all of the companies within that one industry. Indeed, as we consider later on, among all of the more than 350 companies measured by ACSI, customers have the lowest expectations with two airlines.

At the other end of the spectrum, consumers expect far less from a handful of industries. At the very bottom is the internet social media industry—which includes large, industry-leading "new economy" companies like Facebook and Twitter—with a score of 73, more than ten points lower than the leading industries. Consumers of federal and local government services (public administration) have very low expectations as well at 75, but because of the expectations of internet social media consumers, they are spared the very bottom spot. Just slightly above internet service providers (ISPs) at 76 are internet news and opinion websites, internet search engines and information, subscription TV (cable and satellite television) and health insurance, all at 77. Interestingly, four of these seven low-expectations industries come from within and are central to the digital economy, some of the industries at the core of the transformations typically given responsibility (or assigned blame) for creating the rapidly increasing expectations discussed earlier. The other industries—and especially public administration and subscription TV—are widely regarded as some of the least satisfying industries in the economy year in and year out, giving rise to consumers that have come to expect very little from their future experiences.

A similar story emerges for the low-expectations industries vis-a-vis ten-year changes. Not all of these industries have declined (or gained) over the last ten years, with some inspiring their customers to expect much more, and vice versa. For instance, while social media is the lowest scoring industry overall, expectations of social media users have actually risen more than any other industry with just two exceptions (airlines and banks, mentioned above). On the other hand, expectations have declined second-most for internet search engines and information over the same period, showing that even within fairly related categories expectations do not necessarily move in unison.

In sum, ACSI data for the past ten years—a period during which aggregate expectations across the U.S. economy increased 1.6 points, or more than half the total increase since 1994—suggests that expectations are not universally high, nor have they increased equally across industries. For some industries, consumers think they will get very little, and those depressed expectations have either not risen, have risen less rapidly than the aggregate, or have actually moved in the opposite direction and declined significantly. Consumers in other industries, however, expect far more, and for some those expectations are dramatically higher. Given these facts, the fear that runaway expectations are plaguing companies in all industries at the same level and pace of growth is incorrect. As ACSI data suggest, here too the situation is mixed, and companies need to focus on the nuances of cross-industry differences to accurately understand the dynamics of their customers' expectations.

Expectations Leading and Lagging Companies

Among the more than 350 companies measured in the ACSI in the most recent year of data used for this book, whose customers have the highest and lowest expectations? Which companies—through advertising, brand image and reputation, word-of-mouth, a consistent record of strong goods and services, and so forth—have led consumers to believe they will get the most from their experiences?

At the top is Toyota's luxury Lexus automobile brand at 89. Since its debut in the late 1980s, Lexus has cultivated a reputation for offering exceptional quality relative not just to other automakers, but other luxury automakers as well, and this has resulted in buyers with lofty expectations. Second place goes to Apple (for its personal computers like the iMac and the Macbook Air, but not including the iPhone, which is measured in a distinct category), tied with four other companies at 88. Meanwhile, a company often accused of having raised the bar and changing expectations for the entire U.S. (and global) economy, Amazon has expectations only in the top third of measured companies, just inside the top 100 firms with a score of 83.

At the other end, the "award" for the customers with the lowest expectations, those that think they will get the least in terms of quality and satisfaction prior to purchase, goes to Spirit Airlines at 64. While Spirit has pursued and touts its "no-frills" business model that saves travelers money, its bare-bones services and reputation for service failures have left customers with low expectations of what they will experience from the company when they travel. Another airline with essentially the same business model—Frontier Airlines—is second-to-last and has expectations just a touch higher at 65. These low scores on expectation are not necessarily bad; instead they indicate that expectations vis-à-vis delivering on satisfaction, for example, need to be managed (a higher score is not always better; managing more effectively is).

2.3   It's a Trap! Avoid the "We Always Exceed Expectations" Promise

Every consumer comes to their experience with a company and its brands, products, and/or services with some expectations. Even consumers purchasing a category of good or service for the very first time has usually developed some expectations from advertising, conversations with others who have used a similar product or service, their own research prior to purchase, and so forth. These expectations frame the consumer's subsequent experiences, and a long-held theory of consumer behavior and customer satisfaction (called the "expectancy-disconfirmation theory") suggests that a consumer's end-state satisfaction is largely determined by whether their prior expectations were not met ("negative disconfirmation"), met ("confirmed"), or exceeded ("positive disconfirmation"). As such, in trying to satisfy consumers, companies must understand their customer's expectations, manage them carefully, attempt to realize them as often as possible, and even exceed them when possible (and profitable).

Recently, some marketers and companies have set the more ambitious goal that they must "always exceed customers' expectations," or outperform expectations every time a consumer makes a purchase or experiences their services. As the quote above from Virgin Group CEO Richard Branson illustrates, even some large, well-respected business leaders and best-in-class service-providing companies pursue this objective. And to be sure, a customer's expectations can be exceeded, at least at times. An excellent, motivated, and creative customer service representative, a new and novel product with innovative features, or an unexpected price discount or reward for enduring customer loyalty are all means by which a customer might receive more from a firm than originally anticipated. There are limitless stories of companies going above-and-beyond to delight their customers or resolve their problems that have "gone viral" and become exemplars of exceptional customer service. And to be sure, these types of extraordinary experiences will almost always have a positive effect on the consumer's future behaviors in a way valuable to the firm, such as their likelihood to repurchase, up- and cross-selling opportunities, propensity to speak positively about the company, and so on.

But for the customer experience manager or related business executive, is it wise to set a goal to "always exceed expectations?" Should such an objective be the lynch-pin of a customer experience or customer satisfaction system, a goal to actually be measured and tracked, and eventually (hopefully) achieved? For most companies, the answer is a simple and definitive "no." Why? In the first instance, while failures in products or services can certainly be minimized with sufficient attention and investment in quality management, their total elimination is between extremely difficult and impossible, as some probability of failure within even the highest-regulated production processes is likely for most companies in most industries. Failures are even more likely when considering human-delivered customer service, wherein variability of individuals involved in the experience (both the employees and the customers) makes quality control and regulation very complex. Thus, striving just to meet or confirm expectations (in the aggregate) can be difficult or downright impossible, let alone consistently trying to exceed them. In short, "always exceeding expectations" implies near-perfect product and service quality, a state not yet achieved by any company.

Moreover, and perhaps more importantly, a hypothetical company that exceeds expectations at one point in time is going to, inadvertently, create the conditions for its own episodic failures in the future. That is, should a company prove successful in exceeding even just a substantial number of its customers' expectations, it will then have to contend with a future group of consumers who have adjusted their expectations upward, precisely because their earlier prior expectations were exceeded (or positively disconfirmed). As consumers are rational and recall past experiences, their expectations will naturally change over time, and will be adjusted upward after experiencing positive disconfirmation and having expectations exceeded. As such, these consumers will enter their next purchase experience with expectations at least some degree (and probably a good deal) higher than before, making the task of exceeding these new higher expectations even more difficult. And this phenomenon will continue circularly and indefinitely, leading to ever increasing expectations that must always be exceeded in the future. At some point, setting a goal to always exceed what becomes always-increasing expectations is likely to become a drain on the profitability of the company, one that undermines the core economic purpose of measuring and working to improve the customer experience in the first place—to achieve profitable customer satisfaction, retention, and growth.

In fairness to Sir Richard Branson, whose quote to open this section has provided fodder for our investigations, his admonition to "always exceed expectations" contains a very important caveat—seek to exceed expectations, but only after setting "realistic customer expectations" that are aligned between the consumer and supplier. In translated form, what Branson is saying is: "First, make sure the consumer has expectations in line with what you, the company, can actually deliver, and then strive to do just a little better than that." This is a much more realistic perspective on exceeding expectations, as it assumes that the firm and the consumer are critically aligned in their thinking, and that customer expectations are not spiraling upward outside the effective control of the company. Whether expectations can be managed successfully in this way is another matter entirely. But nevertheless, as a practical customer experience management objective, "constantly exceeding expectations" is at best incredibly difficult, and at worst a strategy doomed to frustration and failure, possibly resulting in a self-fulfilling prophecy of defeat for the firm. So, it is more logical to spend some additional resources on managing expectations than only spending resources on delivering higher quality and satisfaction at all times. Customer satisfaction needs to be managed in the fickle social media world we now live in, and it goes far beyond the product or service quality.

2.4   What Can We Expect from Expectations?

Forecasting the future is difficult, even with a vast and detailed wealth of historical data at our disposal. As investment firms love to remind us, "past performance does not necessarily predict future results," and the same holds true for consumer perceptions. While the ACSI project was launched 25 years ago on the basis of developments in the economy that were (correctly) predicted to hold great importance for future relationships between companies and customers, the full breadth and depth of those changes and their enormity and importance were not fully understood. Forecasting can be difficult. Nonetheless, we will consider the above analysis and the trajectory of changes over time as we try to predict what customer expectations will look like in the years ahead. Two future developments in customer expectations, in our estimation, are most likely.

First, given the reactions of many experts and executives over the past decade to the changes transforming the economy and the new consumers within that economy—namely, to point to "sky-rocketing customer expectations" as a justification for difficulties and performance failures—it is safe to anticipate more of the same from business professionals. After all, the advances and innovations that have inspired these warnings and the related hand-wringing are likely to continue, and in some cases develop even faster. If the internet has spawned highly demanding customers with unreasonable expectations, imagine what fully automated, less expensive and more efficient, customized services optimized by machine learning and artificial intelligence will do. As such, it is safe to "expect" more talk of runaway customer expectations.

Our second prediction, however, is that customer expectations are likely to remain rational and grounded in actual consumer experiences, neither rising independent of those experiences nor in ways companies cannot reasonably match. Certainly, customer expectations may increase as perceptions of quality, value, and customer satisfaction improve and consumers adjust expectations of future experiences upward. This is precisely what we have seen over the past 25 years. In this sense, firms must continue to adequately manage expectations and set expectations they are capable of meeting. However, fretting over customers with out-of-control expectations that cannot be met is a waste of time and resources for firms and ultimately allows firms to explain-away deficiencies in the products and services they offer consumers that are hurting their growth relative to competitors.

Notes

1. For just a handful of examples of these dire warnings about skyrocketing customer expectations, see: "Corporate America Under Pressure from Consumers' Rising Expectations," *Lithium*, June 2, 2015; Markovitch, S. and P. Willmott (2014). "Accelerating the Digitization of Business Processes," *McKinsey Group*; Meehan, Mary. "Customer Expectation Trends: They Want It All. So Get Out Of The Way," *Forbes.com*, August 12, 2015.
2. In general, the aggregate, *national-level* ACSI variables we examine in this and the next several chapters have thresholds of significant difference of about 0.1 points, based on the statistical significance testing methods used and the large samples of data collected. Thus, any change over time of ±0.1 or more points are considered statistically meaningful.
3. Research on the alignment between consumer perceptions and manager ideas about those perceptions confirm that managers tend to overestimate the level of many of their customers' perceptions, including their expectations. Hult, G. Tomas M., Forrest V. Morgeson III, Neil A. Morgan, Sunil Mithas and Claes Fornell (2017). "Do Managers Know What Their Customers Think and Why?" *Journal of the Academy of Marketing Science*, 45(1), 37–54.
4. In this chapter and the chapters that follow, we will examine industry-level changes in the ACSI variables over the prior ten-year period, from 2008–2017. While 25-year dynamics at the national level are of greatest interest, to track the changes in consumer perceptions and behaviors over a longer timeline and since the introduction of the ACSI, these more recent comparisons at the industry level will, we hope, add additional insight and context into economic dynamics over this period.
5. Based on the statistical methods used and the industry sample sizes, differences in expectations and the variables examined in the next several chapters at the *industry level* are significantly different at a threshold of roughly 1.0 points. The difference between the significance thresholds between the national- and industry-level variables lies in samples sizes underlying these statistics, which are much larger at the national level.

References and Further Reading

Anderson, E. W., & Sullivan, M. W. (1993). The Antecedents and Consequences of Customer Satisfaction for Firms. *Marketing Science, 12*(2), 125–143.

Cadotte, E. R., Woodruff, R. B., & Jenkins, R. L. (1987). Expectations and Norms in Models of Consumer Satisfaction. *Journal of Marketing Research, 24*(Aug.), 305–314.

Corporate America under Pressure from Consumers' Rising Expectations. (2015, June 2). *Lithium*. Retrieved from https://www.lithium.com/company/news-room/press-releases/2015/corporate-america-under-pressure-from-consumers-rising-expectations

Fornell, C., Johnson, M. D., Anderson, E. W., Cha, J., & Bryant, B. E. (1996). The American Customer Satisfaction Index: Nature, Purpose and Findings. *Journal of Marketing, 60*(4), 7–18.

Hayken, S. (2016, November 12). Today's Customers Demand Customer Service on Their Terms. *Forbes.com*. Retrieved from https://www.forbes.com/sites/she-phyken/2016/11/12/todays-customers-demand-customer-service-on-their-terms/#3fa535cdcaa2

Hult, G. T. M., Morgeson, F. V., III, Morgan, N. A., Mithas, S., & Fornell, C. (2017). Do Managers Know What Their Customers Think and Why? *Journal of the Academy of Marketing Science, 45*(1), 37–54.

Markovitch, S., & Willmott, P. (2014). Accelerating the Digitization of Business Processes. *McKinsey Group*. Retrieved from https://www.mckinsey.com/business-functions/digital-mckinsey/our-insights/accelerating-the-digitization-of-business-processes

Meehan, M. (2015, August 12). Customer Expectation Trends: They Want It All. So Get Out Of The Way. *Forbes.com*. Retrieved from https://www.forbes.com/sites/marymeehan/2015/08/12/customer-expectation-trends-they-want-it-all-so-get-out-of-the-way/#75e18dcb96e3

Morgeson, F. V., III, & Forrest, V. (2013). Expectations, Disconfirmation, and Citizen Satisfaction with the US Federal Government: Testing and Expanding the Model. *Journal of Public Administration Research and Theory, 23*(2), 289–305.

Oliver, R. L. (1980). A Cognitive Model of the Antecedents and Consequences of Satisfaction Decisions. *Journal of Marketing Research, 17*(4), 460–469.

Oliver, R. L. (1997). *Satisfaction: A Behavioral Perspective on the Consumer*. New York: Irwin McGraw-Hill.

Passikoff, R. (2011, November 29). The Final Frontier: Customer Expectations. *Forbes.com*. Retrieved from https://www.forbes.com/sites/marketshare/2011/11/29/the-final-frontier-customer-expectations/#794546581587

Spector, A. J. (1956). Expectations, Fulfillment, and Morale. *The Journal of Abnormal and Social Psychology, 52*(1), 51–56.

3

Perceived Quality: Does Performance Matter?

Chapter Overview

In this chapter, we examine changes in consumer perceptions of the quality of the goods and services provided by companies in the U.S. economy over the last 25 years. Included is a comparison of industries that perform well and poorly on quality, and the changes in those industries over the last decade. We next examine the predominant role of quality in driving customer satisfaction, over and above pricing and consumer perceptions of value. We then proceed to a discussion of two perspectives on what constitutes "quality"—reliability and customizability—and why the latter dominates the former as a predictor of customer satisfaction in today's economy. The chapter closes by examining the prospects for continuing gains in satisfaction in the absence of improved quality.

Key Conclusions

- Over the past quarter-century, consumer perceptions of the quality of economic output in the U.S. have improved, but only very slightly, and far less than one might assume.
- In general, durable and nondurable goods manufacturers tend to provide the highest quality to customers, compared with other industries, though quality with commercial airlines has actually improved the most over the past ten years.
- Contrary to the perceptions of many marketers, quality trumps price and value as an influencing factor on customer satisfaction across almost all industries and sectors of the economy.

© The Author(s) 2020
C. Fornell et al., *The Reign of the Customer*, https://doi.org/10.1007/978-3-030-13562-1_3

- The modern economy is a "mass customization" economy, and thus customer satisfaction is more sensitive to the "personalizability" of goods and services than to their reliability.

3.1 Has Quality Improved?

The last half of the twentieth century saw companies and national economies as a whole focusing more than ever on quality and quality management. This focus came first in manufacturing, production processes, and product quality, and soon thereafter turned to less tangible consumer experiences and customer service quality. Systems and programs like total quality management (TQM), six sigma, and ISO 9000 were (and in some cases, still are) viewed as essential to the financial success of individual firms, to maintaining a healthy domestic economy, and to competing effectively in the global marketplace. The idea that the job of the firm is to "build a great product or service" that the consumer actually wants, rather than forcing suppliers to manipulate demand and attempt to lure customers via pricing, advertising, or creative marketing efforts, is now widely accepted.[1] Most business professionals would say that this level of customer orientation has become widely adopted across most industries.

In addition to these quality improvement programs and the movements they have inspired, the latter part of the twentieth century and the beginning of the twenty-first century also coincide with the dawn of the Information Age and its most recognizable component, the internet. As we discussed in Chap. 1, the internet and related technologies have undoubtedly produced massive changes to the economy, including many that would become synonymous with (or were at least believed to make possible) the improved quality of goods and services across the economy. The ease and efficiency of communications both within companies (e.g., between functional business units, like engineers and marketers) and between companies and their customers (creating new feedback loops beneficial to problem identification) would create opportunities for significant enhancements to both productivity and product quality. The still-developing "Internet of Things (IoT)," enabling seamless connectivity and real-time performance monitoring within production processes, including all phases of the heavily globalized supply chains, promises to further minimize product defects and failures.[2] These same new communication efficiencies, alongside the many related innovations to service (and self-service) via automation and the mining of "big data," would seem to make the delivery of services faster, more efficient, and (potentially) less error prone.

But have these "technology" phenomena resulted in demonstrably better quality of products and services delivered to consumers? Has quality actually improved over the last 25 years? The obvious answer would seem to be yes. Today our phones are wireless, faster, and have much more functionality. We have more television channels and radio stations. Our cars and household appliances are digital and far more efficient. And, we seem to be able to receive faster service from all types of businesses via the internet. Given these advances, we might assume that most consumers also perceive that the goods and services today are of substantially higher quality than they were 25 years ago.

Yet, as we reviewed in Chap. 1, ACSI measures quality not from the perspective of the engineer, the marketing director, or the CEO, but rather from the perspective of the consumer, the final and most important arbiter (at least in a free market economy where consumers have choice and the ability to switch) of the performance of goods and services. And the perceptions of the average consumer do not necessarily mirror those of the engineer or others who may recall a product or service prior to the technological advances that have "changed everything." Likewise, if consumers do not perceive these changes as quality enhancements, either for a particular firm or for the economy as a whole, then the desired outcomes of stronger quality—including elevated customer satisfaction and customer loyalty—may also have failed to materialize. The key is that quality has improved but quality assessments in the minds of the customers are relative to expectations and relative to the alternatives (e.g., today's wireless phones vs. the phone patented by Alexander Graham Bell in 1876). Few customers benchmark the quality of their cars against a 1908 version of a Ford Model T. They perceive the quality relative to today's options in the global marketplace and their expectations. Customers' perceptions, in this regard, also build in a time effect; have companies delivered on the quality expected given the evolution of the marketplace?

According to ACSI data, aggregate national consumer *perceptions* of quality have improved over the last 25 years, but only very slightly. Figure 3.1 shows data for national customer perceptions of quality across all major consumer sectors and industries in the U.S. economy between 1994 and 2017. In 1994, during the first year of ACSI measurement, customer perceptions of quality debuted with a score of 80.2. After falling precipitously between 1994 and 1997, to an all-time low of 77.3, quality increased gradually and consistently until 2013, when it peaked at 81.7. Over the ensuing three years, quality has slipped again; in the most recent year of measurement, 2017, overall consumer perceptions of quality rested at 80.5. This is also a period in which global efficiency (i.e., cross-border trade relative to world production) slipped some. All told, the perceived-quality metric has gained only 0.3 points or

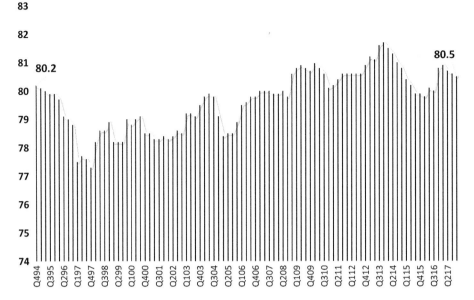

Fig. 3.1 National perceived quality, 1994–2017. (Source: Authors' creation from American Customer Satisfaction Index data and methods)

0.4% over the past 25 years, a statistically significant but marginal improvement, and certainly not representative of a major change in consumer perceptions of quality delivered in the economy. Basically, companies have kept up with the quality improvements in goods and services expected by customers in the global marketplace, relatively speaking not more and not less.

Let us elaborate on this time-dependent quality phenomenon and especially perceptions of quality. Why are American consumers' perceptions of quality virtually unchanged over the past 25 years? To ask the question more pointedly, how can it possibly be that consumers perceive roughly equal quality now as in 1994, given the undeniably dramatic changes and innovations in the economy since that time? A few explanations for this phenomenon are worth considering, some mentioned already and some not so clear-cut or obvious.

First, much of what is often perceived as "better quality" is identified as such by comparing current goods and services to those produced in earlier eras. But not all consumers have this perspective, and the data we are examining here is not "panel data" of the same consumers interviewed in 1994 and again throughout the years. Rather, it is an evolving random sample of all active American consumers (as we described in Chap. 1). So, for example, the roughly 80 million Millennial consumers who were born between 1981 and 1998 are now adults and part of the largest generational cohort in the U.S., representing more than one quarter of the nation's population. Yet no Millennials were adult consumers in 1994, as the oldest members of the Millennial group did not reach adulthood until 1999. As such, virtually no Millennial consumers perceive the current quality of goods and services relative to a time before the Information Age fundamentally changed the economy, at least not based on direct experience as adult consumers. Therefore, current aggregate consumer perceptions of quality will not impound much of this sort of comparative reference to the quality delivered in earlier eras, at least not among a huge proportion of the most active and important consumers today.

Additionally, while the internet has undeniably revolutionized communication in a way that enhances efficiency in both directions—almost always for companies and very often for consumers as well—it also seems to have produced some negative effects on customer service and consumer experiences. Ironically, these negative effects are felt most potently by those consumers—in the Baby Boomer and Generation X cohorts—who *do* remember pre-internet consumerism. More specifically, the internet has been argued to have produced a "dehumanizing" effect on customer service that many consumers have been forced, unhappily, to accept.[3] Automated telephone systems, email communication, "virtual chat" customer support, and so forth have almost completely replaced human-to-human customer service for many large firms. Likewise, internet retail has further limited human interaction for a substantial portion of consumer activity and spending. But what many consumers seem to want, and especially many older consumers, is to speak to a human when comparing goods and services, placing an order, asking a question, or lodging a complaint. These types of interactions are now harder—if not totally impossible—to find. So, while contemporary customer service may be more efficient, it may not create the kinds of experiences that lead to perceptions of higher quality among some consumers and may actually be having the opposite effect for many of them.[4]

A final question remains: If consumer perceptions of quality are basically unchanged over the past 25 years, then how has customer satisfaction increased, as we briefly discussed in the last chapter? After all, quality tends to be the single most important driver of customer satisfaction, and as we pointed out in Chap. 2, both customer expectations and customer satisfaction have increased similarly and significantly over this period. So, if quality is largely unchanged, how has aggregate customer satisfaction improved? In the next chapter, we will examine customer perceptions of value—defined in the ACSI data as the ratio of perceived quality to price perceptions—and show that it, far more so than quality or customer expectations, has driven increased satisfaction over the last 25 years. In that context, we will discuss whether this trend is sustainable over the long term, with companies continuing to offer more satisfaction to consumers primarily via better value, rather than quality. We will also explore the opportunities this opens for companies to beat competitors via quality improvements.

3.2   Quality Leaders and Losers

As we pointed out in Chap. 2 when discussing customer expectations, it is far too common for business and marketing professionals to assume that factors impacting consumer experiences and perceptions in one industry apply equally to all industries. Absent data to suggest otherwise, trends in one industry are far too often assumed to apply to all industries. Yet in reality, industries tend to be differentiated, not only in the types of goods and services provided to customers, but also in how these different goods and services are provided. Given this, it is necessary here to ask as well: Is quality equally high or low, and is it moving in the same direction and at the same magnitude, across all of the many and varied consumer industries? Table 3.1 below shows overall consumer perceptions of quality scores for all of the industries measured in ACSI, ranked from highest to lowest, and with the change (and growth rank) in scores over the last ten years. Over this period, national-level perceptions of quality actually declined slightly (−0.1%).

As we see in Table 3.1, two manufacturing-nondurable goods industries lead in consumer perceptions of overall quality—beer brewers and soft drinks—with scores of 87. Two more manufacturing industries, one in durable goods and another in nondurables—televisions and video players and personal care products, respectively—tie at second with scores of 86. All told, six of the ten highest-quality-producing industries are producers of physical goods rather than service providers, a common result in ACSI data since the project's inception. This is the case for a variety of reasons. In the first instance, when measuring quality in manufacturing industries where only product quality is under the direct control of the supplying company—including the top-performing beer, soft drinks, televisions and video players, and personal care products industries, which are mostly sold by the manufacturer to a large number of retailers who then provide most or all of the pre- and post-consumption "service"—ACSI is only measuring consumer perceptions of the goods themselves, and not the services. As such, the consumer is asked to rate only the quality of the product, not the retail experience through which it was purchased, and all of the aforementioned manufacturing goods tend to be produced via highly regulated, meticulously monitored production processes that limit defects.

Table 3.1 Industry quality perceptions, ten-year changes, and growth rank

Sector	Industry	Overall quality 2017 (0–100)	Ten-year change (%)	Growth rank
Manufacturing-nondurables	Breweries	87	−2	24
Manufacturing-nondurables	Soft drinks	87	−4	40
Manufacturing-durables	Televisions & video players	86	−2	26
Manufacturing-nondurables	Personal care products	86	−3	34
Retail trade	Internet retail	85	−1	19
Manufacturing-nondurables	Food processing	85	−3	35
Finance & insurance	Banks	84	8	5
Finance & insurance	Credit unions	84	−2	27
Manufacturing-durables	Automobiles & light vehicles	84	−5	41
Telecommunications & information	Computer software	83	9	2
Accommodation & food services	Limited service restaurants	83	8	4
Retail trade	Specialty retail stores	83	6	6
Accommodation & food services	Full service restaurants	83	1	15
Finance & insurance	Property & casualty insurance	83	−2	28
Manufacturing-nondurables	Apparel	83	−3	36
Manufacturing-durables	Household appliances	83	−3	37
Transportation & warehousing	Consumer shipping	83	−7	42
Retail trade	Supermarkets	82	4	10
Manufacturing-durables	Wireless telephones	82	4	11
Accommodation & food services	Internet travel services	82	3	13
Retail trade	Health & personal care stores	82	0	16
Manufacturing-nondurables	Athletic shoes	82	−2	29
Finance & insurance	Internet investment services	81	3	12
Energy utilities	Municipal utilities	81	1	14
Finance & insurance	Life insurance	81	−2	30
Health care & social assistance	Ambulatory care	81	−4	38
Energy utilities	Cooperative utilities	81	−7	43
Manufacturing-durables	Personal computers	80	0	17

(*continued*)

Table 3.1 (continued)

Sector	Industry	Overall quality 2017 (0–100)	Ten-year change (%)	Growth rank
Accommodation & food services	Hotels	80	−1	20
Energy utilities	Investor-owned utilities	80	−2	31
Health care & social assistance	Hospitals	80	−2	32
Retail trade	Gasoline stations	80	−4	39
Retail trade	Department & discount stores	79	5	9
Telecommunications & information	Wireless telephone service	78	8	3
Telecommunications & information	Internet news & opinion	78	−1	21
Telecommunications & information	Internet search engines & information	78	−7	44
Transportation & warehousing	Airlines	77	17	1
Finance & insurance	Health insurance	77	0	18
Transportation & warehousing	U.S. postal service	77	−1	22
Telecommunications & information	Fixed-line telephone	76	−3	33
Telecommunications & information	Internet social media	75	6	8
Public administration	Public administration	75	−2	25
Telecommunications & information	Subscription TV	72	6	7
Telecommunications & information	ISPs	71	−1	23

Source: Authors' creation from American Customer Satisfaction Index data and methods

Beer, soft drinks, and personal care products also share other traits as products experienced by consumers that tend to result in higher consumer perceptions of quality. They are all sold at a fairly low price point, variety is strong, competition is high, and switching is frictionless. Consumers who typically make a choice with these products at some point in their customer life cycle are able to quickly switch to another product without losing much if the product does not meet their quality needs (or quality deteriorates over time), and ultimately settle on (i.e., become loyal to) a brand or brands they like the most. In other words, most of these consumers are providing quality perceptions regarding a good they consume precisely because they find it, perhaps after some trial and error, to be of high quality and the most desirable among competitors.

Down at the bottom, two interconnected industries—both service providers—come in at the bottom in terms of perceptions of quality: internet service providers (ISPs) at 71, and subscription TV (cable and satellite services) at 72. Here too, the finding that the cable companies that often provide both TV and ISP services are not seen by their customers to provide strong service quality will probably not come as much of a surprise. These companies are notoriously unpopular with their customers, to the point that the industry is regularly used as an exemplar of poor services. Service disruptions caused by both preventable and uncontrollable phenomena, such as weather, are common. Stories of consumers waiting days or weeks for service at their residence—services often provided by "independent contractors" not directly employed by the company—are common as well. As we will discuss in each of the next two chapters, these industries have added insult to injury: poor service with dramatically higher prices and numerous mega-mergers, the latter often leading to service problems and diminished customer satisfaction.

In terms of improvements in quality over the last decade, one industry clearly stands out as the most improved, paralleling earlier results regarding changing customer expectations. Up 17.0% to a score of 77, airlines have seen the largest improvements in customer perceptions of quality, nearly doubling the improvement of the next closest industry (computer software, up 9–83%). Because the quality of commercial airlines remains in the bottom 25% of all industries in terms of overall ranking in 2017, it would be incorrect to suggest the industry now delivers "exceptional" quality. But it is vastly improved over this period. Pressure on the largest legacy carriers (e.g., Delta, United, and American Airlines) by smaller, newer companies like Southwest and JetBlue, both of which regularly provide stronger quality and satisfaction than their competitors according to customers, has seemed to lift the performance of all the carriers to more respectable levels.

The industry where quality has declined the most over this period is surprising: internet search engines and information. Consumer perceptions of quality with search engines and similar information-seeking web portals have declined 7.0% since 2008, more than any other industry measured in ACSI. Much of the quality decline is attributable to market share leader Google, which has gone from exceptional quality (and satisfaction) to merely good (and closer to average) quality. The company has focused much more on revenue growth over this period, via advertising and related monetization strategies, which seem to have disrupted the consumer experience at least to some extent. Cooperative electric utilities (−7.0%) and consumer shipping companies (such as UPS and FedEx, −7.0%) decline in quality nearly as much as internet search engines and information and show that here, too, quality levels and changes are not constant across industries.

Quality Leading and Lagging Companies

Which companies provide the highest overall quality, from the perspective of their customers? Among all of the firms measured by ACSI, three companies tie for the lead in customer perceived overall quality in the most recent data available—chocolate bar icon Hershey Foods, fast food chicken sandwich leader Chick-fil-A, and supermarket/grocery store Publix, each registering a score of 89. Coming from three very distinct industries (food processing, limited-service restaurants, and supermarkets), these three companies with very different business models, products, and services illustrate that delivering high quality to consumers need not be isolated to only a limited or a select few industries.

At the other end of the spectrum, the two companies anchoring the bottom, tied for lowest customer perceived overall quality at 62, come from the same industry and offer the same services in (roughly) the same way—Frontier Communications and Windstream Communications, both for their ISP services. While Subscription TV providers are often lambasted for their notoriously poor quality, in both customer service and product offerings, it appears that these same companies do even worse by their customers when offering them ISP services than cable TV. As new media for delivering internet services emerge, become more widely available, and gain popularity, one would expect these companies to suffer.

3.3   What Matters Most? It's Quality, Stupid

Perhaps the single most ubiquitous marketing approach (and undoubtedly also one of the oldest) is to lure new customers or secure existing customer's loyalty via price promotions. Among the four traditional "P's" of marketing (product, place, price, and promotion), "price" has long held a position of prominence for many companies, often beating out product (i.e., quality), promotion (advertising), and place (channel) as a marketing strategy. Seasonal or holiday shopping specials, limited-time price promotions, discounts or exclusive offers for new or repeat purchasers, and "going out of business" sales are an unavoidable feature of the consumer landscape, and are often very successful in driving traffic into stores, onto websites, and so on. Taken by itself, there is nothing wrong with marketing to consumers on price—assuming that sufficient attention is paid to profitability, of course—and nothing we will write here will dissuade companies from doing so in the future. But how important is price to consumers, exactly? If the manipulation of price is sufficient to both bring in new customers and keep existing customers from leaving, does a company really need to focus on any other marketing strategy or metrics when analyzing the customer experience?

Based on analysis of data from ACSI—which looks at not only performance on quality and value, but also relative importance in driving satisfaction—one result has appeared repeatedly over the last quarter of a century, and this finding is important to any discussion of marketing strategy and competition on price: While price and the value proposition certainly matter, quality is consistently found to be a more important driver or influencing factor of customer satisfaction and customer loyalty in virtually every consumer industry. In other words, consumer perceptions of quality tend to matter more than price—somewhere between a little and a lot more, depending on the consumer industry being considered—in driving customer satisfaction, and thus propensity for the customer to return to the company (remain loyal) in the future.

There are a handful of exceptions where the consumer's perception of value matters more in terms of its impact on customer satisfaction, and these deserve mention. More precisely, of the 48 consumer industries measured in ACSI, about a half-dozen regularly show consumer perceptions of value as a more influential predictor of satisfaction than quality. To give a few examples, the list of the most value-sensitive industries includes fixed-line telephone, subscription television service, and internet service providers. These three industries are, of course, virtually interchangeable today; for many consumers, their cable TV, landline telephone, and internet service are all provided by the same company via the same delivery mechanism and paid for via the same bill. Because of the near-monopoly status of these companies in many local markets, options are limited and price is more critical to consumers. Given that prices have increased for cable TV service far above the rate of inflation since telecommunications deregulation in the mid-1990s, as exemplified by these three industries having the three lowest value perception scores among all private sector industries measured by ACSI (see Chap. 4), consumer price sensitivity as a driver of satisfaction is not surprising. Two more examples are gasoline service stations and electric utility providers, two "credence good" industries that are highly commoditized and in which perceptions of price are far easier to form than perceptions of quality. Another is credit unions, and here the preeminence of value is understandable too; while credit unions score very well on the value proposition in the eyes of consumers, they are often the choice of those seeking better rates and prices than traditional banks, thus making value a primary driver of satisfaction.

Nevertheless, for a vast majority of companies in B2C industries, consumers' perceptions of performance or quality, whether with a product or a service, are between slightly and substantially more important than value in driving the consumer's end-state satisfaction, and through it their loyalty. Most likely, this finding will make sense to experienced marketers; consumers may be drawn in by a promotion and an attractive price, but if that discounted price entails a product or service that fails to perform at a basic level relative to competitive offerings, the customer will be unhappy and leave, or at least seek-out alternatives. In some cases, marketing primarily on price, as in the case of Walmart and its "Always Low Prices" promise, can send a signal to the marketplace that quality may be low, thereby confounding efforts to boost customer satisfaction by calling quality into question from the start. With this in mind, it is wise to remember that customers can be temporarily attracted by low prices, but enduring satisfaction and long-term loyalty is won via high quality. To stress this notion, here we are again talking about perceptions of quality relative to the times we live in, not relative to some historical benchmark (i.e., any new car of today is better than the 1908 version of a Ford Model T that we mentioned earlier, which was a great innovation at the time, but relatively speaking compared with today's cars, is the car a customer is considering of the quality expected).

In the next chapter, we will expand on the issue of "quality versus price" as a driver of customers' satisfaction. Specifically, following a discussion of the finding that improvements in satisfaction over the last 25 years have been largely value-driven, to some extent contrary to the lessons presented above, we ask whether value can continue to drive higher satisfaction. Can the economy continue to remain highly and increasingly satisfying without improving quality in the minds of consumers? Or, have consumers become more value-focused, and/or are companies so much better at providing value that quality simply matters less today?

3.4   Customization Trumps Reliability

There are many ways to define quality as it is perceived by the consumer of a good or service, and if asked, different consumers will often define quality differently. For example, the popular SERVQUAL model used to measure the service quality delivered by firms identifies five differentiated generic items and more than a dozen sub-items included in most customer service experiences (such as tangibles, reliability, empathy).[5] Similar models for measuring the quality of products tend to be even more complex, and they typically differ significantly across the type of good or product being investigated. Furthermore, consumer perceptions of quality and what constitutes quality are themselves complex and evolving. Taken together, the broadness intrinsic to the quality concept can complicate efforts to understand consumer perceptions. But intrinsic to virtually every good or service is a tension between two broad yet essential quality dimensions that sometimes complement and sometimes conflict with one another: quality as reliability and quality as customization.

Defined briefly, quality-as-reliability refers to the consumer's perception that the product or service experienced was free from observable defects, and that when consuming it nothing significant went wrong. On the other hand, quality-as-customization refers to the perception that the good or service meets consumers' particular, personal needs, or that it is appropriate to what they want as individual consumers. Thinking of quality perceptions from any consumer experience in a simplified four-box matrix form, a product (for instance) can be both highly reliable and highly customized (the optimal outcome), achieve high quality on one dimension (reliable or customizable, but not both), or exhibit low reliability and low customization (the worst outcome). Sometimes, of course, a trade-off is necessary between these two values for companies, with high reliability being chosen at the cost of lesser customizability. For example, manufacturing a highly standardized product may allow a firm to simplify and improve production processes and virtually eliminate defects, but there is an opportunity cost for the company (or the customer) in not offering customized goods, and vice versa. This begs the question: What is more important to the consumer, customization or reliability?

Basing our conclusions on the data from ACSI over the last quarter of a century, we find that in every industry measured (with almost no exceptions over time), and regardless of price structure, competitive environment, or whether the consumer is purchasing a good or a service, quality-as-customization trumps quality-as-reliability as a driver of customer satisfaction and loyalty. This result is perhaps not terribly surprising, as the past few decades have seen the principle of prioritizing customization become commonplace for companies in many industries, with most consumers now expecting that goods or services will optimally meet their unique, particular needs.

At the same time, improvements in production processes, customer service training and management, and in some cases service delivery automation have resulted in increasing levels of reliability across the board, to the point that it is often taken as a given, a basic barrier to entry into any competitive market rather than a primary driver of satisfaction. Yet regardless of the particular explanation for this phenomenon (and there are certainly others), companies must now compete first and foremost on their ability to customize for their customers. Providing a reliable product or service is important, but not as important as offering a product or service tailored to customers' unique desires. The "production-centric" era of Henry Ford, where the supplier wielded substantial power over the consumer and could often control their choice set, is long gone, and has been replaced by the customer-centric economy; customers now demand customization, and will turn elsewhere if they do not get it.

Notes

1. In a poignant comment along these lines, Amazon CEO Jeff Bezos once said: "The right way to respond to this [increased consumer power] if you are a company is to put the vast majority of your energy, attention and dollars into building a great product or service and put a smaller amount into shouting about it, marketing it."
2. For a brief review of how IoT promises to change the economy, see: "5 Areas Where The IoT is Having The Most Business Impact," *Forbes.com*, June 12, 2018.
3. For a good discussion of these trends, see: LeBret, Jabez. "Your Customer Service is Missing One Critical Piece," *Forbes.com*, March 10, 2016. Accessed online at: https://www.forbes.com/sites/jabezlebret/2016/03/10/your-customer-service-is-missing-one-critical-piece/#3801f97b3ee7
4. As we observe below when discussing industry-level changes in quality over the past decade, there is some evidence for the "product vs. service quality" divide. Three of the four biggest drops in quality among industries over this period are observed for pure service providers, with the fourth being automobiles and light vehicles, where both product and service quality are measured. ACSI does not produce national-level product and service quality variables for analysis, however, as only a smaller percentage of industries (as defined by ACSI) include both distinct product and service quality components, making sample available for analysis an issue.
5. For more on the SERVQUAL model, see: Parasuraman, A., V. A. Zeithaml and L. L. Berry (1988). "SERVQUAL: A Multi-Item Scale for Measuring Consumer Perceptions of Service Quality," *Journal of Retailing*, 64(1), 12–40.

References and Further Reading

5 Areas Where the IoT Is Having The Most Business Impact. (2018, June 12). *Forbes.com*. Retrieved from https://www.forbes.com/sites/insights-hitachi/2017/12/18/5-areas-where-the-iot-is-having-the-most-business-impact/#1a6691404396

Finch, B. J., & Luebbe, R. L. (1997). Using Internet Conversations to Improve Product Quality: An Exploratory Study. *International Journal of Quality and Reliability Management, 14*(8), 849–865.

Foremski, T. (2010, July 30). Jeff Bezos: Put Your Energy into Making Great Products and Not Marketing…. *ZDNet.com*. Retrieved from https://www.zdnet.com/article/jeff-bezos-put-your-energy-into-making-great-products-and-not-marketing/

Fornell, C. (2007). *The Satisfied Customer: Winners and Losers in the Battle for Buyer Preference*. New York, NY: Palgrave Macmillan.

Gilmore, J. H., & Pine, B. J. (1996). The Four Faces of Mass Customization. *Harvard Business Review, 75*(1), 91–101.

Hult, G. T. M., Morgeson, F. V., III, Morgan, N. A., Mithas, S., & Fornell, C. (2017). Do Managers Know What Their Customers Think and Why? *Journal of the Academy of Marketing Science, 45*(1), 37–54.

Johnson, M. D., & Ettlie, J. E. (2001). Technology, Customization, and Reliability. *Journal of Quality Management, 6*(2), 193–210.

LeBret, J. (2016, March 10). Your Customer Service is Missing One Critical Piece. *Forbes.com*. Retrieved from https://www.forbes.com/sites/jabezlebret/2016/03/10/your-customer-service-is-missing-one-critical-piece/#3801f97b3ee7

Parasuraman, A., Zeithaml, V. A., & Berry, L. L. (1988). SERVQUAL: A Multi-Item Scale for Measuring Consumer Perceptions of Service Quality. *Journal of Retailing, 64*(1), 12–40.

Thatcher, M. E., & Pingry, D. E. (2004). An Economic Model of Product Quality and IT Value. *Information Systems Research, 15*(3), 268–286.

4

Perceived Value: Is It Really All About Price?

Chapter Overview

In this chapter, we examine variation in consumer perceptions of the value of the goods and services provided by the U.S. economy over the last 25 years. During this period, perceptions of value have improved enormously, more so than for any of the other drivers of customer satisfaction. While in Chap. 3 we discussed the primacy of consumer perceptions of quality in driving satisfaction across nearly all firms and industries, national-level satisfaction improvements over the last quarter of a century have been driven mostly by a stronger value proposition. Following a discussion of industry and company leaders and laggards, we close this chapter with a discussion on the feasibility—for both individual companies and the economy as a whole—of a continued focus on the value proposition as the primary driver of customer satisfaction.

Key Conclusions

- For the past 25 years, consumer perceptions of value have improved significantly, more so than any other driver of customer satisfaction included in the ACSI model.
- As with customer expectations and perceived quality, value varies widely across industries, with a handful of manufacturing companies leading and a few telecommunications industries at the bottom.
- While value is up strongly at the national level, over both the past 10 and 25 years, not all industries have strong and improving value, and some are offering a significantly worse value proposition to consumers.

© The Author(s) 2020
C. Fornell et al., *The Reign of the Customer*, https://doi.org/10.1007/978-3-030-13562-1_4

- We conclude the chapter with a discussion of the pros and cons of continuing to drive aggregate customer satisfaction and economic growth via a price-based value proposition rather than quality, and suggest that this may not be possible over the long term.

4.1   Are Consumers Seeing Better Value?

Today, companies have the tools at their disposal to achieve greater efficiency throughout their operations than ever before, producing and delivering goods and services far more cost-effectively. As discussed in each of the chapters we have covered so far, the Information Age and its new communications technologies that have changed so much about the modern economy have also played an outsized role in these cost-efficiency-related developments. To give a few examples, ICT has given rise to easier and more effective communication within firms, more efficient communications between customers and companies, real-time performance measurement and monitoring designed to pre-emptively detect and eliminate costly defects (e.g., during the production process), and more effective automation of both physical goods production and service delivery.

In parallel, a related development has grown more and more prevalent over the past few decades—namely, economic globalization. Companies have been able to provide substantial additional cost savings on top of those realized via new technologies. Through globalization, companies not only can acquire the raw materials and labor needed to produce their goods and provide their services at dramatically lower prices, but are also required to spend far less on capital investment (for either real property or facilities), can take advantage of lucrative tax benefits and other local government incentives, and can realize hugely profitable economies of scale, all of which help keep costs low (Chap. 9 covers more on globalization and international trade).

Companies have continued to battle for customers via one of the oldest and best-known business and marketing strategies—price competition. In part by using the cost savings gleaned through both efficiency-enhancing new technologies and globalization, companies are working to undercut their competitors and win buyers by offering the best price to the consumer, just as they always have. Yet the game is different now, in ways beneficial to those same consumers. Information about pricing is now more available and transparent than ever before, and this allows the consumer to price-compare and find the best deal. Companies also have the means to better discover and act on this information. That is, readily available information about competitors' pricing—alongside related "big data" and the computing power needed to analyze such competitor data effectively and rapidly—permit companies to anticipate, track, and match the price promotions of these competitors more effectively. Dynamic and algorithm-based pricing models allow price changes to happen automatically and nearly in real-time, speeding up the pace with which customers realize these savings.[1] Increasingly, and particularly in e-commerce, e-retail, and similar industries, price wars are bringing goods and services to consumers at incredible, almost unbelievable savings. This constant equilibrium-seeking of supply and demand creates efficiencies in the market that were largely unheard of when the ACSI project started in 1994 (e.g., today when a Delta Airbus 330 airplane takes off, the 234 passengers represent dozens of ticket prices depending on when their tickets were bought).

Unsurprisingly, the convergence of more efficient operations and other means of operational cost savings (e.g., globalization), alongside traditional but far more effective, timely, and prolific price competition, has proven beneficial for customers and their pocketbooks. This fact is perhaps best illustrated in the recent growth—or more correctly, the relative lack thereof—of inflation. Price inflation over about the last three decades—the 1990s, the 2000s, and the 2010s—has been exceptionally low, less than half (roughly) of the comparable annual average rates of the 1970s and 1980s.[2] In fact, prices have not grown this slowly since the 1950s. In effect, consumers are benefitting from the new technologies and other innovations that have allowed companies to produce goods and services more efficiently and pass those (savings) along to consumers via price competition.

But have these efficiencies trickled down to the customer in a way that is actually noticed by them? Have consumers' *perceptions* of the value they receive from their economic transactions improved over the past 25 years, in line with what the enhanced efficiencies, greater price competition, and the lower inflation would suggest? As we saw in the last two chapters (on customer expectations and perceived quality), consumers do not always behave as prognosticators anticipate or experts believe, nor do they necessarily take notice when economic conditions are objectively deemed "far better than before." They may not recall or may not have directly experienced earlier eras used as reference points. To elaborate, companies with longevity in the marketplace often have different pricing (and efficiency) benchmarks based on history than many customers who have engaged in the market fewer years. Consequently, consumers may not necessarily view this as a time of lower prices and better value given different reference points. That said, on a positive, ACSI data suggest that consumers do in fact perceive far greater value from the economy over the last 25 years.

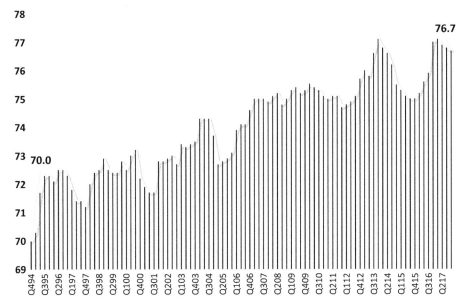

Fig. 4.1 National perceived value, 1994–2017. (Source: Authors' creation from American Customer Satisfaction Index data and methods)

Figure 4.1 shows national aggregate consumer perceptions of value between 1994 and 2017, measured on the same 100-point scale referenced in the previous chapters (for easy comparisons). As the figure shows, customer perceptions of value debuted with a score of 70.0 in 1994. Like the other macro-level variables discussed thus far, value perceptions have generally trended upward over time, but excluding a handful of moments where declines were observed—such as in 2001 during the brief recession that year, in 2004 when energy and gas prices spiked due to the war in Iraq, and in 2014–2015 when all consumer perceptions of the economy waned—they have done so both more rapidly and more extensively than the other ACSI variables. Interestingly, only a small dip in value metrics was seen in the 2008 period during the most recent recession. In total, value has increased 6.7 points to 76.7, a very large and statistically highly significant 9.6% increase over the period. In fact, of the three crucial left-hand-side driver variables included in the ACSI model—including the three drivers of satisfaction, expectations, quality, and value—none has improved more than customer perceptions of value.

Figure 2.2, first introduced in Chap. 2, graphically illustrates these insights and compares changes in consumer perceptions of expectations, quality, value, and satisfaction since 1994. Here we see the results discussed in the last two chapters illustrated, including the sizable 25-year growth in expectations (+3.0) and the very small gain in quality (+0.3) over the same period. The 6.7-

point improvement in national perceptions of value stands out, as discussed, especially relative to the growth in aggregate customer satisfaction or ACSI (+2.5). Customer satisfaction—often labeled the ACSI score—is the focus of Chap. 5. Taken together, these observations lead to a definitive conclusion: Gains in customer satisfaction across the economy over the last quarter-century have been *driven largely by a stronger value proposition*. Expectations have gained substantially but tend to have only a small impact on satisfaction, and quality typically has the largest impact on satisfaction but is virtually unchanged over the time series. While quality tends to be most strongly related to satisfaction for almost all industries and companies, as we discussed in the last chapter, offering better value led companies to push satisfaction higher for the economy as a whole. Later on, we come back to examining both the tenability and the desirability of continuing to seek gains in satisfaction via continuous value improvements over the long term.

4.2 Who Are the Value Leaders?

As we discussed in Chap. 1, perceived value as measured in the ACSI survey and statistical model is not a simple metric of consumer "happiness" with the prices they have paid for a good or service. There are a host of reasons for not focusing on ratings of price or "price satisfaction" in this fashion, as is often-times done. Most significantly, to measure value as direct perceptions of price paid results in raw data and mean scores heavily skewed by industry characteristics and respondent subjectivity, with higher scores for lower-priced goods, and lower scores for higher-priced goods. These scores are also heavily influenced by consumer characteristics and idiosyncrasies, like income. In turn, ratings of price conducted in this way have little meaning when trying to compare across industries, companies, or even brands within a single company's portfolio. In scientific terminology, we also lose variance, explanatory means, and prediction possibilities with such a coarse-grained "happiness" score. ACSI measures value more rigorously, with more validity and reliability.

To better facilitate cross-respondent and cross-category comparisons, ACSI measures value as the ratio and relationship between perceptions of price paid relative to quality, and quality relative to price paid. As such, results on this variable—when comparing two industries, for example—mean something different and more than just "Industry X has a lower price," and instead refer to what marketers call the "value proposition." A higher score on this summated variable for one company relative to a competitor could actually indicate a higher price for a good combined with substantially higher quality, for example, the marketing mix strategy used by luxury goods providers. Likewise, a company could outperform a competitor on this value variable by offering slightly lower quality (as product quality, selection and variety, aftersales customer service, or along some other quality dimension) but at far lower prices, the strategic mix used by discount retailers. Both cases would provide superior value.

We reiterate this definition of consumer value perceptions as the price-quality ratio central to the value proposition to reaffirm that this measure of value should not to be confused with a simplistic ranking of price across industries from high to low. While price is a central component of the value metric, we should not necessarily expect industries with lower average prices to score better, or vice versa. This is confirmed in Table 4.1, which shows industry value scores from high to low, with changes over the last ten years and growth rank over the same period. During this period, national consumer perceptions of value across the entire economy increased 2.3%.

Beginning with value scores and leaders, and very similar to the case of the expectations and quality variables discussed in Chaps. 2 and 3, one manufacturing industry (in this case, durable goods) sits undisputed at the top of the rankings—televisions and video players, with a score of 87. While it may seem odd for the value-leading industry to sell products costing, in some cases, thousands of dollars per unit, it is actually unsurprising. Because value perceptions are the ratio of price to quality and quality to price, as we described earlier, and this (and related) manufacturing industries are generally very strong in quality, it stands to reason they would also perform well in consumer value perceptions too, at least so long as prices are not excessively high or rising unreasonably. In fact, not only does the televisions and video players industry have very high quality, but prices for these goods have actually declined as quality has increased. For example, while it is undeniable that televisions have evolved radically over the past few decades—and all for the better, becoming smaller and lighter and clearer and brighter and of far higher overall quality—they have also declined dramatically in price, selling for one quarter of what was paid in the mid−1990s.[3]

The second-place group includes three manufacturing industries—soft drinks, breweries, and personal care products, each at 84—all nondurable goods suppliers selling mostly "old economy" products at fairly low prices, with easy switching for unhappy customers to one of many preferred alternatives. These industry conditions are conducive to both strong quality, as we described in Chap. 3, and competitive pricing. The one entrant in the second-place group just below televisions and video players that does not emerge from within the manufacturing sectors is internet retail. As we discussed to open the chapter, internet retailers—with e-commerce giant Amazon leading

Table 4.1 Industry perceptions of value, ten-year changes, and growth rank[a]

Sector	Industry	Perceived value 2017 (0–100)	Ten-year change (%)	Growth rank
Manufacturing-durables	Televisions & video players	87	1	21
Manufacturing-nondurables	Soft drinks	84	2	18
Manufacturing-nondurables	Breweries	84	−1	28
Manufacturing-nondurables	Personal care products	84	−1	29
Retail trade	Internet retail	84	−2	32
Finance & insurance	Credit unions	83	−5	40
Manufacturing-nondurables	Apparel	82	−2	33
Manufacturing-durables	Automobiles & light vehicles	82	−4	37
Telecommunications & information	Computer software	81	17	2
Retail trade	Department & discount stores	81	5	11
Manufacturing-durables	Personal computers	81	0	22
Manufacturing-nondurables	Food manufacturing	81	−1	30
Manufacturing-durables	Household appliances	81	−4	38
Finance & insurance	Banks	80	7	7
Retail trade	Supermarkets	80	5	8
Accommodation & food services	Limited service restaurants	80	5	9
Accommodation & food services	Internet travel services	80	5	10
Manufacturing-nondurables	Athletic shoes	80	3	17
Retail trade	Specialty retail stores	80	1	20
Finance & insurance	Internet investment services	79	7	6
Retail trade	Health & personal care stores	79	4	13
Finance & insurance	Property & casualty insurance	79	0	23
Accommodation & food services	Full service restaurants	79	0	24
Manufacturing-durables	Wireless telephones	79	0	25
Finance & insurance	Life insurance	79	−1	31
Transportation	Consumer shipping	79	−2	34

(continued)

Table 4.1 (continued)

Sector	Industry	Perceived value 2017 (0–100)	Ten-year change (%)	Growth rank
Health care & social assistance	Ambulatory care	79	−2	35
Accommodation & food services	Hotels	78	3	16
Transportation & warehousing	Airlines	76	21	1
Retail trade	Gasoline service stations	75	9	4
Energy utilities	Cooperative utilities	75	−5	41
Transportation & warehousing	U.S. postal service	74	3	15
Health care & social assistance	Hospitals	74	0	26
Finance & insurance	Health insurance	73	0	27
Energy utilities	Municipal utilities	72	9	3
Telecommunications & information	Wireless telephone service	72	7	5
Energy utilities	Investor-owned utilities	72	3	14
Telecommunications & information	Fixed-line telephone service	69	−4	39
Public administration	Public administration	68	2	19
Telecommunications & information	ISPs	63	−3	36
Telecommunications & information	Subscription TV	62	5	12

Source: Authors' creation from American Customer Satisfaction Index data and methods
[a]Because ACSI does not measure value perceptions for industries that generally do not charge a fee for customers to receive their services—such as internet search engines and news and information websites—the total number of industries included in Table 4.1 is slightly lower than for the other variables, at only 41

the way in both innovation and sheer size—have played a significant role in changing the game for consumers overall in the recent past, and especially vis-à-vis pricing. Not only does Amazon excel at offering virtually everything the consumer might want and shipping it to them rapidly, but they do so at very low prices, oftentimes far lower than competitors. Moreover, anyone hoping to compete with Amazon, even if for only a tiny share of the market or in a niche segment, must still price-competitively to do so. Given this, it is understandable that consumers find the value proposition provided by this industry to be near the top economy-wide.

Down at the very bottom, the value laggards should not be particularly surprising either, as we have seen them in earlier chapters at or near these same undesirable positions on other ACSI metrics. At 63 for ISPs and 62 for subscription TV, these cellar-dwellers score a full 24 and 25 points lower, respectively, than the televisions and video players industry in value perceptions. In some way, it is fascinating that the television and video products score so high relative to the subscription TV service. The gap between the top and bottom performers on perceived value is far larger than we have observed for either the expectations or quality variables, suggesting that even though consumer value perceptions are most-improved among the drivers of customer satisfaction, there remains substantial variance between industries, with some unable or unwilling to keep pace with these trends (logically, TV products and TV subscription services should be more value-aligned to maximize positive overall customer sentiments). As mentioned in Chap. 3, where we also found ISPs and subscription TV to anchor the bottom in customer perceptions of quality (though in reverse order), these two industries are largely undifferentiated as services in the minds of consumers, and a majority receive both from the same company via the same delivery channel and pay via the same bill. We also noted that prices have increased far above the rate of inflation for the telecommunications sector as a whole, and especially in these industries, since deregulation in the 1990s. Consumers feel this pricing pain and, when combined with the notoriously low quality also seen in ACSI data, they respond by rating these industries lowest in perceived value.

We turn now to the most recent ten-year changes, and here too the results in terms of gains or losses in customer perceptions of value largely make sense. For example, the commercial airlines industry—up 21% in value perceptions since 2008, more so than any other industry—has undergone enormous change during this period. In particular, the fastest-growing segment within the industry are the no-frills, low-cost air carriers, companies that have worked their way into the market and grown rapidly to challenge the large "legacy carriers" with bargain-basement prices. While these carriers score poorly on both quality and satisfaction, their overall value propositions are much stronger. For instance, Spirit and Frontier score lower on expectations than all other companies, and lower than almost all on quality, but they sit near the middle of the pack on perceptions of value. By necessity, this finding can only be due to their very low prices, and while customers may cringe when buying tickets, the low prices keep them coming back. Moreover, the existence of these price-focused competitors has forced the larger carriers to themselves lower prices on many routes to keep pace and prevent defections. Overall the result is a dramatically improved value proposition for air travelers.

The second largest gain in consumer perceptions of value, at +17%, is for the computer software industry. This result is likely driven by the open-source software movement and the proliferation of free or low-cost software "apps" that are putting pressure on the prices that can be demanded by traditional software suppliers like Microsoft. The third and fourth biggest gains in consumer value perceptions are in two energy industries, municipal (publicly owned) energy utilities (+9.0%) and gasoline service stations (+9.0%). Given that these industries tend to be almost fully commoditized, any perceived quality changes are most likely taking a back seat to improved price perceptions in driving value improvements; the substantial drop in crude oil prices since 2010 and their continued lower cost (historically speaking) provides support for this conclusion.

Finally, the industry that has declined the most in terms of consumer perceptions of value is cooperative electric utilities (−5%). While energy prices across all types of suppliers were generally lower over this period, reflected in the fact that both municipal and investor-owned energy suppliers saw substantial gains in consumer perceptions of value, it appears customers of smaller, mostly rural electricity and gas suppliers are finding a significantly lower value proposition. Most likely, the lack of options in the rural areas and customers knowing about more competitive prices in urban areas combine to form more negatively slanted value perceptions in the minds of rural customers. The next largest decline in value is somewhat surprising—credit unions, also down −5%—in that credit unions often position themselves as providing substantially better value than their large commercial bank competitors. This ten-year decline in value for credit unions might serve as a warning sign that large banks are doing a better job competing with better rates and lower fees. It may be that larger banks have the pulse on the customer clientele better than the traditionally no-frills oriented credit unions and this approach is now catching up to the value proposition for credit unions.

Leading and Lagging Companies

Which companies provide the highest perceived value in the minds of consumers? Based on ACSI data, one company has sole claim to the award—ALDI, the German discount supermarket chain renowned for slashing prices, with a score of 89. Just below ALDI at 87 are two Japanese automakers, Toyota and Subaru, companies renowned for offering exceptional quality at solid, competitive prices.

On the other hand, a slew of companies we have talked about in this and other chapters hold the "honor" of worst-in-class value—cable TV and ISP providers like Comcast (for subscription TV, at 55), Windstream (for ISP, at 56), and Mediacom (for ISP, at 57). As mentioned, the large price increases over the last few decades on top of the reputation for poor quality of both products and services make it unnecessary to give further attention to this finding. It is an industry-wide value problem that needs to be solved.

4.3   Toward a Post-Quality Economy?

In Chap. 3, we reviewed changes in consumer perceptions of quality since 1994. We briefly discussed the relationship between consumer perceptions of quality, perceived value, and customer satisfaction. In virtually every industry measured in the ACSI, consumers' perceptions of quality, for all types of goods and all types of services, are more important than their perceptions of value in driving customer satisfaction and loyalty. We concluded the discussion in Chap. 3 with a reminder to marketers that "customers can be temporarily attracted by low prices, but enduring satisfaction and long-term loyalty is won via high quality." Yet based on what we have discussed in this chapter, vis-à-vis national-level changes in expectations, quality, value, and customer satisfaction since 1994, we concluded that the 25-year customer satisfaction improvement has been driven mostly by an improved value proposition, and very little by improved quality. In other words, recommendations regarding the stronger effect of quality on customer satisfaction relative to value notwithstanding, individual firms and the economy as a whole have been focusing predominantly on price to drive satisfaction higher over this period.

To clarify, the most recent ACSI data confirms that quality remains primary for consumers as a driver of customer satisfaction across virtually all companies and industries. That is, in a multi-variable statistical model including all of these factors, customers' perceptions of quality are more strongly related to their satisfaction than value perceptions, and little has changed in this regard since ACSI began measuring data in 1994. As such, a long-running recommendation for firms to focus on quality above value in driving satisfaction remains. But does this finding really matter, either to individual companies or to policymakers seeking to improve national customer satisfaction and guarantee the competitiveness of a national market in the globalized economy (e.g., China)? Have we entered a "post-quality economy" where constantly increasing consumer perceptions of value and stagnant quality drive satisfaction and total economic growth?

Perhaps most importantly, can this trend continue on into the foreseeable future, or will improvements in value flatten out at some point, as the new technological innovations that have made lower prices possible taper off? This question is, of course, nearly impossible to answer without a proverbial crystal ball. It is tempting to suggest that the price and value-enhancing technological innovations that have driven prices lower and satisfaction higher for decades are bound to emerge more slowly (or halt entirely) in the near future. Yet those who have predicted a "slow-down" in technological advancement, either in its pace or in the boundaries of what can be achieved, have so far always been proven wrong. But even a fairly small slow-down could be enough. As the data show, it required a relatively massive 6.7-point improvement in value (along with a 3.0-point improvement in expectations) to push national-aggregate customer satisfaction in the U.S. economy a relatively small 2.5 points higher over a 25-year period. According to the ACSI model, a gain in quality similar to this gain in value would have resulted in a much larger gain in satisfaction; in many industries, consumer perceptions of quality have more than twice the effect on satisfaction than does value. Therefore, should the future hold even a small setback in value-improving technology relative to the frenetic pace of the last two-plus decades, and quality continues to remain stagnant, customer satisfaction with firms and the national economy overall may fail to increase or could even decline.

In Chap. 5, we will provide some finality to this topic, examining how low-cost advances in quality via technology may provide both the solution for stagnant quality, help national economies overcome the value dilemma, and lead to more robust growth in customer satisfaction in the future.

Notes

1. While economists continue to debate the root cause of slower inflation, it is difficult to argue against the impact of new technologies, which are ultimately what allow Walmart (via its logistics) and Amazon to have the downward effect on prices that they do. The article by Brush, "6 reasons why inflation will stay low—and how to capitalize on it," provides a good and simple discussion of the new technology-low prices relationship.
2. All pricing data referenced in this chapter focuses on the U.S. market and its economy and come from the Bureau of Labor Statistics (BLS). The phenomenon is global, however, and these insights are relevant to almost all developed, advanced economies.
3. One 2017 analysis found that TVs had declined from $5.83 per inch to $1.78 between 1997 and 2017. The top-end TVs in 1997 were more than $30 per inch. https://www.cnet.com/news/are-tvs-really-cheaper-than-ever-we-go-back-a-few-decades-to-see/

References and Further Reading

Anderson, E. W., & Fornell, C. (2000). Foundations of the American Customer Satisfaction Index. *Total Quality Management, 11*(7), 869–882.

Billige, M. Rethinking Price Wars: Disruptive Forces Are Reshaping How They Start, Get Fought, and Get Resolved. Retrieved from https://www.simon-kucher.com/en/blog/rethinking-price-wars-disruptive-forces-are-reshaping-how-they-start-get-fought-and-get-resolved

Brush, M. (2017, September 27). 6 Reasons Why Inflation Will Stay Low—And How to Capitalize on It. *Marketwatch.com*. Retrieved from https://www.market-watch.com/story/6-reasons-why-inflation-will-stay-low-and-how-to-capitalize-on-it-2017-09-26

Fornell, C. (2007). *The Satisfied Customer: Winners and Losers in the Battle for Buyer Preference*. New York, NY: Palgrave Macmillan.

Fornell, C., Johnson, M. D., Anderson, E. W., Cha, J., & Bryant, B. E. (1996). The American Customer Satisfaction Index: Nature, Purpose and Findings. *Journal of Marketing, 60*(4), 7–18.

Heda, S., Mewborn, S., & Caine, S.. (2017, January 3). How Customers Perceive a Price Is as Important as the Price Itself. *Harvard Business Review*.

Hult, G. T. M., Morgeson, F. V., III, Morgan, N. A., Mithas, S., & Fornell, C. (2017). Do Managers Know What Their Customers Think and Why? *Journal of the Academy of Marketing Science, 45*(1), 37–54.

Morgeson, F. V., III, Sharma, P. N., Tomas, G., & Hult, M. (2015). Cross-National Differences in Consumer Satisfaction: Mobile Services in Emerging and Developed Markets. *Journal of International Marketing, 23*(2), 1–24.

Morrison, G. (2017, November 23). Are TVs Really Cheaper Than Ever? We Go Back a Few Decades to See. *CNET.com*. Retrieved from https://www.cnet.com/news/are-tvs-really-cheaper-than-ever-we-go-back-a-few-decades-to-see/

5

ACSI: Is Satisfaction Guaranteed?

Chapter Overview

In this chapter, we focus on the central, most critical metric for understanding the customer experience and the health of the customer-firm relationship—customer satisfaction—and examine the evolution of the satisfaction of American consumers over the last 25 years. In the process, we identify the most and least satisfying industries across the entire U.S. economy, and the changes in those industries over the last ten years. We next discuss customer satisfaction as an important predictor of macroeconomic growth and changes in the economy, one that can help us both forecast and understand changes in the economy better. We then turn to a consideration of those rare cases in which satisfaction itself can provide a misleading indicator of a firm's health, and the potential effects of merger and acquisition (M&A) activity on the customer experience and customer satisfaction. Finally, we discuss the future of customer satisfaction, focusing on how artificial intelligence and technological advances could have a revolutionary impact on customer service.

Key Conclusions

- Over the last 25 years, the satisfaction of the average American consumer has improved significantly, much more so than consumer perceptions of quality. Improved satisfaction is being driven primarily via pricing and the value proposition.
- Similar to the findings vis-à-vis consumer perceptions of quality, a few manufacturing industries tend to best satisfy customers, while information sector industries like subscription TV and ISP companies lag behind.

© The Author(s) 2020
C. Fornell et al., *The Reign of the Customer*, https://doi.org/10.1007/978-3-030-13562-1_5

- National customer satisfaction is related to traditional indicators of macroeconomic performance and growth, reinforcing the importance of this metric for both firms and national economies as a whole.
- Although popular as a growth strategy, mergers and acquisitions are often detrimental to the satisfaction of consumers and must be undertaken cautiously.
- While vitally important for firms to track, caution must be taken when interpreting satisfaction data, as the data is not without interpretational challenges and can at times be deceiving.
- Near-future advances in artificial intelligence and machine learning could boost consumer perceptions of quality while still allowing improvements in price and value, boosting future customer satisfaction even higher.

5.1   Are Consumers More Satisfied?

In Chap. 1, we began the book with a review of the history of the American Customer Satisfaction Index (ACSI). We discussed the genesis of the ACSI project, arising in large part due to a recognition of a new kind of customer in a new kind of economy, a more empowered and more demanding consumer requiring more careful monitoring and management in order to secure loyalty and profitability for the firm. Yet the concept of "customer satisfaction"—its importance and its benefits to a company—is certainly more than 25 years old. Indeed, "satisfying customers" has been a focus and core objective of American companies—and companies all around the world, large and small—for nearly a century and a half. Montgomery Ward's famous promise— "satisfaction guaranteed or your money back"—still resonates in the minds of consumers today, nearly 150 years after it first appeared in 1875. And herein lies the enduring power of the customer satisfaction concept; while marketing metrics have come and gone over the years, the satisfaction concept has endured. This is precisely because satisfaction exists in the minds of consumers—both consciously and unconsciously—as the most critical, comprehensive, and final evaluation of a company and its brands, products, and services.

As we also discussed in Chap. 1, at the time the ACSI project was founded in 1994 the stakes for companies to satisfy customers were becoming greater than ever before, and those stakes have only risen in the last quarter of a century. Indeed, consumers themselves are even more powerful today than they were just 25, 20, 10, or even only 5 years ago. Due to the rapidly changing consumer landscape, and particularly the innovations in information and communications technology that we have discussed in various ways in other chapters as well, today's consumers are: better able to research goods and services before buying, and thus better informed; better able to identify and select goods and services that meet their particular needs and that (at least potentially) prove more satisfying; in a position to more effectively air grievances to both companies and other consumers when dissatisfied; and better able to identify alternative suppliers of a good or service and defect to a competitor when displeased. Given these customer-empowering circumstances, it could be argued that now, finally, the consumer is truly "sovereign"—or at least more so than ever before.[1] And companies, or at least those with any hope of surviving, are aware of the increased power consumers have in the international marketplace. Whereas in the past, one dissatisfied customer was unlikely to have much of an effect on the marketplace, that one customer today could potentially have significant impact on companies' production, other consumers' sentiments, and the longevity of the company as a competitor in the market.

Given the greater and still-growing power of consumers, one might expect companies to have responded over time by providing increasingly satisfying goods and services, over both the longer and the nearer-terms. That is, as goal-driven organizations seek to maintain their market share relative to competitors (via defensive marketing) and to grow it wherever possible (via offensive marketing), providing a more powerful type of consumer with more of what they want (satisfaction) as a means for achieving either goal is the rational response. Yet companies do not or cannot always act rationally. Sometimes they cannot discern the correct response to dynamic conditions evolving around them, and at other times that response is too expensive or otherwise impossible to enact. This raises the question: Has customer satisfaction actually improved since the ACSI project started in 1994? A quarter of a century of ACSI data provide an interesting story, one that has significant implications for the likely mass customization, individualized customer approach expected in the future.

According to ACSI data, aggregate national customer satisfaction (ACSI) has improved significantly over the last quarter of a century. Figure 5.1 shows data for the ACSI index—our customer satisfaction metric—across all major economic sectors and industries in the U.S. economy between 1994 and 2017. In 1994, ACSI registered an initial score of 74.2. After dropping significantly from 1994 to 1997 to an all-time low of 70.7, much like consumer perceptions of quality over the same period, ACSI followed a mostly upward trajectory—with the exception of only a few significant setbacks in 2001 and 2004, and a fairly large and sustained decline that began in 2013. ACSI rapidly rebounded from that last large dip and peaked at a score of 77.0 in early

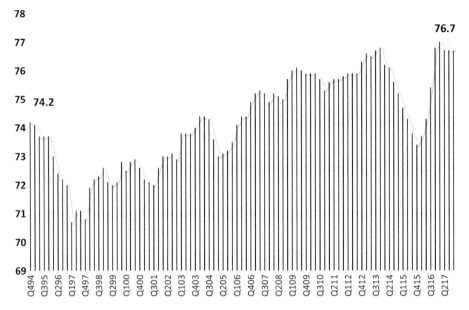

Fig. 5.1 National customer satisfaction (ACSI), 1994–2017. (Source: Authors' creation from American Customer Satisfaction Index data and methods)

2017, the same year consumer perceptions of value peaked (see more on perceptions of value in Chap. 4). Over the full time series, national ACSI has gained 2.5 points or 3.4%, a statistically significant and relatively sizable improvement in the satisfaction of the average American consumer.

In Chaps. 2, 3 and 4, we have discussed national-level changes in consumer perceptions of expectations, quality and value, and how those perceptions have varied over time. Additionally, in Chap. 3 we discussed in some detail a perennial finding from the ACSI data—that across virtually all measured industries and a substantial majority of companies, consumer perceptions of quality outweigh perceptions of value as a driver or determinant of customer satisfaction. In other words, with few exceptions, customer satisfaction responds most noticeably and significantly to improvements in the performance of goods and services (quality) than to strategies centered in discounting and price manipulation (value). Furthermore, while expectations are certainly important for framing consumers' experiences and how satisfaction judgments are formed, they have little direct effect on customer satisfaction, at least relative to quality or value. The quarterly national-level results for these variables over the past 25 years confirm that these findings apply to the aggregate level of data as well; both quarterly changes and levels of these variables (either contemporaneously or as lagged/leading indicators) show that the most important driver of ACSI is quality, with value next and expectations bringing up the rear.

However, in Chap. 4 we focused on how, over the last quarter-century, perceived value has grown the most among the national ACSI model variables, while consumer perceptions of quality have been virtually unchanged. We asserted that companies appear to be passing savings from new efficiencies in production and operations along to consumers, and consumers view this as a significant improvement to the value proposition. These 25-year-changes are reproduced again in Fig. 2.2.

The national-level changes in quality, value, and satisfaction since 1994 lead to a fairly straightforward—but vitally important—conclusion about what firms, and the economy as a whole, have focused on toward improving customer satisfaction over this time. That is, given that customer expectations have a small effect on customer satisfaction, especially when compared with quality and value, and that quality is nearly flat over the 25-year period, gains in satisfaction have been driven almost exclusively by stronger customer perceptions of value. Quality, as we said before, has the potential to have a greater effect on satisfaction (technically, the econometric results strongly support this cause-and-effect logic), but given the relative flatness of the level of quality perceptions among customers in the last 25 years, value has been the variable with the most impact on satisfaction. And since consumer perceptions of value in ACSI (as we described in Chaps. 1 and 4) are measured as the ratio of price paid to quality received, and consumer perceptions of quality are unchanged, these results suggest that companies have focused first and foremost on pricing as a means for better satisfying consumers.

There are a variety of explanations for why the improvement in satisfaction over the last 25 years has been predominantly value-driven. Yet one stands out as the most likely. As discussed in Chap. 4, changes in the efficiency of production, operations, and both product and service delivery, along with the oft-discussed advantages of globalization, have created opportunities for companies to pass cost savings on to customers in the form of lower prices without harming profitability. The two most important and oft-mentioned firms in this regard are Amazon and Walmart, both of which have, at various times, been credited with almost-singlehandedly suppressing inflation in the U.S. economy, both by cutting prices and by forcing competitors to respond in kind with lower prices. The result of this, when combined with other factors, of course, has been pronounced; average annual inflation has been historically low over the past 30 years.

The fact that price and value improvements are mostly responsible for improvements in customer satisfaction over the past 25 years, and not improvements to product or service quality (which would be more logically expected, and in some way is assumed by managers in many companies), raises questions about the future. Most critically, we should ask: Is this source of improved customer satisfaction sustainable? Or will the efficiencies that made controlling prices possible eventually reach a plateau, forcing companies to once again raise prices to maintain financial performance goals and keep shareholders and investors happy? And if customer satisfaction cannot be further increased or even maintained via this particular value driver, what are the potential consequences for the economy? It is this final, extremely important question that we address at the end of Chap. 5.

5.2   Satisfaction Gainers and Leaders, Losers and Laggards

Based on what we have learned in Chaps. 2, 3 and 4, there is little reason to believe that customer satisfaction is equally high or low, or increasing or declining equally, across distinct industries. The marketplace is dynamic and so are economic sectors and, especially, industries. There are oftentimes stark contrasts across industries and companies vis-à-vis customer expectations, perceptions of quality, and perceptions of value, as we have seen, and it is reasonable to suspect that the same exists in regard to customer satisfaction. But even considering only our discussions so far in Chap. 5, the fact that improvements in consumer perceptions of price and value have been largely responsible for driving gains in aggregate customer satisfaction suggests that satisfaction has evolved differently across distinct industries, as not all industries have experienced the same structural changes that have held prices in check and enhanced consumer perceptions of value. So where is customer satisfaction highest and lowest, and where has it increased (or declined) the most over the past decade, a period during which aggregate national-level satisfaction increased 1.3%? Table 5.1 shows customer satisfaction scores for all of the industries currently measured in ACSI, ranked from highest to lowest, and with the change (and growth rank) in score over the last ten years.

A few industries that should be familiar at this point sit atop the heap and lead the others in ACSI. Indeed, while the order is slightly different, the top three industries in customer satisfaction are the same top three that lead in both quality and value: one durable goods manufacturer, televisions and video players at 85, and two nondurable goods manufacturers, breweries and soft drinks, both at 84. Of the 14 industries that make-up the top (roughly)

Table 5.1 Industry customer satisfaction, ten-year changes, and growth rank

Sector	Industry	Customer satisfaction (ACSI) 2017 (0–100)	Ten-Year change (%)	Growth rank
Manufacturing-durables	Televisions & video players	85	2	14
Manufacturing-nondurables	Breweries	84	1	20
Manufacturing-nondurables	Soft drinks	84	1	21
Retail trade	Internet retail	82	0	22
Finance & insurance	Credit unions	82	−2	37
Finance & insurance	Banks	81	8	4
Transportation & warehousing	Consumer shipping	81	−1	32
Manufacturing-durables	Automobiles & light vehicles	81	−1	33
Manufacturing-nondurables	Food processing	81	−2	38
Manufacturing-nondurables	Athletic shoes	80	1	19
Manufacturing-nondurables	Apparel	80	0	23
Manufacturing-durables	Household appliances	80	0	24
Finance & insurance	Property & casualty insurance	80	−1	34
Manufacturing-nondurables	Personal care products	80	−6	44
Manufacturing-durables	Wireless telephones	79	11	2
Finance & insurance	Internet investment services	79	7	6
Accommodation & food services	Internet travel services	79	5	7
Retail trade	Supermarkets	79	4	11
Retail trade	Specialty retail stores	79	4	12
Retail trade	Health & personal care stores	79	1	17
Accommodation & food services	Limited service restaurants	79	1	18
Telecommunications & information	Computer software	78	10	3
Finance & insurance	Life insurance	78	0	25
Accommodation & food services	Full service restaurants	78	−3	39
Energy utilities	Cooperative utilities	78	−5	41
Retail trade	Department & discount stores	77	4	9
Manufacturing-durables	Personal computers	77	4	10

(continued)

Table 5.1 (continued)

Sector	Industry	Customer satisfaction (ACSI) 2017 (0–100)	Ten-Year change (%)	Growth rank
Health care & social assistance	Ambulatory care	77	−5	42
Retail trade	Gasoline service stations	76	3	13
Accommodation & food services	Hotels	76	1	16
Telecommunications & information	Internet search engines & information	76	−5	43
Transportation & warehousing	Airlines	75	21	1
Health care & social assistance	Hospitals	75	0	26
Telecommunications & information	Internet news & opinion	75	0	27
Energy utilities	Municipal utilities	74	1	15
Energy utilities	Investor-owned utilities	74	0	28
Telecommunications & information	Wireless telephone service	73	7	5
Telecommunications & information	Internet social media	73	4	8
Finance & insurance	Health insurance	73	0	29
Transportation & warehousing	U.S. postal service	73	−1	35
Public administration	Public administration	71	0	31
Telecommunications & information	Fixed-line telephone service	70	−4	40
Telecommunications & information	Subscription TV	64	0	30
Telecommunications & information	Internet service providers (ISPs)	64	−2	36

Source: Authors' creation from American Customer Satisfaction Index data and methods

third in customer satisfaction, with scores of 80 or higher, nine are manufacturing industries, an even stronger concentration of this particular sub-set of industries at the top in customer satisfaction than we observed vis-à-vis consumer perceptions of quality. In Chap. 3 we suggested reasons why these industries excel in offering high quality—a focus on (often automated) production processes, rather than customer service delivery where quality is less "controllable"—and these same explanations (along with the lower price-point, greater competition, and easier switching in some of these industries) explain the stronger customer satisfaction as well.

The bottom-performers in customer satisfaction should look familiar at this point as well, as the two "basement spots" in ACSI are occupied once again by two oft-reviled industries: internet service providers (ISPs) and subscription TV (cable and satellite), both with ACSI scores of 64. These two industries also score at the bottom for both customer perceptions of quality and value, and when coupled with their general reputation as poor performers—for reasons discussed in earlier chapters, including regular service disruptions, dramatic increases in prices, widespread merger activity, and decentralized customer service delivery—seeing them at the bottom in customer satisfaction comes as little surprise.

In terms of changes and improvements over the last ten years, one industry stands out as the most improved, nearly doubling the second-largest improvement by an industry: commercial airlines, an industry that has gained a whopping 21% in the ACSI index since 2008. Because airlines improved the most in both quality and value as well, this huge leap in customer satisfaction is likewise not shocking. The wireless telephones industry experienced the second largest growth in ACSI over this ten-year period, improving 11% to an ACSI score of 79. This rapid and dramatic growth is not surprising either, given that this period coincides almost perfectly with the introduction of modern smartphones to the mass consumer market (the first Apple iPhone having been released in late 2007), which dramatically changed (and improved and expanded) user interactions with their mobile devices and changed the products all manufacturers now offer. There is also more flexibility to start and end wireless services between competitors, giving customers more options as well as opportunities to be satisfied in their own unique ways.

Finally, the industries where ACSI has declined the most over this decade is personal care and cleaning products, down 6% to an ACSI score of 80. While still in the top-third of all measured industries, consumers are far less pleased with these household products—such as soap, shampoo, household cleaning products, among myriad products in this category—than they were a decade ago. The second largest decline for an industry is somewhat more surprising, coming for internet search engines and information, which falls to a score of 76. Given that the same company dominated the industry in 2008 as does now—Google—deteriorating satisfaction for this one company is responsible for most of the decline. Perhaps the monopolistic tendencies (few search options) and privacy concerns in the online search engine and information industry create uneasiness today that customers did not think about or know of a decade ago.

Who Can (and Can't) Get Some Satisfaction?

Which companies provide the most satisfaction to their customers? The leader in customer satisfaction is chicken sandwich-maker Chick-fil-A, with a score of 87. While controversial with some segments of the population for its outspoken stand on social and religious issues (and the fact that it is closed on Sundays), the fast food restaurant is best known for its great food and outstanding customer service. This strong satisfaction has resulted in far-better-than-industry growth over the last several years. Three companies are tied for second in satisfaction at 86: chocolate giant Hershey, supermarket Publix, and Toyota (for Toyota and Lexus brands).

At the other end of the spectrum, the two companies anchoring the bottom— tied for the lowest customer satisfaction at 56—come from the same industry and offer similar services in (roughly) the same way: Mediacom and Frontier Communications, the former for its subscription TV service, the latter for its ISP offerings. Given what we have seen in prior chapters on the bottom-basement quality and value for these companies and industries as a whole, and will see in Chap. 6 on complaints, we are on solid ground declaring the subscription TV and ISP companies, taken together, as those that consumers most love to hate.

5.3 Customer Satisfaction as a Macroeconomic Indicator

How important is customer satisfaction and satisfaction measurement, really? As we have discussed, we know satisfaction measurement is used by innumerable companies in the U.S. and around the world as an important metric of consumer perceptions of their experiences, one that has been tracked by many companies for decades and remains a key piece of information for companies' decision-makers.[2] In Chaps. 7 and 8, we will also examine more thoroughly the links between customer satisfaction and repeat business, and through it to central financial performance metrics for companies and industries, such as market share, revenue growth, earnings, and stock market returns. But here let us ask a slightly different question: Does customer satisfaction matter to the economy as a whole? Should anyone beyond market and customer-centric researchers working inside a company—and that company's leadership, shareholders, and customers—care about the satisfaction of private sector companies? The answers to these questions require us to examine the value of aggregate customer satisfaction for understanding macroeconomic phenomena.

As such, in what follows we examine the relationship between national customer satisfaction as measured by ACSI and consumer spending growth (and relatedly, gross domestic product growth), and between ACSI and the national unemployment rate. In both of these cases, the relationship between customer satisfaction and these crucial macroeconomic indicators for a country points to customer satisfaction's importance not only for companies seeking long-term financial success, but also as a leading macroeconomic indicator with significant consequences for understanding the health and prospects of entire national economies. We begin with economic growth and the customer satisfaction-consumer spending relationship.

The economic importance of consumer spending growth can hardly be overstated. In the U.S., consumer spending represents about 70% of total gross domestic product (GDP). Given this massive connection between consumer spending and the economy, it is logical that changes in consumer spending are closely monitored by public policymakers, economists, and companies large and small. Indeed, even fairly small changes in consumer spending can have substantial implications not only for the health of the economy, but also for the innumerable companies and industries that rely mostly or entirely on consumer expenditures to survive. Reports of declining or potentially slowing consumer expenditures will often cause managers and firms to adapt their strategies in several ways. For instance, concerns about future consumer spending may cause an organization to be reluctant to make long-term commitments to new product development or new advertising campaigns, switching instead to tactics they believe will drive short-term sales while consumers struggle (e.g., price discounting). Likewise, retailers might adjust not only their pricing strategy but also their product portfolio in the wake of an anticipated reduction in consumer spending, paring-back on higher-priced brands and models for increased production of less expensive "basics." As consumer spending improves or is expected to grow more rapidly, managers might be disposed to make the opposite adjustments.

Given this, it is critical for a variety of actors to be able to anticipate movements in consumer spending. However, consumer spending growth has proven very difficult to predict. For many years, starting in the middle of the twentieth century, the most renowned economists working in this area had come to believe that consumer spending was a "random walk," with no exogenous variable reliably able to predict and forecast its changes. This implied that future consumer spending was a function only of current consumption and that all other information was irrelevant. Some studies of consumer-related variables, such as consumer sentiment, contradicted this argument and showed some ability to forecast spending growth, leading economists and marketers to attempt to do so.[3] Importantly, one variable—customer satisfaction—has been found to be positively predictive of spending growth—that is, as satisfaction improves in one quarter, spending tends to also improve (or improve more strongly) in the next quarter. This relationship is illustrated in Fig. 5.2.[4]

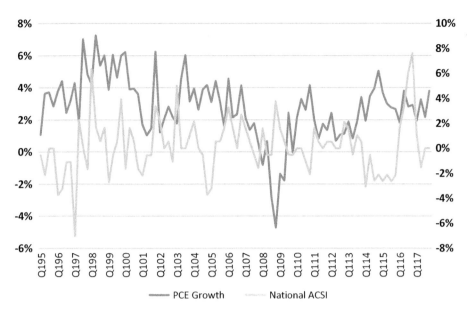

Fig. 5.2 National ACSI and PCE (consumer spending, lagged) growth. (Source: Authors' creation from American Customer Satisfaction Index data and methods)

Why does improving customer satisfaction tend to result in stronger consumer spending growth? The answer to this question is straightforward, intuitive, and difficult to deny. In short, a consumer's level of anticipated (future) satisfaction with goods and services, estimated based on past experiences with those goods and services, is positively related to their willingness to pay for them again in the future, and perhaps even to purchase more frequently and/or to buy other goods. A positive outcome from a buyer-seller transaction makes both parties in the exchange more inclined to repeat the experience, leading to both more production and more consumption, while a negative outcome is likely to have the opposite effect. As such, changes in customer satisfaction do not merely shift consumer preferences from one company to another, but they also affect the general willingness of households to "open their wallets" and spend more. Since its inception, national customer satisfaction as measured by ACSI has accounted for more of the variation in future spending growth than any other factor, including widely tracked metrics like consumer sentiment. Therefore, not only is customer satisfaction vital to measure at the company and industry levels, to understand success with a company's customers and success relative to competitors, but also in the aggregate, as it can help understand what is coming for the economy at large.

And the story does not end there. Not only has the national ACSI customer satisfaction variable been shown to be predictive of spending growth, it is also

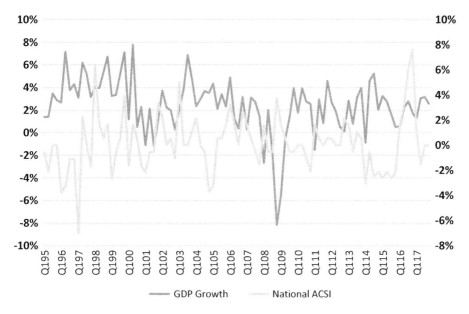

Fig. 5.3 National ACSI and GDP (gross domestic product) growth. (Source: Authors' creation from American Customer Satisfaction Index data and methods)

related to the broader gross domestic product of total national economic growth. Obviously, the explanation for ACSI as a predictor of GDP growth lies in the relationship between ACSI and consumer spending. Consumer spending is a component of GDP and accounts for some 70% of it, and thus aggregate customer satisfaction is likely to be correlated with GDP, even though GDP contains components (like government spending and international accounts) that are only loosely related to consumer perceptions of their domestic private sector experiences. Figure 5.3, now showing contemporaneous changes in customers' satisfaction and GDP, illustrates this relationship.

Taking these two sets of findings together (consumer spending growth and national economic growth), they reveal that the importance of customer satisfaction and satisfaction measurement extends well beyond the micro level or the interests of any one individual firm. Rather, satisfaction is critical for both marketers and public policymakers in forecasting future consumer behavior, and through this overall economic growth. The implications of these findings for actors at all levels of the economy cannot be overstated. In the final chapter, Chap. 9, we will extend upon this finding (among others) when discussing the future of customer satisfaction and satisfaction measurement as a national imperative in a highly competitive, increasingly globalized and interconnected economic ecosystem.

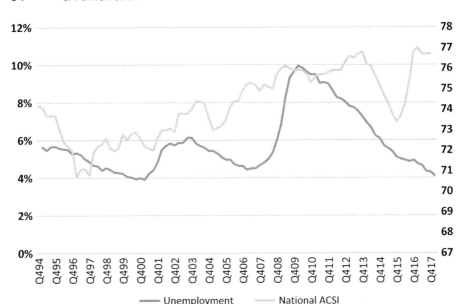

Fig. 5.4 National ACSI and unemployment (lagged). (Source: Authors' creation from American Customer Satisfaction Index data and methods)

Let us turn now to another interesting and important finding from the national ACSI customer satisfaction data collected over the last 25 years: the relationship between unemployment and customer satisfaction. To begin, Fig. 5.4 shows this relationship—in this case, between levels of national ACSI and levels of (lagged) unemployment—since 1994.

As we discussed earlier, customer satisfaction tends to precede and predict economic growth. More satisfied customers tend to be more likely to open their wallets and spend; even absent rising income, low interest rates and "cheap money" allow consumers to debt-finance goods and services when interested in spending, and conversely to refuse to do so when unhappy with their experiences. Companies respond to this increased desire to spend rationally, producing more goods and more satisfying goods to meet these demands, leading to even more satisfaction and spending. One might expect, then, that improvements in customer satisfaction lead to a never-ending positive feedback loop, with more satisfaction leading to more and better and cheaper products, in turn leading to more satisfaction, and so on ad infinitum. Yet ACSI data show that this is not always the case, and that an important external factor tends to intervene and interrupt this positive feedback loop at some point: the unemployment rate. More directly, ACSI data show that when the unemployment rate begins to decrease—when fewer people are unemployed and unable to find work—and is driven to significantly lower levels (typically by economic growth), aggregate customer satisfaction begins to decline as a consequence.

Why does lower unemployment lead to declining customer satisfaction? After all, low unemployment and a tighter labor market are usually praised as positives for an economy and a society, as signs of general social prosperity and a strong economy. For many companies, however, they also present challenges. When the labor market tightens, many workers leave their jobs to seek new, better positions. It is typically the case that, as unemployment declines, the number of people quitting their job spikes. Many of these "quitters" do so because they already have or think they can more easily find better pay at a more "prestigious" and higher-paying position, a position more aligned with their long-term career goals, and so forth. And this is where things begin to get difficult for firms trying to satisfy consumers, and in the aggregate for the economy as a whole.

When workers leave one position for another, it is oftentimes bad for consumers. Many lower-paying and less prestigious jobs are customer-facing (e.g., cashiers, retail personnel, call center staff), and thus many of the job-quitters come from this category of job position. These employees need to be replaced, of course, but because of the already tight labor market, options are limited. These workers are then often replaced by new employees with less (or no) experience, and in many cases, with general qualifications that leave them less-well-prepared to offer strong service to customers. In many cases, these open positions also go unfulfilled for extended periods. The job-hoppers moving up also enter their new positions in need of training, a process that always takes some time, and if these new positions are customer-facing, this too can have negative effects for customer service and consumers.

So, a strong economy driven by more satisfied consumers can sometimes contain the seeds for its own (if only temporary) demise, a victim of its own success, driving unemployment down and planting and creating the conditions for customer dissatisfaction. Yet it should be noted that the economy today is markedly different than it was over the first 10 or 15 years of ACSI measurement, and the massive changes it has undergone could forestall some of the historically observed negative effects of low unemployment on customer service and satisfaction in the future. For instance, many companies have dramatically improved their employee training programs. Likewise, automation and other self-service technologies have eliminated many customer-facing positions entirely, and this too may soften the blow of the glut of new, inexperienced employees across the economy in the future.

In the final section of this chapter, when pondering the future of customer satisfaction, we will discuss how advances in automation and artificial intelligence may provide better consumer perceptions of quality alongside the already extant better prices and value. This phenomenon might also counteract the negative effect unemployment has been observed to have on customer satisfaction over the years ahead. But for the time being, a strong labor market should serve as a warning to firms that they may have difficulty maintaining the same level of customer service and satisfaction that has allowed them to prosper in the recent past, with effects that can be felt across the whole of an economy.

5.4   Mergers and Acquisitions and Satisfaction

Mergers and acquisitions (M&A) are a ubiquitous feature of the modern economic landscape. M&A activity has a huge impact on economic growth worldwide. While less common in the years following the Great Recession (2008–2009), M&A activity rapidly rebounded thereafter, and the total value of M&A in 2015 nearly topped the record set in 2007. Though not quite as robust over the next two years, M&A continued at a very brisk pace in both 2016 and 2017. While mergers are appealing to firms for a number of reasons, the most basic and common objective for companies that pursue this growth strategy is to increase economies of scale, that is, to improve profitability by offering products and/or services to a larger number of customers while holding fixed costs constant, or actually decreasing them due to the same economies of scale. In short, M&As allow a company to instantly add a significant number of new customers to its customer base (i.e., customer acquisition) while avoiding traditional customer acquisition costs, and ideally to improve its total revenue, its profit margin, its market share, and its market value.

But while mostly adored in the corporate world, mergers are not always loved by consumers. Indeed, many of the consequences of M&As can be seen as detrimental to the consumer experience and, as illustrated nicely by the ultimately failed Comcast-Time Warner merger example from 2015, are sometimes actively opposed by consumers and consumer advocacy groups, along with politicians and anti-trust regulators.[5] This anti-merger impulse has been validated from a financial perspective in some studies as well, with one indicating that more than 60% of M&As actually *destroy value* for investors and shareholders.[6] Likewise, it has been borne out by customer satisfaction data. Analyses of ACSI data have shown that satisfaction does indeed tend to decline significantly for customers of all of the companies involved in a merger in its wake (for several years thereafter), with the effect being most pronounced in services industries. The "why" of this effect is less certain, but most likely has to do with a number of interconnected factors.

First, some of the deleterious effects of M&A on customer satisfaction may be only temporary, with satisfaction dropping as the two companies work to integrate core systems and production processes, or while consumers grow accustomed to their status as a customer of a new company or brand through no choice of their own (e.g., Northwest Airlines customers having to adopt Delta as their airline frequent-flyer brand after the companies merged in 2008). Yet some of the effects seem to be longer-term, causing tangible problems with the goods and services companies deliver. For example, the gain in economies of scale in an M&A scenario can also result in *dis*-economies of scale that impact the consumer, where increased organizational complexity negatively impacts the consumer experience. Moreover, mergers often result in the permanent scaling-back of some services; when two brick-and-mortar retailers or two banks merge, for example, they often shutter a number of physical locations to improve efficiency and profitability, leaving a larger number of customers with a smaller number of locations from which to receive services.

Declining customer satisfaction following a merger may also be related to the kinds of companies that tend to merge in the first place. As in the example of the proposed though ultimately unsuccessful Comcast-Time Warner merger, these amalgamations often involve two companies that both offer poor customer service to begin with. Facing high customer churn and high customer acquisition costs, these poor performing companies use M&A as a relatively inexpensive strategy for "buying" a large number of new captive customers, rather than winning them through marketing and advertising spending, or retaining them with good, satisfying service. Consequently, rather than improving the situation over the long term, the merger usually only exacerbates the problems. There is little reason to believe that two dissatisfying companies merged into one would be anything more than the sum of their parts, and ACSI data provide no evidence to the contrary.

But going beyond the somewhat unique case of merging firms and the effect of M&A activity on satisfaction, these lessons can also be applied more broadly. Any company that plans to expand or is already expanding organically (i.e., is adding a substantial number of new customers to its portfolio) should be mindful of maintaining customer satisfaction performance during this process. This is especially true if growth is happening rapidly. As the number of customers to be served increases for any company, whether that company is making a product or providing a service, the increase in demand can often lead to system load beyond the capacity of the company, and consequently degrade the customer experience and consumer satisfaction. In sum, carefully minding the consumer experience as new customers are added is vital, whether this comes via organic growth or M&A.

5.5 Customer Satisfaction "Death Rattle" and Other Interpretational Challenges

While customer satisfaction measurement is vital for almost every firm—except for the rare case of the pure monopolist perhaps—and while its results can be very useful for aiding with strategic decision-making, there are times when the data gleaned from this measurement can be deceiving. Indeed, there are circumstances when customer satisfaction scores can fool those analyzing the data into drawing bad conclusions that paint a picture from reality, at least if the data is not viewed in the proper context. We briefly examine some of these pitfalls here. While these are certainly not all of the pitfalls that a firm can experience when measuring and managing customer satisfaction, they are easy-to-understand examples that reinforce the importance of considering context when interpreting customer satisfaction data.

Let us start with our first pitfall, which we can call the "When Better Is Bad" problem. Put another way, our question is: Can improving customer satisfaction scores ever be indicative of a bad or worsening situation? Superficially, the answer to this question would seem to be "absolutely not!", as the goal of virtually every company with growth and prosperity in mind is to at least maintain their existing level of satisfaction, if not improve it incrementally over time. Indeed, much of what we have written to this point in the book and will write hereafter has given the impression that every company should always prefer better satisfaction results, as typically this is indicative of stronger performance in those consumer perceptions that drive satisfaction (such as quality and value), and in turn predictive through satisfaction of stronger customer loyalty and financial performance (see Chaps. 7 and 8). But this is not always true. Indeed, and as strange as this might sound to the broader mission and theme of this book, a company in enormous trouble, and sometimes even a dying company that is facing bankruptcy and possible dissolution in the near future, can sometimes see its satisfaction performance *improve*, even if only temporarily. The explanation for this rare occurrence is quite simple.

When a company is losing market share rapidly and substantially, it is most often the case that the least satisfied customers are the customers leaving first. Conversely, the customers who stay the longest (even as others are leaving in droves) tend to be the most satisfied and/or the most brand-loyal (e.g., BlackBerry customers). Yet in most satisfaction surveys, only current or recent customers are interviewed regarding their satisfaction, as these are the consumers that matter most. For most firms, it makes little sense to survey an ex-customer who has not purchased from the company in years, as they cannot tell you much about the products/services you are now offering with which you are trying to improve perceptions. So, customers who have already defected are not interviewed in most surveys, and as mentioned, they tend to be the least satisfied. And with these least happy customers gone, and the smaller aggregate of customers that remains tending to be the diehard loyalists, oftentimes companies that are seeing a rapid decrease in their market share will simultaneously see an upward spike in their satisfaction performance based on nothing more than the changing composition and size of their customer portfolio.

On top of this, and often in addition to it, dying companies will often attempt a last-ditch effort to stave off financial ruin and raise revenue through more extreme price-cutting, which can likewise have a positive short-term effect on satisfaction (as a driver from perceptions of value). As an example of this phenomenon, consider one-time retailing juggernaut Kmart. While being one of the revenue-leading discount retailers when ACSI measurement began in 1994, the company typically underperformed in satisfaction and sat near the bottom of the industry. Then in 2001, the company's satisfaction performance as measured by ACSI leapt to an all-time high, a huge and statistically significant improvement. But total sales and revenue were already beginning to suffer in 2001, and the Kmart found itself unable to pay its vendors. Early in 2002, Kmart was forced to declare bankruptcy, the largest retail bankruptcy in U.S. history at the time. How did these two events, Kmart's leaping satisfaction score and its entry into bankruptcy, coincide?

As executives inside Kmart began to notice slowing sales and many customers being lost to faster-growing competitor Walmart, Kmart responded by slashing prices in order to maintain revenue and hopefully pay its vendors. For those diehard Kmart lovers who had stuck by the company, the effect was a double-positive—lower prices for their merchandise, and emptier stores in which to buy and receive customer service. Satisfaction increased, but this was only illusory. Kmart would emerge from bankruptcy 16 months later, merge with Sears soon thereafter, and the combined company continues to shrink and struggle mightily today (with hundreds of store closings announced as this book goes to print).

Our second pitfall is more a truism than anything else, one that will likely make most customer-experience researchers and managers cringe, because it makes their job more difficult: "The Satisfaction Target is always Moving." While goals can be set based on some initial starting point for customer satisfaction, with target levels to be achieved identified relative to the performance of competitors, there are times when the target moves mid-stream. Sometimes, a company might improve its satisfaction to a new level that had represented the goal at the beginning, only to find that all of its competitors have improved as well, leaving it no better off (relatively speaking) than before. Conversely, a company may find its satisfaction flat when improvement had been the goal, but based on declining scores among its key competitors, its relative performance is now better (this phenomenon was seen with perceptions of quality in Chap. 3). In this latter case, while the goal of realizing improvement in satisfaction is not realized, the most important goal of improving relative to competitors has happened, nonetheless.

In short, customer satisfaction measurement is almost never a static process that exists within a vacuum. The notion of levels, changes, and impacts that we discussed in the Appendix to Chap. 1 on the science of customer satisfaction is critically important to achieve reliability and validity in measurement, implications, and astute strategic decision-making. As in virtually any real-world application, the context within which that customer satisfaction measurement is occurring is vital to understand. And more than anything else, these realities require more than one-time, one-off measurement projects, at least for big firms servicing large, complex, diverse, and evolving groups of consumers. Rather, measurement must be an ongoing process based on flexible goals and near-constant attention.

5.6   Perfect Satisfaction: Future Fact or Science Fiction?

"Futurists" are everywhere today. Most of them focus on the impending upheaval to society soon to be unleashed by dramatic new technological developments, and particularly machine learning and artificial intelligence (AI). The most optimistic of these thinkers believe that we are just a few years away from creating machines as smart as humans—that is, to achieving computers with "human-level general intelligence".[7] Even the least optimistic experts working in this area point to the twenty-first century as the time when we are likely to achieve artificial general intelligence, spawning "thinking machines" that are at first as smart as the average human, and probably very soon thereafter, substantially smarter.[8] Setting aside the imagined scenario where these smart machines become "self-aware" and immediately seek to eliminate their human creators—what we might call the "Terminator Scenario"—the prospect of thinking machines and true artificial intelligence holds incredible promise vis-à-vis the business world in general and in providing satisfying goods and services to consumers. Customer service professionals are already keenly aware of this fact and are therefore giving it increased attention.[9]

Already today, humans are enjoying the fruits of technological innovation, as we have discussed at various points throughout this book. The enhanced efficiencies and information transparency spawned by the Information Age has allowed companies to offer better prices to consumers and better compete with other companies on price. We have likewise discussed, however, how some of these innovations have had a downward effect on consumer perceptions of quality. We love our better and cheaper goods—our thinner and lighter and cheaper-but-higher-quality TVs, for example—but many consumers are less pleased with how technology has impacted customer service delivery. Anyone that has tried to contact a company with a problem and reached only an automated call center and a "virtual agent" software system that can neither understand the nuances and complexity of our questions nor adequately reply to them will understand why many consumers have come to conclude that technology has demonstrably *worsened* customer service. These automated services may be cheaper for companies, and that may allow them to offer consumers better prices, but in the eyes of many consumers the experience is far worse.

In Chaps. 3 and 4, we discussed how price and consumer perceptions of value, rather than either improved customer expectations or, most importantly, consumer perceptions of quality, have driven improved satisfaction over the last 25 years. In the last chapter in particular, we wondered if this phenomenon was sustainable, if the economy could continue to provide even modest, incremental improvements in satisfaction via solely improvements to value and continue to pass these cost savings from new efficiencies on to consumers. Surely, at some point price-driven improvements in satisfaction will begin to drag on corporate profitability and lead to deteriorating satisfaction, absent concurrent improvements in quality. What might help the economy out of this dilemma? Like so many futurists suggest for all manner of dilemmas, the answer may very well lie in AI and machine learning.

AI and machine learning—and more specifically, forthcoming dramatic advances therein—could soon begin to deliver improved quality via better customer service and might do so without drastically undermining the improved price and value consumers are already seeing from technology. That is, most of the complaints consumers have with receiving customer service from a "damned machine" revolve not around the fact that the service provider is a computer per se, but rather because these automated systems are, relatively speaking, quite primitive. To put it bluntly, many of the AI systems used to deliver customer service today are actually pretty dumb. They are unable to understand many commands, often route the consumer to the wrong menu or person, and rarely anticipate new problems that may emerge for the customer during the interaction. Interactions with these systems regularly result in even more frustrated consumers demanding to "please, PLEASE, just let me talk to a person" after having already expended 10 or 20 minutes with nothing to show for it. While not universally true, certainly a substantial portion of automated customer service tools available today are poor and ineffective at resolving customer problems.

As a related example, consider what is perhaps the most ubiquitous and famous AI currently operating in the world today—Siri, the "virtual assistant" that comes standard with the Apple iPhone. For those of us that pre-date the iPhone as consumers, Siri is actually pretty amazing, capable of answering a bevy of questions via voice-prompted automated internet searches and performing other simple tasks for the user. Yet very few customer experience professionals (or anyone else for that matter) would suggest completely replacing human customer service personnel with Siri or anything like it. This is because, while an amazing innovation, especially compared to computer technology even just a decade ago, Siri is still very limited in what "she" can do; "she" often misunderstands the speaker, and even when understanding correctly, she is unable to provide an answer or provides irrelevant (and sometimes hilarious) responses to questions. Siri is an example of a very limited, "narrow" kind of AI that is typical of the systems now available and being deployed in customer service settings.

But now let us imagine Future Siri, a new version released 5 or 10 or 20 years from now. Future Siri has been updated with the latest advances coming out of AI and machine learning research. "She" is now as smart as you or I. Indeed, Future Siri is maybe even a little smarter, at least vis-à-vis completing a particular set of processes, rapidly and accurately understanding and responding to common questions, offering advice on how to resolve more complex problems (maybe with a product and service), and so forth. Future Siri is even able to think critically, understanding not only the nature of a problem someone is experiencing, but also anticipating how one possible solution could in fact exacerbate rather than solve the problem, or lead to new problems the customer has not considered. Maybe, for example, we are able to tell Future Siri our plans for the day—the things we have to do, the order we intend to do them in, and the time we have to complete them all—and ask her if the plan will work. Future Siri is smart enough to tell us that we will not have sufficient time, and then instruct us on how to reorder our plans and successfully accomplish everything we need to do in the time we have. In short, at this point Future Siri will have become at least as smart and, perhaps smarter than the average person, able to provide answers and assistance that is superior to what the person is able to do for themselves.

Now, what would it be like to receive customer service from Future Siri? Certainly, at the very least, to do so would be far superior to the automated voice recognition software with very limited capabilities available today. AI could—and according to those that specialize in this area, almost certainly will—advance enough to change how we as consumers perceive automated customer service. As AI advances to human-level intelligence, these applications will allow customer service to be delivered by programs that are at least as good as those delivered by a person, and in many cases probably significantly better, as Future Siri will not get tired, will not have an "off day," and will not suffer downtime due to illness.

Combining together what we have discussed vis-à-vis technology's positive effect on prices for consumers with the near-future improvements to the customer services it can offer, let us now ask a question: Could we be heading toward a world of "perfect customer satisfaction," one in which companies provide incrementally better pricing via enhanced efficiencies, but are also able to offer better and better services via smarter and smarter machines, and do so without having to spend substantially more on this improved quality or undermine the value proposition? Returning to our discussion of how declining unemployment often results in weakening customer satisfaction, here too AI could provide a solution. That is, because of better AI, a tightening labor market may no longer result in worsening service, with AI filling the gaps—even if only temporarily—caused by employees' job-hopping. AI does not quit when the market is good, and it would not need extensive training when replacing human service providers. While we cannot know for sure, certainly it appears that humans are closer to "perfect" customer satisfaction today than during any earlier economic era. But perfect customer satisfaction is also a function of customer expectations (and other variables), as the ACSI model in Fig. 1.1 indicates, so the reality of "perfect" customer satisfaction may sound too perfect!

Notes

1. The term "consumer sovereignty" was introduced in 1936 by economist William Harold Hutt in his book *Economists and the Public: A Study of Competition and Opinion*, to illustrate the ultimate power of consumers to control what goods and services capitalistic firms produce.
2. In one recent study, customer satisfaction was found to be the most-used marketing metric by managers when making decisions across a selection of large companies in multiple nations. Mintz, O., I. S. Currim, J. B. Steenkamp and M. de Jong (2020). "Managerial Metric Use in Marketing Decisions across 16 Countries: A Cultural Perspective," *Journal of International Business Studies*, Forthcoming.
3. See: Carroll, C. D., J. C. Fuhrer and D.W. Wilcox (1994). "Does Consumer Spending Forecast Household Spending? If So, Why?" *The American Economic Review*, 84(5), 1397–1408.
4. See: Fornell, Claes, Roland T. Rust and Marnik G. Dekimpe 2010. "The Effect of Customer Satisfaction on Consumer Spending Growth," *Journal of Marketing Research*, 47(1), 28–35.
5. Griswold, Alison. "The Most Hated Merger in America," *Slate.com*, April 24, 2015.
6. See: Lewis, A. and D. McKone. "So Many M&A Deals Fail Because Companies Overlook This Simple Strategy," *Harvard Business Review*, May 10, 2016. Accessed online at: https://hbr.org/2016/05/so-many-ma-deals-fail-because-companies-overlook-this-simple-strategy
7. For an example of an optimistic futurist, see: Kurzweil, Ray (2005). *The Singularity is Near: When Humans Transcend Biology*, Penguin Books: New York.
8. In 2013, a group of world-leading experts in AI were surveyed and asked to give an "optimistic," "realistic," and "pessimistic" estimate of when humanity would achieve "human-level machine intelligence," or computers as smart as the average human. The median "optimistic" estimate was 2020; the median "realistic" estimate was 2040; the median "pessimistic" estimate was 2075. Barrat, James (2013). *Our Final Invention: Artificial Intelligence and the End of the Human Era*, St. Martin's Press: New York.
9. For some examples, see: Kerravala, Z. "Why Customer Service Needs Artificial Intelligence," *CIO.com*, May 2, 2018. Accessed online at: https://www.cio.com/article/3269498/why-customer-service-needs-artificial-intelligence.html

References and Further Reading

Anderson, E. W., & Fornell, C. (2000). Foundations of the American Customer Satisfaction Index. *Total Quality Management, 11*(7), 869–882.

Anderson, E. W., Fornell, C., & Rust, R. T. (1997). Customer Satisfaction, Productivity and Profitability: Differences between Goods and Services. *Marketing Science, 16*(2), 129–145.

Anderson, E. W., & Sullivan, M. W. (1993). The Antecedents and Consequences of Customer Satisfaction for Firms. *Marketing Science, 12*(2), 125–143.

Carroll, C. D., Fuhrer, J. C., & Wilcox, D. W. (1994). Does Consumer Spending Forecast Household Spending? If So, Why? *The American Economic Review, 84*(5), 1397–1408.

Fornell, C. (1992). A National Customer Satisfaction Barometer: The Swedish Experience. *The Journal of Marketing, 56*(1), 6–21.

Fornell, C. (2001). The Science of Satisfaction. *Harvard Business Review, 79*(3), 120–121.

Fornell, C., Johnson, M. D., Anderson, E. W., Cha, J., & Bryant, B. E. (1996). The American Customer Satisfaction Index: Nature, Purpose and Findings. *Journal of Marketing, 60*(4), 7–18.

Fornell, C., Mithas, S., & Krishnan, M. S. (2005). Why Do Customer Relationship Management Applications Affect Customer Satisfaction? *Journal of Marketing, 69*(4), 201–209.

Fornell, C., Mithas, S., Morgeson, F. V., III, & Krishnan, M. S. (2006). Customer Satisfaction and Stock Price: High Returns, Low Risk. *Journal of Marketing, 70*(1), 3–14.

Griswold, A. (2015, April 24). The Most Hated Merger in America. *Slate.com.* Retrieved from https://slate.com/business/2015/04/comcast-time-warner-cable-merger-why-it-fell-apart.html

Hult, G. T. M., Morgeson, F. V., III, Morgan, N. A., Mithas, S., & Fornell, C. (2017). Do Managers Know What Their Customers Think and Why? *Journal of the Academy of Marketing Science, 45*(1), 37–54.

Hutt, W. H. (1936). *Economists and the Public: A Study of Competition and Opinion.* London: Jonathan Cape, Ltd.

Johnson, M. D., Hermann, A., & Gustafsson, A. (2002). Comparing Customer Satisfaction across Industries and Countries. *Journal of Economic Psychology, 23*(6), 749–769.

Keiningham, T. L., Cooil, B., Andreassen, T. W., & Aksoy, L. (2007). A Longitudinal Examination of Net Promoter and Firm Revenue Growth. *Journal of Marketing, 71*(3), 39–51.

Kerravala, Z. (2018, May 2). Why Customer Service Needs Artificial Intelligence, *CIO.com.* Retrieved from https://www.cio.com/article/3269498/why-customer-service-needs-artificial-intelligence.html

Kurzweil, R. (2005). *The Singularity is Near: When Humans Transcend Biology.* New York: Penguin Books.

Lewis, A., & McKone, D. (2016). So Many M&A Deals Fail Because Companies Overlook This Simple Strategy. *Harvard Business Review.* Retrieved from https://hbr.org/2016/05/so-many-ma-deals-fail-because-companies-overlook-this-simple-strategy

Mintz, O., Currim, I. S., Steenkamp, J. B., & de Jong, M. (2020). Managerial Metric Use in Marketing Decisions Across 16 Countries: A Cultural Perspective. *Journal of International Business Studies.* https://doi.org/10.1057/s41267-019-00259-z

Morgeson, F. V., III, Mithas, S., Keiningham, T. L., & Aksoy, L. (2011). An Investigation of the Cross-National Determinants of Customer Satisfaction. *Journal of the Academy of Marketing Science, 29*(2), 198–215.

Morgeson, F. V., III, Sharma, P. N., Tomas, G., & Hult, M. (2015). Cross-National Differences in Consumer Satisfaction: Mobile Services in Emerging and Developed Markets. *Journal of International Marketing, 23*(2), 1–24.

Oliver, R. L. (1997). *Satisfaction: A Behavioral Perspective on the Consumer*. New York: Irwin McGraw-Hill.

Solomon, M. (2018, December 11). AI (Artificial Intelligence) and The Customer Service Experience: 3 Key Principles. *Forbes.com*. Retrieved from https://www.forbes.com/sites/micahsolomon/2018/12/11/ai-artificial-intelligence-and-the-customer-service-experience-3-key-principles/#43815473e566

6

Customer Complaints: Learning to Love Your Angry Customers

Chapter Overview

In this chapter, we start by discussing changes in customer complaint behavior and the aggregate national complaint rate over the last 25 years. We test the premise that the internet, social media, and related channels have made complaining easier and more impactful, and thus complaint rates higher. We then turn to a detailed discussion of cross-industry differences in customer complaint rates and highlight how the nature of distinct economic sectors and the products and services consumed helps explain variations in complaint likelihood. This is followed by a review of why many (or most) dissatisfied customers choose not to complain at all, and the negative consequences of this fact for companies. Finally, we discuss the importance of complaint management for firms, a practice critical to converting dissatisfied customers into enduringly loyal ones and examine whether companies have improved their complaint management practices over the past decade. The chapter concludes with a brief discussion of the potential benefits for companies of maximizing customer complaint rates.

Key Conclusions

- While complaining may be easier than ever, since 1994 the national average complaint rate has declined dramatically, falling from 21.3% to 11.7% over the last 25 years—a 45.1% decline.
- Complaint rates vary dramatically across diverse economic industries, more so than for the other variables in the ACSI model. This variance can be

© The Author(s) 2020
C. Fornell et al., *The Reign of the Customer*, https://doi.org/10.1007/978-3-030-13562-1_6

explained by industry context, price, the perceived advantages of complaining, and related factors.

- Many dissatisfied customers—and in all likelihood, a majority of them across most companies and industries—fail to complain when unhappy, a fact that presents a significant risk to companies.
- Complaint handling by companies has improved over the last decade, perhaps suggesting that firms recognize the importance of complaint management in a more competitive economic landscape and have responded accordingly.

6.1 Are Customers Complaining More?

As we have discussed in earlier chapters, innovations in communications technology have fundamentally changed the modern economy. While we need not review the nature of these changes again, suffice it to say that they have resulted in an almost total restructuring of how companies identify, communicate with, advertise, and market to their customers. They have also changed how customers contact and interact with companies. For example, though once viewed primarily as avenues for informal personal interactions, social media websites—such as Facebook, Instagram, and Twitter—have fast become important vehicles for customers to communicate with companies about their experiences. When unhappy, these and other websites have made it dramatically easier for consumers to lodge "formal" complaints directly to a company via official and verified pages on the sites. When combined with channels like email and virtual chat, and a generally easier time finding corporate contact information and a venue by which to complain to a company because of the internet, it would certainly seem that the modern economy is more conducive to customer complaints than ever before. The days of hunting for a company's address, typing or hand-writing a "strongly worded" letter to a company that has made us mad, buying a stamp, mailing it, and then waiting on the off chance something comes of it are long gone.

Additionally, and maybe even more importantly, these same internet social media websites have made it far easier and decidedly more effective for dissatisfied customers to "informally" but publicly complain—via an amplified type of negative word-of-mouth—about companies when unhappy. Companies have come to expect this feedback and have developed strategies for managing these episodes when they do occur.[1] This is because today, unlike in years past, an angry customer can complain to a firm and also simultaneously to *millions of other consumers* about their dissatisfaction. Occasionally, this amplified complaining can create an "online firestorm" of negative pub-licity with immense financial consequences for a firm.[2] Indeed, the presence of social media has allowed complaining customers—or at the very least influ-ential ones like Kylie Jenner along with less famous consumers able to craft a compelling online story about a service failure, such as the "United Airlines Broke My Guitar Guy"[3]—to have an enormous impact on the economic for-tunes of companies they are displeased with. In early 2018, Jenner, with only a brief message to her millions of followers of just 18 words—"sooo does anyone else not open Snapchat anymore? Or is it just me… ugh this is so sad"—was able to eliminate billions of dollars of market value from a publicly traded company in a few hours.[4]

As recently as 15 or 20 years ago, marketers and market researchers largely agreed that customer complaints were, at best, an inconsistent and, at worst, a very imprecise indicator of consumer dissatisfaction. This is because research has shown that, at least in many cases and contexts, most dissatisfied custom-ers do not actually complain, a phenomenon and its consequences we will examine more fully in this chapter.[5] Thus while companies in many industries have long tracked and monitored complaints, and rightly so, market research-ers were always cautious when interpreting high or low or changing rates of complaints. But has this changed? Has the greater ease of lodging customer complaints, alongside a perceived increase in efficacy and value to the indi-vidual consumer of doing so in an era of amplified communication, changed this situation? Indeed, it might seem safe to conclude, given the ease with which consumers can now contact companies for any number of reasons, that more customers are complaining than ever before.

Figure 6.1 shows data for aggregate customer complaints across all major consumer sectors and industries in the U.S. economy between 1994 and 2017, measured in this case as a simple percentage of customers indicating that they "complained to the company" of which they were a customer.[6] In 1994, 21.3% of consumers reported complaining to the company they had purchased from and about which they were being interviewed. After a three-year period during which complaints steadily increased to a high of almost 25%, the national complaint rate has rapidly and steadily declined, resting at a mere 11.7%—or almost 10% points lower—at the end of 2017. This 45.1% decline in the complaint rate is by far the largest change among any of the ACSI model variables, even taking into consideration the different scale on which the customer complaint rate is measured relative to the others. In short, while customers may have far more efficient and simpler mechanisms through which to lodge complaints, and at least in some cases the activity could be viewed as more efficacious than ever before, it appears that these changes have

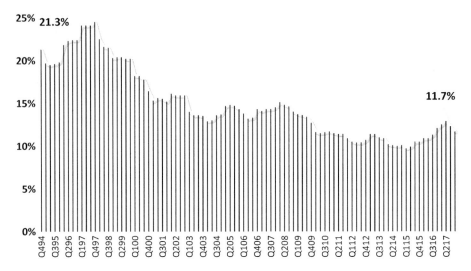

Fig. 6.1 National customer complaints, 1994–2017. (Source: Authors' creation from American Customer Satisfaction Index data and methods)

not resulted in a tsunami of consumer complaints. In fact, far fewer consumers are complaining today when compared to a quarter-century ago.

So why, contrary to what we might have expected, has the national customer complaint rate declined? In the first instance, some of this decline is almost certainly due to the improvement in customer satisfaction since 1994, as we discussed in Chap. 5. In the ACSI model, customer satisfaction tends to have a strong negative effect on the customer complaint rate, with happier, more satisfied customers less likely to complain. Therefore, improved satisfaction is predicted to and does result in fewer complaints. However, while the relatively modest improvement in satisfaction over this period likely explains some of the dip in complaints, it is insufficient to explain all of it. Simply put, it is virtually impossible that a 2.5-point improvement in customer satisfaction is responsible for a nearly 10%-point drop in the complaint rate, at either the company or the national aggregate level.

Alternatively, it is possible that consumers do not view the greater ease with which they can complain, mentioned above, as a reason to do so, but quite the opposite. That is, the ease with which consumers can now complain to companies might be perceived as a disincentive rather than an incentive to do so, precisely because "anyone can do it" and can do it easily. Thus, consumers view their one additional complaint in a (perceived) giant sea of complaints as little more than meaningless noise with little chance of having an effect. Finally, perhaps the improvement in the value proposition discussed in Chap. 4 is itself depressing complaints, as consumers are so much happier with the prices that they are paying that they feel a lesser need to seek redress and recompense when displeased, an important phenomenon we discuss more fully in this chapter.

Yet whatever the reason for the declining complaint rate, and the suggested causes that likely combine in some way to explain this phenomenon, we might nevertheless proceed to view it is a good thing, a positive development for the economy. After all, many or even most companies would regard a lower complaint rate as a positive development. Fewer complaining customers mean fewer contact centers and other resources devoted to managing these displeased consumers, and it could also indicate fewer service failures and stronger satisfaction. But is this really the case? Is it a good thing for firms, and the economy as a whole, to have fewer complaining customers? After examining and explaining cross-industry differences in complaint rates, we discuss the proportion of dissatisfied customers that actually take the time to complain, and how for companies in many industries a low and declining complaint rate should be viewed as a *negative* phenomenon.

6.2   Which Customers Complain Most, and Why?

While the aggregate national customer complaint rate has dipped substantially over the past 25 years, it would be wrong to assume that all economic industries are built alike, either in their absolute rate of complaint or in changes over the recent past. As we have seen in earlier chapters, consumer perceptions and behaviors tend to differ significantly across industries and do so for a variety of reasons. This is confirmed to be the case for customer complaints as well, as we see in Table 6.1, which shows industry complaint rates from low to high. Also included are changes over the last ten years, a period during which the national aggregate complaint rate declined more than 16%.

We will focus our analysis only on the percentage of complaints from low to high across industries, as both ten-year changes and the growth rank (excluded entirely from the table) are somewhat less meaningful due to the larger cross-industry variance and the yes-no (0–1) scale of the variable.[7] Doing so, we observe a huge range in the rate of complaints across industries. For two industries—internet social media and personal care products—virtually no customers complain, with just 1% of respondents indicating doing so over the prior 12 months. At the other end of the spectrum, for some industries

Table 6.1 Industry customer complaints and ten-year changes

Sector	Industry	Customer complaint rate 2017 (0–100%) (%)	Ten-Year change (%)
Telecommunications & information	Internet social media	1	−75
Manufacturing-nondurables	Personal care products	1	0
Telecommunications & information	Internet news & opinion	2	100
Manufacturing-nondurables	Food processing	3	0
Telecommunications & information	Internet search engines & information	4	0
Accommodation & food services	Full-service restaurants	5	−38
Retail trade	Gasoline service stations	5	−29
Manufacturing-nondurables	Soft drinks	5	150
Manufacturing-nondurables	Breweries	5	400
Telecommunications & information	Computer software	6	−67
Retail trade	Department & discount stores	6	−54
Health care & social assistance	Ambulatory care	6	−54
Manufacturing-durables	Televisions & video players	6	20
Manufacturing-nondurables	Apparel	6	200
Retail trade	Specialty retail stores	7	−42
Manufacturing-durables	Personal computers	8	−62
Energy utilities	Municipal utilities	8	−56
Retail trade	Supermarkets	8	−43
Retail trade	Health & personal care stores	8	−33
Health care & social assistance	Hospitals	8	−33
Finance & insurance	Property & casualty insurance	8	−27
Accommodation & food services	Limited service restaurants	8	−27
Finance & insurance	Life insurance	8	33
Manufacturing-nondurables	Athletic shoes	8	167
Finance & insurance	Credit unions	9	−25

(*continued*)

Table 6.1 (continued)

Sector	Industry	Customer complaint rate 2017 (0–100%) (%)	Ten-Year change (%)
Accommodation & food services	Internet travel services	9	13
Finance & insurance	Internet investment services	10	11
Finance & insurance	Health insurance	11	−45
Manufacturing-durables	Major appliances	11	−24
Retail trade	Internet retail	11	22
Energy utilities	Cooperative utilities	12	−14
Accommodation & food services	Hotels	12	−8
Energy utilities	Investor-owned utilities	13	−19
Finance & insurance	Banks	15	−48
Manufacturing-durables	Wireless telephones	15	−12
Public administration	Public administration	15	40
Transportation & warehousing	Consumer shipping	15	50
Transportation & warehousing	Airlines	16	−6
Transportation & warehousing	U.S. postal service	17	0
Telecommunications & information	Wireless telephone service	18	−47
Manufacturing-durables	Automobiles & light vehicles	19	0
Telecommunications & information	Fixed-line telephone service	27	−13
Telecommunications & information	Internet service providers	35	−3
Telecommunications & information	Subscription TV	37	−21

Source: Authors' creation from American Customer Satisfaction Index data and methods

more than one-third of all customers indicate having complained, such as internet service providers (35%) and subscription TV companies (37%). As mentioned earlier, complaint rates range very widely and far more so than the other measured ACSI variables, even when considering the different nature of the question (a no-yes question) and the scale used to measure it (0–1 rather than a 1–10 scale converted to 0–100 as for the other ACSI model variables).

To be sure, some of the variance from low to high complaint rates across both companies and industries is driven by satisfaction—with higher satisfaction generally pushing complaint rates lower, and vice versa. Yet satisfaction is certainly not the only source of variance at play. This is clear from the results in Table 6.1, as the industry with the very lowest complaint rate at just 1%—internet social media—is far from the most satisfying industry in the U.S. economy. Indeed, although virtually no customers complain about their experiences with social media websites, the industry comes in seventh from last in satisfaction across all measured industries (at 73). On the other hand, one of the top-ten industries in satisfaction, automobiles and light vehicles at 81, has the fourth-highest complaint rate of any industry at 19%, showing that just as lower satisfaction does not always mean more complaints, higher satisfaction does not always mean fewer. And to complicate matters further, the two industries with the lowest customer satisfaction scores—internet service providers and subscription TV—do indeed have the highest complaint rates, at 35% and 37%, respectively.

These results beg a question: Why do some dissatisfying industries have very high complaint rates, and others virtually none, while some very satisfying industries still have high complaint rates, and vice versa? Put differently, why do customer satisfaction and customer complaint rate *not* move together more closely or equally across distinct industries? The answer to this question is actually straightforward: While customer satisfaction is a strong predictor of complaint rate in most cases at the individual and company level, industry-dependent economic factors vary enormously across industries and are also strongly predictive.

Marketers and economists have long understood that many factors influence the individual consumer's decision about whether or not to complain to a company when dissatisfied. These include the consumer's demographic profile, psychological factors, and related individual characteristics. Nearly 50 years ago, groundbreaking work by economist Albert Hirschman focused on the economic foundations of customer complaints and generated the "exit-voice-loyalty" theory, and his work subsequently inspired voluminous research on the topic.[8] Both this academic literature and the tests of these theories have generally pointed to a handful of most important influencing factors that cause complaint rates to vary across industries. These factors include the degree of competition and number of competitors in an industry, the price paid for a good or service, the switching costs (or the costs associated with defecting from one company to another), real or perceived obstacles to complaining, and perceived likelihood (and benefit) of recovery or redress.

To begin, dissatisfied consumers are less likely to complain when an industry's economic landscape is more competitive (i.e., includes more alternative suppliers or companies), as under these conditions defecting from one company to another is easier, and unlike complaining, defecting itself does not require additional cost (such as a time and effort expenditure) from the consumer. Also, the price paid for a product or service about which the consumer is dissatisfied and considering complaining will often influence the decision to complain, as failures with more expensive goods in which the consumer has invested a larger share of disposable income create a stronger motivation in the consumer to seek redress and some form of recompense from the company.

Moreover, higher switching costs, or the tangible and intangible difficulties a consumer might experience after leaving one company for another—such as a greater distance to a new retail outlet, fewer or less convenient automated teller machines (ATMs), learning a new computer or wireless phone system, the psychological discomfort of abandoning a known and trusted brand, and so forth—will often make consumers more likely to complain rather than just exit. Likewise, if consumers perceive little or no opportunity to realistically achieve significant redress (i.e., some form of compensation from the firm) from a company via the act of making a complaint, or if the time-cost of complaining outweighs the expected benefit, dissatisfied customers are less likely to complain. And finally, significant barriers to complaint, such as limited information about how to complain (difficult-to-find contact center telephone numbers or email addresses) or whom to complain to (the manufacturer of a product vs. the retailer selling the product), are often predictive of lower complaint rates. In sum, the nature of an economic exchange and the context within which it takes place—and typically some combination of the factors we have described—directly and strongly impact the likelihood that a consumer will complain to a company about their experience, and as these factors differ significantly across industries so too does the customer's incentive to complain.

Based on the above arguments, certain industries can be reasonably predicted to have relatively low complaint rates, regardless of levels of satisfaction, both in an absolute sense and relative to other economic industries. Take, for example, two industries in the same economic sector, food processing (which includes all of the different types of processed and packaged foods purchased by consumers in supermarkets and similar retail outlets) and personal care products (e.g., soaps, shampoos, shaving cream). Regarding competition, both industries have very low economic concentration scores, meaning the markets are highly competitive and offer consumers many alternatives.[9] This means that for consumers defection is relatively easy and a viable option when dissatisfied with their experiences, which in turn minimizes complaint likelihood. These industries also tend to have a relatively low price-point for the individual products sold, which also minimizes complaint likelihood and aggregate complaint rates, as the consumer has only a relatively small "investment" in the product. Furthermore, while brand loyalty may play a role in increasing perceived switching costs to some degree, given the number of alternative suppliers and the "ease of use" of products in this industry (it does not require a significant time-cost to "learn to eat" a new breakfast cereal, or to "learn to use" a new bar of soap), switching costs offer little resistance for customers seeking to defect to a competitor, and this too decreases the likelihood of complaint.

Additionally, because in almost all cases the products in food processing and personal care products are sold in retail outlets not directly affiliated with the actual manufacturer of the product (store-branded products being the exception), at least some barriers to complaining exist (to whom should the customer complain, the manufacturer or the retailer?), and this too results in lower complaint rates. Finally, because of the aforementioned low price-point for the typical good purchased in these industry categories, while consumers might anticipate a benefit in terms of redress from the act of complaining when dissatisfied, that benefit is likely perceived to be limited to the price paid for the good itself, and since that price is relatively low, it diminishes the perceived benefit relative to the cost of complaining.

These predictions regarding low complaint rates in the food processing and personal care products industries are substantiated in Table 6.1. According to the results, personal care products (1%) and food processing (3%) have the second and fourth lowest complaint rates of all the industries measured and included in ACSI data. Yet, to show that the higher satisfaction scores for these two industries are not entirely responsible for the low complaint rates, the two other industries with similarly low complaint rates—internet news and opinion (online news media content) at 1% and internet social media websites at 2%, both have much lower satisfaction, but are in reasonably competitive industries—provide completely free services, have moderate to low switching costs, moderate-to-high barriers to complaint, and limited (or no) compensation for redress to those who do complain. On the other hand, the industries with the highest complaint rates—subscription TV at 37% and internet service providers at 35%—are marked by: very limited competition, with near-monopoly power for companies in both industries in many geographic regions; a relatively high price-point that has increased rapidly[10]; in many cases, significant switching costs (e.g., learning a new service platform or remote control); limited barriers to complaint; and, in some cases, opportunities to receive significant discounts via the act of complaining.

In sum, it is important for marketers, market researchers, and anyone involved in customer relationship management and complaint monitoring to understand that not only do complaints vary across different economic contexts and types of consumer products, but that this variance is not entirely explainable solely by variations in customer satisfaction. Indeed, as we have discussed, the economic causes of complaint rate variation are a prime reason why customer satisfaction measurement and complaint rate monitoring cannot be considered equivalent, with one used as a proxy for the other (and, by extension, why simply measuring customer satisfaction as a function of how likely a customer is to recommend a good or service to another potential customer does not capture the full variance of satisfaction, nor its predictive impact, level, and change over time). And as we will see next, it appears to be the case that, regardless of industry or context, not even a majority of dissatisfied customers complain, limiting the ability of firms to both learn from customer complaints and mitigate the loss of customers due to disloyalty.

And the Award for "Most Complaints" Goes To

Which companies have the lowest and highest complaint rates in the U.S. economy? The award for lowest complaint rate is shared by more than two-dozen companies, all with complaint rates of 0%, or literally no customers lodging formal complaints whatsoever. This includes companies with fairly low customer satisfaction, like Facebook and LinkedIn, and those with some of the highest customer satisfaction economy-wide, like famed chocolate candy maker Hershey Foods.

The two companies with the highest complaint rates are likewise diverse and include one of the most dissatisfying and one of the more satisfying companies across the U.S. economy. The highest complaint rate, at 49%, is achieved by Mediacom, the internet service provider whose customer satisfaction is near the bottom of the pack. Interestingly, though, the second highest complaint rate of 47% comes for BMW, the luxury automaker whose customer satisfaction is near the top of ACSI measurement year in and year out. Again, these company-level findings confirm that complaint behavior is driven by economic and other factors beyond just customer satisfaction, and that this fact must be incorporated when analyzing complaint data.

6.3   Do All Dissatisfied Customers Complain?

When rigorous studies of consumer complaint behavior began in the 1970s and 1980s, an important early finding changed how researchers and businesspeople understood consumers and consumer behavior in general, and complaint behavior in particular: A very small proportion of customers dissatisfied with a company and the goods/services they have consumed actually expend the time and effort to complain. In these studies, conservative estimates suggested that as many as two-thirds (66%) of dissatisfied consumers failed to complain about their experience, leaving only one-in-three (33%) as complainants to a company.[11] Other, more "shocking" estimates indicated that only one dissatisfied customer in 20—or only 5% of them—formally complained when experiencing a problem and anger with a company. Over the next 30 years, especially this second "only 5% complain" finding would be cited as a truism about customer behavior, and confirmation of the fact that customer dissatisfaction and customer complaint rates are not always correlated. But is it still the case today that relatively (or very) few dissatisfied customers complain? And if indeed still true, what are the implications for companies?

To answer the first question, we again analyze the latest sample of ACSI data referenced in earlier chapters, the most recent full year of reliable data available for analysis (2017) at the time of this book's completion, and all of the respondents across more than 350 companies measured in this sample. Put simply, and looking across a selection of diverse ACSI-measured industries, including those with both high and low average satisfaction and both high and low aggregate complaint rates, and defining "dissatisfaction" in multiple ways, we find that in all cases a relatively small (though variable) percentage of dissatisfied customers actually complain. These results are shown in Table 6.2.

In Table 6.2, we begin with the aggregate sample of all respondents across all companies and industries, including all of the consumer survey respondents from 2017 answering about experiences with companies in 48 distinct industries across diverse economic sectors. In the aggregate, among consumers reporting average satisfaction, 11.7% of all customers complain about their experiences with their companies. Taking the same sample but parsing it to include only those customers who indicate below average satisfaction with their experience—that is, defining "dissatisfaction" as anyone below the full sample average satisfaction—the complaint rate rises to 18.9% of customers. Parsing the sample again but now defining "dissatisfaction" more strictly as only those respondents giving a response about their customer satisfaction that is more than one standard deviation below average (or one unit of "average variance" in satisfaction below average), the complaint rate jumps to 33.3%. Finally, most strictly defining dissatisfaction as only a small percentage of respondents in the bottom half (1–5) of the raw 1–10 customer satisfaction variable scale, the complaint rate rises to 40.2%. The final column shows the change in "probability of complaint" between average respondents and the least satisfied group, and in the case of the aggregate sample, it shows that these least satisfied customers are 2.9 times more likely to complain than the average consumer.

Table 6.2 Complaint rates among dissatisfied customers

Industry[a]	Complaint rate—all customers (average satisfaction) (%)[b]	Complaint rate—all below-average satisfaction customers (%)	Complaint rate—all one SD below-average satisfaction customers (%)	Complaint rate—all in bottom half of satisfaction scale (1–5 of 1–10) customers (%)	Complaint probability change from average to least satisfied customers ×
Full sample	11.7	18.9	33.3	40.2	2.9
Television & video players	5.8	9.4	15.9	0	0
Breweries	5.1	6.4	9.3	12.5	2.5
Automobiles & light vehicles	21.4	32.7	41.9	52.2	2.4
Wireless telephones	15.7	25.4	41.0	46.0	2.9
Limited service restaurants	9.9	14.3	26.7	32.6	3.3
Airlines	14.0	15.9	21.3	24.2	1.7
Wireless telephone service	15.7	25.4	41.0	46.0	2.9
Subscription TV	36.8	54.3	66.5	66.5	1.8

Source: Authors' creation from American Customer Satisfaction Index data and methods
[a]Industries sorted by high to low customer satisfaction score
[b]Some overall industry complaint rates may not perfectly match the numbers in Table 6.1 above, as those results reflect weighted averages based on company market shares, while these scores are unweighted to allow for selection of cases based on different types of dissatisfaction

Focusing on the strictest definition of customer dissatisfaction as our reference point, we see that while complaint rate and complaint probability vary across industries, in most cases less than half of even the least satisfied customers complain. For two typically very satisfying industries, television and video players and breweries, only a tiny fraction (0% and 12.5%, respectively) of even the very least satisfied customers complain. That is, in these industries and even in cases of relatively extreme dissatisfaction, between absolutely no customers and only one-in-eight dissatisfied customers actually lodge a complaint. Moreover, for only two industries in this sample of industries—automobiles and light trucks and subscription TV service—do more than half of the least satisfied customers complain. The subscription TV industry, which leads all industries with the highest complaint rate at 37% and has the second lowest satisfaction score behind only ISPs, has only about two-thirds of its very least satisfied customers complaining.

To integrate these findings with the earlier findings, we have now seen three interconnected phenomena and reached several conclusions. First, the national, aggregate complaint rate is relatively low and has declined substantially since 1994. Second, complaint rates range across industries due to economic conditions, and in some cases, even very dissatisfying industries have virtually no complaining customers because of these exogenous economic factors. Third, in general across industries, a relatively small percentage of even very dissatisfied customers complain, from a low of 0% to a high of 66% of dissatisfied consumers in the representative sample of industries examined. Taken together, these interrelated phenomena lead to some important conclusions, all of which could be viewed as potentially troubling for companies.

First, if customers are complaining less in the aggregate, complain little in some industries, and even very dissatisfied customers often fail to complain, then at least some of these customers—and most likely a substantial portion—are "silently defecting." That is, instead of even bothering to complain to a company and attempting to seek redress or compensation, these customers are simply leaving the company and switching to a competitor without saying a word. As we will see in the next section, this kind of silent defection indicates that companies are losing repeat business, a vital source of profitability for most companies, by missing an opportunity to turn these dissatisfied customers into loyal ones. Furthermore, this lack of complaining means that firms are also missing valuable opportunities to use complaint information and feedback from customers to improve their goods and services, and thus to prevent future dissatisfaction among the same or different customers. In short, most firms ought to view a lack of complaints from consumers as missed opportunities. In fact, some managers thrive on their companies not receiving complaints at the level of their competitors, but it may in fact be an indication that their own companies are facing trouble in the future. Customer engagement is a critically important issue in today's marketplace, and customers complaining is one form of such engagement. Lacking a healthy rate of complaints likely means your company's customers are not as engaged as they should be.

In the next section, we discuss how successful companies are at managing complaints, and whether or not firms have fully recognized the importance of complaint handling and improved their practices over time. We then conclude with a lesson about customer complaints and "complaint maximization." In Chap. 7, which looks at customer loyalty and retention, we fully consider the "service recovery paradox," the notion that customers who complain and have their complaint managed very well actually become more loyal than the average non-complaining customer.

6.4   Complaint Management Is Critical. Is It Improving?

Customer complaints and the consequences of poor complaint management—dissatisfied and potentially disloyal customers—are as old as business itself. Recently, researchers "discovered" (or rediscovered, in a museum) what is believed to be the oldest written customer complaint on the nearly 4000-year-old Babylonian "Complaint Tablet of Ea-Nasir." The tablet reads in part:

> Now, when you had come, you spoke saying thus: 'I will give good ingots to Gimil-Sin'; this you said to me when you had come, but you have not done it. You have offered bad ingots to my messenger, saying 'If you will take it, take it; if you will not take it, go away.'… You will learn that here in Ur I will not accept from you copper that is not good.

With this evidence, we know that not only have customers long complained when dissatisfied, but they have also used threats of disloyalty to achieve acceptable recompense via a firm's complaint handling and complaint management.

Modern research on the relationships between customer complaints, a firm's complaint management (or recovery) system, and customer loyalty is diverse and well established. As with a variety of topics relating to the linkages between consumer perceptions, consumer behaviors, and external performance metrics, the idea of customer complaint handling as an important phenomenon with a tangible financial impact requiring significant attention has grown over the last two decades. In this context, much of the scholarly marketing literature takes as its starting point the relatively recent "service recovery paradox," the proposition that customers who experience a failure and complain to a firm might (empirically) remain as satisfied or become even more satisfied and/or as likely or more likely to remain loyal to the firm than non-complaining customers (or pre-complaint customers). The driver of such "increased loyalty scenarios," of course, is that the complaints are handled very well by the firm. As the researchers who initiated the SRP research agenda—which we will investigate more fully in Chap. 7—succinctly noted at the time, "a good recovery can turn angry, frustrated customers into loyal ones. It can, in fact, create more goodwill than if things had gone smoothly in the first place."[12]

The existence of the service recovery paradox and the importance of complaint handling by companies have been relatively common knowledge for almost three decades, with many marketing and business professionals understanding clearly that this practice can be critical to maintaining customer loyalty. But have companies really taken these imperatives to heart and focused on improving complaint management? Figure 6.2 provides data on aggregate consumer perceptions of complaint handling by the companies these customers have complained to, using all ACSI sample data for each year and a 0–100 scale, as in previous examples.

As the data in Fig. 6.2 show, complaint handling has improved economy-wide over the last ten years, and substantially so. In fact, in only two of the ten years of data did customers' ratings of complaint handling decline from the prior year, though one of those did occur between 2016 and 2017, the most recent two years of data available for this book. Nonetheless, given the large samples we are examining, and similar to the national-level ACSI variable results discussed earlier (and in each chapter of this book), even very small changes in the complaint handling variable are statistically significant. Therefore, the 6.1-point, 10.7% growth in the national-level complaint handling rating over the last decade indicates very real improvement in the eyes of consumers in how well firms are responding to customer complaints over this period.

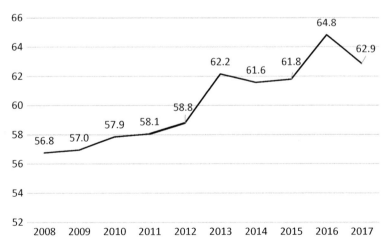

Fig. 6.2 National customer complaint handling, 2008–2017. (Source: Authors' creation from American Customer Satisfaction Index data and methods)

Two explanations—one very much positive, the other more ambiguous—for firms' improvement in complaint handling seem most plausible. First, companies have finally "gotten the message," and now managers are recognizing the importance of complaint management for transforming dissatisfied customers into enduringly loyal ones and are responding accordingly. The service recovery paradox and its admonition to manage complaints aggressively may have actually driven this message home, at least for many companies. And technologies like websites, email, and social media, which we have discussed extensively, may have aided in these efforts. Just as these technologies have made it easier for consumers to find and contact companies, they have also made it easier for firms to respond to complaint inquiries.

Second, but somewhat less positive, it may be the case that companies have done very little to improve their complaint management, but rather that the improvement in complaint management is due solely to the declining aggregate complaint rate. That is, if fewer customers are complaining, as the ACSI data suggests, it may just be easier for firms to handle a smaller number of total complaints more effectively with no additional effort. It is even possible that companies are doing less today to manage complaints, but because of the lower total system load consumers perceive it as companies are actually improving their complaint handling efforts.

This second explanation for improved complaint handling delivered to U.S. consumers—as an unintended but positive artifact of lower complaint rates—raises an important issue, one that has "reared its head" at several points throughout the chapter, and one that provides a good lesson upon which to close the chapter. That lesson is: Whenever possible, companies that want to maximize customer loyalty need to find means for inspiring dissatisfied customers to complain, and then need to manage those complaints well. Whether we are considering the declining aggregate complaint rates caused (possibly) by lesser perceived efficacy among consumers, industry conditions that lessen complaints, or the simple fact that a fairly small percentage of even very dissatisfied customers' complaint is unimportant, as the negative outcomes for the companies are the same. In each case, companies are losing opportunities to turn unhappy customers into loyal customers via strong complaint handling and are unable to use complaints as a source of information for making goods and services better for all customers in the future. Thus, for any company willing to truly invest in managing complaints and building customer loyalty, finding strategies to encourage displeased customers to complain is imperative. Such efforts can simply be focused on "give us your feedback," which may or may not be a real complaint, per se, nor a dissatisfied customer. It may just be a customer willing to share what they think are areas of opportunity for improvement as a more general take on a good, service, or company. In Chap. 7, the strong relationship between effective complaint management and future customer loyalty is more clearly revealed.

Notes

1. For example, see: Bortz, Daniel. "5 Social Media Hacks for Better Customer Service," *Time.com*. Accessed online at: http://time.com/money/4672443/social-media-hacks-customer-service/
2. See: Pfeffer, J., T. Zorbach and K. M. Carley (2014). "Understanding Online Firestorms: Negative Word-of-Mouth Dynamics in Social Media Networks," *Journal of Marketing Communications*, 20 (1–2), 117–128.
3. See: Nasaw, Daniel. "YouTube video on wrecked guitar gets United Airlines to Pay Up," *theguardian.com*. Accessed online at: https://www.theguardian.com/world/2009/jul/23/united-airlines-guitar-dave-carroll
4. Vasquez, Justina (2018). "Kylie Jenner Tweeted About Snapchat. Then Its Stock Lost $1.3 Billion in Value," *Time.com*, February 22, 2018.
5. See: Chebat, J. C., M. Davidow and I. Codjovi (2005). "Silent Voices: Why Some Dissatisfied Consumers Fail to Complain," *Journal of Service Research*, 7(4), 328–342.
6. Some caution should be taken in comparing ACSI's complaint rates before and after 2000, as in this year a slight adjustment to the metric to specify only "formal" complaints to companies (rather than informal complaints) was made. Even with this questionnaire change having some potential effect, however, the downward trend in the complaint rate before and after 2000 is clear.
7. In the case of customer complaints, both the ten-year change and the growth rank should be viewed with caution, as changes in percentages tend to be "inflated" due to the scale, and the rank in changes likewise reflects this.
8. See: Hirschman, A. O. (1970). *Exit, Voice, and Loyalty: Responses to Decline in Firms, Organizations, and States*, Boston, MA: Harvard University Press.
9. HHI is a well-known metric of industry concentration that serves as a proxy for industry competitiveness. We use the accepted calculation—sum of the squared company-level market share percentages of the companies measured in the industry—to calculate HHI.
10. "See: Cable TV Prices Keep Going Up as More People Cut the Cord," *Associated Press*, January 5, 2018.

11. See: Chebat, J. C., M. Davidow and I. Codjovi (2005). "Silent Voices: Why Some Dissatisfied Consumers Fail to Complain," *Journal of Service Research*, 7(4), 328–342; TARP (1986), "Consumer Complaint Handling in America: An Update Study," Washington, DC: Technical Assistance Research Programs, U.S. Office of Consumer Affairs, Contract HHS-100-84-0065.

12. Hart, Christopher W., James L. Heskett and W. Earl Sasser, Jr. (1990). "The Profitable Art of Service Recovery," *Harvard Business Review*, 68(4), 148–156.

References and Further Reading

Aydin, S., Özer, G., & Arasil, Ö. (2005). Customer Loyalty and the Effect of Switching Costs as a Moderator Variable: A Case in the Turkish Mobile Phone Market. *Marketing Intelligence & Planning, 23*(1), 89–103.

Balasubramanian, S. K., & Cole, C. A. (2002). Consumers' Search and Use of Nutrition Information: The Challenge and Promise of the Nutrition Labeling and Education Act. *Journal of Marketing, 66*, 112–127.

Bortz, D. (2017, February 16). 5 Social Media Hacks for Better Customer Service. *Time.com*. Retrieved from http://time.com/money/4672443/social-media-hacks-customer-service/

Cable TV Prices Keep Going Up as More People Cut the Cord. (2018, January 5). *Associated Press*.

Chebat, J. C., Davidow, M., & Codjovi, I. (2005). Silent Voices: Why Some Dissatisfied Consumers Fail to Complain. *Journal of Service Research, 7*(4), 328–342.

Cole, C. A., & Balasubramanian, S. K. (1993). Age Differences in Consumers' Search for Information: Public Policy Implications. *Journal of Consumer Research, 20*(1), 157–169.

Davidow, M., & Dacin, P. A. (1997). Understanding and Influencing Consumer Complaint Behavior: Improving Organizational Complaint Management. In M. Brucks & D. J. MacInnis (Eds.), *NA—Advances in Consumer Research* (Vol. 24). Provo, UT: Association for Consumer Research.

Dickson, P. R., & Sawyer, A. G. (1990). The Price Knowledge and Search of Supermarket Shoppers. *Journal of Marketing, 54*, 42–53.

Folkes, V., & Matta, S. (2004). The Effect of Package Shape on Consumers' Judgments of Product Volume: Attention as a Mental Contaminant. *Journal of Consumer Research, 31*, 391–401.

Fornell, C., & Davidow, N. M. (1980). Economic Constraints on Consumer Complaining Behavior. In J. C. Olson (Ed.), *NA—Advances in Consumer Research* (Vol. 07). Ann Arbor, MI: Association for Consumer Research.

Fornell, C., & Westbrook, R. A. (1984). The Vicious Circle of Consumer Complaints. *Journal of Marketing, 48*(3), 68–78.

Hart, C. W., Heskett, J. L., & Earl Sasser, W., Jr. (1990). The Profitable Art of Service Recovery. *Harvard Business Review, 68*(4), 148–156.

Hirschman, A. O. (1970). *Exit, Voice, and Loyalty: Responses to Decline in Firms, Organizations, and States*. Boston, MA: Harvard University Press.

Kilgrove, K. (2018, May 11). Meet the Worst Businessman of the 18th Century BC, *Forbes.com*. Retrieved from https://www.forbes.com/sites/kristinakillgrove/ 2018/05/11/meet-the-worst-businessman-of-the-18th-century/#5cb1f89a2d5d

Lee, J., Lee, J., & Feick, L. (2001). The Impact of Switching Costs on the Customer Satisfaction-Loyalty Link: Mobile Phone Service in France. *Journal of Services Marketing, 15*(1), 35–48.

Pfeffer, J., Zorbach, T., & Carley, K. M. (2014). Understanding Online Firestorms: Negative Word-of-Mouth Dynamics in Social Media Networks. *Journal of Marketing Communications, 20*(1–2), 117–128.

TARP. (1986). Consumer Complaint Handling in America: An Update Study. Washington, DC: Technical Assistance Research Programs, U.S. Office of Consumer Affairs, Contract HHS-100-84-0065.

Vasquez, J. (2018, February 22). Kylie Jenner Tweeted About Snapchat. Then Its Stock Lost $1.3 Billion in Value. *Time.com*. Retrieved from http://time.com/5170990/kylie-jenner-snapchat-stock-value/

Williams, T. D., Drake, M. F., & Morgan, J. D. (1993). Complaint Behavior, Price Paid and the Store Patronized. *International Journal of Retail & Distribution Management, 21*(5), 3–9.

7

Customer Loyalty: Hey, Stick Around for a While!

Chapter Overview

In this chapter, we consider changes in the loyalty of consumers over the last 25 years and the resulting implications. We find that customer loyalty, when measured as an estimate of customer retention, has increased substantially to the brands customers opt to engage with since 1994. Contrary to the many warnings of businesspeople and marketers, we find that Millennials are among the most loyal customers across the generational cohorts included in the ACSI data, behind only the rapidly dwindling Silent Generation in their loyalty. After considering industries with the strongest and weakest customer loyalty, we examine the service recovery paradox, the finding that customers who experience a problem with a good or service but receive highly effective complaint management end up with stronger-than-average loyalty, even stronger than those customers with a problem-free experience. Chapter 7 closes with a discussion of the future of customer loyalty measurement—and in some sense, measurement of the entire consumer experience—with an examination of recently popularized (but highly flawed) measurement methods.

Key Conclusions

- Contrary to the dire warnings by some business professionals of an impending "collapse in brand loyalty," loyalty has not declined, and it has in fact increased dramatically, over the past quarter-century.
- While Millennial consumers are often accused of rampant disloyalty to companies and brands, ACSI data show that Millennials are one of the most loyal generational cohorts.

© The Author(s) 2020
C. Fornell et al., *The Reign of the Customer*, https://doi.org/10.1007/978-3-030-13562-1_7

- The service recovery paradox, where companies manage failures and complaints very effectively, does in fact lead to stronger customer loyalty among consumers. Companies in most contexts should therefore implement and maintain effective complaint recovery systems.
- Many popularized alternative measures of customer loyalty, like Net Promoter Score™, are highly flawed and should not be considered as viable alternatives to customer satisfaction and loyalty measurement.

7.1   Is Customer Loyalty Dying? Or Dead Already?

In many ways, consumers have more choice than ever before and more convenient ways of evaluating those choices before, during, and after the purchasing process. The Information Revolution, the internet, and the consequent rise of electronic commerce (e-commerce) have brought with them seemingly limitless alternatives for consumers, as well as other advantages. These new technologies provide consumers myriad new powers, such as the ability to more easily learn about alternative products, the ability to compare quality attributes and features between these more numerous options, compare prices, and then buy what they prefer from suppliers almost anywhere in the international marketplace. Under these new and more dynamic market conditions, worries among business professionals and others about the potential death of consumer loyalty are understandable. Put simply, consumers with more power and choice than ever before are better able to exhibit disloyalty and better able to abandon one company for another, resulting in reasonable concerns about the future of customer loyalty.

Yet worries about the death of customer loyalty in an era of greater choice are not necessarily universal and aimed at all consumers. Indeed, these worries have been focused on particular groups of consumers. For a variety of reasons, both related and unrelated to their behavior as consumers, the generations coming-of-age as the Information Age first began to truly materialize (Millennials) and then after its effects had already transformed society (Generation Z) have become the source of particular attention and consternation. As consumers, these two generations, we are often told, are fundamentally different than their predecessors in the Silent Generation, Baby Boomer, or Generation X cohorts. Millennials and Generation Z consumers either barely remember, or recall not at all, a time before the internet, smartphones, e-commerce, social media, and retail giants like Amazon.com.[1] While the behavior of Baby Boomers and Generation X consumers may have been *changed* by the Information Age, Millennial and Generation Z consumers have been *shaped* by it. These recent generations are, for far too many reasons to list here, the product of a radically new age and are fundamentally different in their ideas, opinions, and consumer behavior. Their consumer power is also growing quickly and requires the full, undivided attention of companies.

Just about the same time as we are required to send our book manuscript to the publisher for type-setting and publication, projections indicate that Millennials will surpass Baby Boomers as the largest generational cohort in the U.S. in 2019.[2] Since all individuals in both the Boomer and the Millennial groups are now adult consumers, with the youngest Millennials set to turn 23 in 2019, the latter will surpass the former as the largest group of adult consumers in the U.S.. But Millennials will not hold their title as "largest generational cohort" for very long. Projections suggest that Generation Z will pass Millennials as the largest cohort in total number later in 2020 as well, and as those consumers reach adulthood (which the youngest in Generation Z will do in 2028), their combined importance as consumers will be truly unmatched.[3] Consequently, we think our book on the reign of the customer is very timely, as a roadmap for customer-centric issues in an era of generational and dynamic market shifts. Together, Millennials and Generation Z consumers will soon dominate the economy—and thus the fates of most companies—over the next decade. And it is unlikely that all companies are fully ready for this onslaught of tastes, needs, and wants likely to be exhibited by Millennials and Generation Z consumers.

Taken together, all the aforementioned changes could be viewed as detrimental—and potentially deadly—to customer loyalty. Given that many companies rely heavily on loyal customers and repeat business to drive revenue and profitability, the potential effects of systematically less loyal customers, should this materialize, would be catastrophic.[4] Without being too technical, a company has two choices to have sustainable performance success: repeat customers and/or developing new products continually (the latter is a function of the product life cycle theory, albeit beyond the scope of this book). Needless to say, continually developing new products at a high rate to maintain success in the marketplace is typically more costly and ineffective than strategically working on and implementing measures to obtain repeat customer (i.e., customer loyalty).

Unfortunately, if all consumers have the ability to more intelligently and easily choose from among a larger number of alternatives, they are at a minimum also better able to exhibit disloyalty than ever before, regardless of their actual behavior. And if this behavior is centered in and most potently exhibited by the youngest and soon-to-be largest generational cohorts driving the economy, the effects could be even worse. This begs the question: Has the proliferation of choice and the Information Age, and the gradual emergence of new and different generational cohorts of consumers that exhibit different ideas and behaviors, resulted in the "death of brand loyalty," or has customer loyalty actually improved over the last 25 years?

According to ACSI data and as we see in Fig. 7.1, aggregate national customer loyalty—measured here as an estimate of customer retention on a 0–100% scale[5]—has improved significantly over the last 25 years. Indeed, but for a few brief periods of decline, customers have gradually and consistently become more and more loyal since 1994. In 1994, estimated economy-wide customer retention posted an initial and relatively low score of 68.8%. By 2017, the retention estimate had increased 8.1 percentage points to 76.9%, an 11.8% gain. Near an all-time high, customers are now more likely to remain loyal to their chosen companies than at almost any point since 1994. In short, while customer satisfaction has increased moderately over the past 25 years, with bigger and more dramatic changes for expectations and value, customer loyalty and retention has leapt far higher than them all.

Yet the aggregate growth in customer retention notwithstanding, it is certainly still possible that trouble lies ahead. For instance, it is possible that the

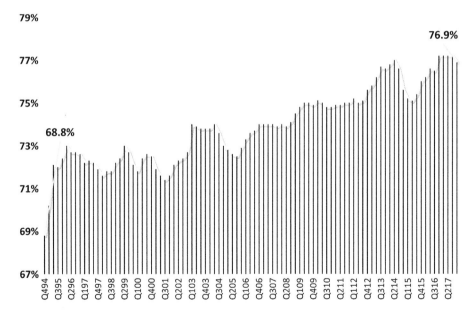

Fig. 7.1 National customer retention, 1994–2017. (Source: Authors' creation from American Customer Satisfaction Index data and methods)

gains in customer retention from 1994 to 2017 are isolated to improvements only (or mostly) among the older generations, and that younger consumers—those Millennial and Generation Z consumers causing so much hand-wringing—will indeed turn out to be "problematic" customers. Are there differences across these generational cohorts that should make us worry about the death of customer loyalty in the near future, even if it has increased since 1994? Put differently, which generational groups of consumers are most loyal—those from the Silent Generation, Baby Boomers, Generation X, Millennials, or Generation Z? In Table 7.1, we answer these questions, analyzing the same aggregate sample of respondents across all companies and industries from the most recent available ACSI data, or nearly 175,000 consumer survey respondents answering about experiences with companies in 48 distinct industries across diverse economic sectors.

As the ACSI data show, customer loyalty measured as an estimate of retained customers does not behave as popular opinion suggests. Indeed, there is very little differentiation in customer retention across the generations, and the differences that do exist mostly run contrary to the warnings being issued. Silent Generation consumers exhibit the highest customer loyalty at 78%, suggesting that the oldest consumers (at least as of 2017), those ranging in age from 72 to 89 years old at the time, are least likely to leave their current provider for a competitor and most likely to stay with their current company. Loyalty dips to 76% for Baby Boomers and 75% for Generation Xers, with consumers aged 53–71 and 37–52, respectively, somewhat less loyal than the oldest cohort in the sample. This decline in loyalty among Boomers and Gen Xers is perhaps not surprising, as these consumers also tend (in general and in the aggregate) to have greater wealth and access to resources, with most in the prime of their careers or early in retirement, and thus more financially able to switch between companies easily.

But something surprising happens when we get to the Millennial generation, the primary source of consternation among businesses needing customer loyalty for financial success. The customer retention estimate for this group rebounds to 77%, with Millennials having *higher* loyalty than either of the

Table 7.1 Customer retention across generations

Generation	Customer retention (%)
Silent Generation (1928–1945)	78
Baby Boomers (1946–1964)	76
Generation X (1965–1980)	75
Millennials (1981–1996)	77
Generation Z (1997–2012)	73

Source: Authors' creation from American Customer Satisfaction Index data and methods

two generations preceding them, and nearly as high as their Silent Generation parents, grandparents, and great grandparents. In short, not only are Millennials *not* demonstrably less loyal than most of their predecessors, they indicate being more loyal than most of them, and in a statistical sense significantly so.

Importantly, however, customer loyalty does take a big dip with the generation following Millennials, a generation that also represents a source of concern for marketers, plunging down to 73% for the Generation Z cohort. This score is, by a significant margin, the lowest customer retention score. While the Generation Z finding could portend trouble ahead for companies vis-à-vis customer loyalty, it is important to note that in 2017, the year from which this sample was drawn, only a very small percentage of the Generation Z customers had actually reached adulthood[6] and thus appear in the sample. As of 2017, the only Generation Z consumers in the sample were either 18, 19, or 20 years old, and thus this sub-sample of respondents is comparatively quite small and demographically narrower than the more than 20 years of data used as a comparison. Given this, it is too soon to declare Generation Z consumers as definitively "less loyal," and until a larger proportion comes of age as adult consumers, we should withhold judgment on their loyalty behavior. Perhaps, though, the ACSI data provide some early warning signs for firms.

In sum, based on the analysis of customer retention across generations and the earlier finding that loyalty has not declined substantially between 1994 and the present, but has in fact improved substantially, it appears that the rumors of the "death of customer loyalty" have been greatly exaggerated. Loyalty still appears to be alive and well, and Millennials and Generation Z customers have not (or have not yet) killed it.

7.2   Which Customers Are Most Loyal?

Much like the other variables in the ACSI model that we have discussed thus far in the book, customer loyalty and retention might be expected to vary across industries, both in levels and in changes over time. While strongly correlated with and driven by customer satisfaction, customer loyalty is highly sensitive to both firm and industry effects, similar to the case of customer complaints that we described in Chap. 6. For example, customers can be highly satisfied with a good or service but indicate lower loyalty than satisfaction alone might predict due to a particularly high price point. Consumers are typically more satisfied with luxury goods but cannot always afford to buy them on every purchase occasion, leading to a disconnect between satisfaction and loyalty. Conversely, consumers are sometimes highly loyal to a good or service about which they have only lukewarm satisfaction (e.g., the fast food restaurant closest to a customer's home). In many cases, strong loyalty despite lower satisfaction can be driven by some companies offering mediocre goods and services, but offering them at very low price points that consumers cannot afford or even want to reject.

Regarding exogenous influences, changes in income or employment situation, among other macroeconomic effects, can make consumers more or less loyal to certain brands than they would be otherwise, and these effects are likely to impact different industries differently. Cross-industry variance in levels and changes are thus to be expected, and this is confirmed to be the case for customer retention as well. This variance is visible in the results provided in Table 7.2, which shows industry-level customer retention rates from low to high in 2017, with changes over the previous ten years, a period during which the aggregate national customer retention rate increased 3.2%.

The leader in customer loyalty is the supermarkets industry, with a customer retention estimate of 83%. Close behind, two nondurable goods industries, breweries (beer) and soft drinks, share second place with two retailers, health and personal care stores and internet retailers at 82%. The strong customer retention enjoyed by companies in all of these industries is understandable. Retailers like supermarkets and health and personal care stores are often chosen by consumers based on proximity to the consumer's residence (similar to our fast food example earlier). While these consumers may stray from time to time and drive some distance to shop at an "exotic" alternative, most supermarkets and health and personal care stores enjoy strong "convenience-based" customer loyalty. Beers and soft drinks, on the other hand, are the type of products where there is a large variety of alternatives at similarly low prices, but for which consumers—through an evolving process of trial and error over time—often settle on a favorite and purchase it almost instinctively time and time again, a fact to which many bartenders across the country would attest.

At this juncture in the book, the worst performing industries should come as little surprise and almost deserve no further mention. Internet service providers come in near the bottom at 64% retention, only slightly better than their basement-dwelling cousins in Subscription TV, at 63%. While at one point the companies in these industries had near-monopoly power and little real reason to fear consumer dissatisfaction and disloyalty, due to government regulation and the importance of delivery infrastructure in these industries, as alternatives (to subscription TV, especially) finally arrive, many consumers are becoming "cord cutters" and leaving them behind at the first opportunity.

Table 7.2 Industry customer retention, ten-year changes, and growth rank

Sector	Industry	Customer retention 2017 (0–100%) (%)	Ten-year change (%)	Growth rank
Retail trade	Supermarkets	83	2.5	23
Manufacturing-nondurables	Breweries	82	5.1	17
Retail trade	Health & personal care stores	82	1.2	27
Retail trade	Internet retail	82	1.2	28
Manufacturing-nondurables	Soft drinks	82	0.0	29
Manufacturing-nondurables	Apparel	81	6.6	12
Retail trade	Department & discount stores	81	3.8	20
Retail trade	Gasoline service stations	81	1.3	26
Manufacturing-nondurables	Food processing	81	0.0	30
Transportation & warehousing	Consumer shipping	81	−1.2	36
Transportation & warehousing	U.S. postal service	81	−1.2	37
Health care & social assistance	Ambulatory care	81	−2.4	40
Manufacturing-durables	Televisions & video players	80	14.3	4
Accommodation & food services	Limited service restaurants	80	8.1	8
Accommodation & food services	Internet travel services	80	8.1	9
Retail trade	Specialty retail stores	80	0.0	31
Finance & insurance	Property & casualty insurance	80	−1.2	38
Manufacturing-nondurables	Personal care products	80	−3.6	41
Manufacturing-durables	Wireless telephones	79	19.7	2
Telecommunications & information	Computer software	79	5.3	16
Telecommunications & information	Internet news & opinion	79	3.9	19
Finance & insurance	Credit unions	79	−1.3	39
Telecommunications & information	Internet search engines & information	79	−4.8	43
Finance & insurance	Banks	78	18.2	3
Manufacturing-nondurables	Athletic shoes	78	8.3	7
Finance & insurance	Internet investment services	78	5.4	15

(*continued*)

Table 7.2 (continued)

Sector	Industry	Customer retention 2017 (0–100%) (%)	Ten-year change (%)	Growth rank
Telecommunications & information	Internet social media	78	4.0	18
Transportation & warehousing	Airlines	77	20.3	1
Manufacturing-durables	Automobiles & light vehicles	77	6.9	11
Telecommunications & information	Wireless telephone service	74	12.1	6
Accommodation & food services	Full-service restaurants	74	7.2	10
Finance & insurance	Health insurance	74	2.8	22
Energy utilities	Cooperative utilities	74	−5.1	44
Public administration	Public administration	74	−0.6	35
Finance & insurance	Life insurance	73	5.8	14
Health care & social assistance	Hospitals	73	−3.9	42
Manufacturing-durables	Personal computers	72	5.9	13
Energy utilities	Investor-owned utilities	72	0.0	32
Accommodation & food services	Hotels	71	2.9	21
Telecommunications & information	Fixed-line telephone service	71	1.4	25
Manufacturing-durables	Household appliances	71	−0.3	34
Energy utilities	Municipal utilities	70	0.0	33
Telecommunications & information	Internet service providers	64	1.6	24
Telecommunications & information	Subscription TV	63	12.5	5

Source: Authors' creation from American Customer Satisfaction Index data and methods

Regarding ten-year changes, the biggest gain in customer loyalty comes for airlines, increasing a whopping 20.3% over this period. This dramatic improvement in customer retention should not come as a shock either. The airlines industry has also gained the most over this ten-year period in expectations, quality, value, and satisfaction, and thus most of the companies in this industry are enjoying dramatic improvements in the loyalty of their customers. In turn, this is evidence that improvements in the experiences of consumers provide financial benefits for companies. The second largest gain in loyalty among the industries comes for wireless telephones, gaining 19.7% since 2008. As we saw in Chap. 5, the wireless telephones industry has also gained the second most in customer satisfaction over the past decade, and it has paid-off in more loyal customers.

The biggest drops in loyalty appear in cooperative energy utilities (−5.3%), and more interestingly, internet search engines and information (−4.8%). The latter industry has the second largest decline in satisfaction over this period as well. While Google is clearly the dominant player in this industry and has grown from a "smaller" $18 billion annual revenue company to a $140 billion revenue company over this period, or a more than 670% growth in revenue, it has done so through an aggressive advertising model that appears to have alienated some customers and caused them to seek alternatives and display disloyalty.

Leading in Loyalty

As a whole, the supermarket industry leads the measured industries in customer loyalty, and three individual supermarkets likewise lead in customer retention. Publix comes in first with a retention rate of 86%, with Aldi and HEB close behind and both at 85%. Amazon also scores in this top group at 85%, showing the power and endurance of one of the world's largest companies to continue to grow rapidly even as innumerable smaller competitors seek to pick away at their customers.

At the very bottom and lagging behind in loyalty are—surprise, surprise—two internet service providers—Windstream at a mere 54% and Frontier even lower at 53%. Not only do these companies need to be particularly concerned about their ability to keep customers over the long term, but the industry as a whole should be worried. As real practical choice arrives for consumers in this space, they are likely to defect en masse.

7.3   The Service Recovery Paradox Is Real!

There has long been a suspected relationship between customer complaints, complaint management (i.e., complaint recovery or complaint handling) by a company, and a complaining customer's continued loyalty to that firm. Because of this relationship, economic benefits are assumed to exist for a company that operates a complaint management system (e.g., a Customer Relationship Management or CRM system) that minimizes customer dissatisfaction and maintains loyalty (or even increases satisfaction and customer loyalty likelihood) among displeased customers. Indeed, a significant majority of the academic studies on the topic have found that complaint behavior itself is not fatal to a complainant customer's satisfaction and loyalty, so long as firms manage and handle the complaints of customers very well.[7] As we briefly mentioned in the last chapter on customer complaints, most of the studies in this area take as their starting point the "service recovery paradox (SRP)," the notion that customers who experience a failure and complain to the company can remain as or even more satisfied, and as or even more likely to remain loyal, to the firm than non-complaining customers. Of course, this increased loyalty is dependent on complaints being managed really well by a firm.

But is the service recovery paradox real? After all, business professionals, marketers, and market researchers sometimes fall victim to sensational and convincing marketing truisms—such as the oft-repeated yet highly dubious claim that "every dissatisfied customer will tell 10 (or 15, or 20) people about their experience"—that are disconnected from any empirical evidence or apply only to some very limited contexts.

To confirm the existence of the service recovery paradox (SRP), we analyze a large sample of ACSI data across multiple industries and sectors and over the same, most recent ten-year period used throughout the chapter, to establish both the existence and the durability of this relationship, should it exist. The results are presented in Figs. 7.2 and 7.3. Figure 7.2 compares aggregate responses among consumers to the 1–10 scaled "repurchase likelihood" survey question discussed earlier, splitting the sample between those customers who did and those who did not complain. These results bring into sharp focus just how important customer complaints are to firms, revealing the substantial differences in loyalty intention between consumers who complain and those who do not. For example, while only 3% of non-complainants indicate

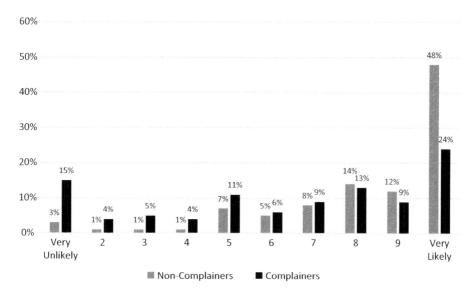

Fig. 7.2 Customer retention among complainers and non-complainers. (Source: Authors' creation from American Customer Satisfaction Index data and methods)

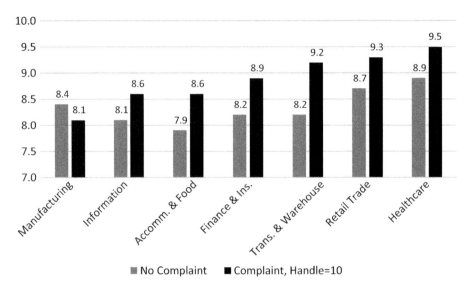

Fig. 7.3 Customer retention for non-complainers versus complainers with perfectly managed complaints. (Source: Authors' creation from American Customer Satisfaction Index data and methods)

that they are "very unlikely" to repurchase from the same firm again in the future, among complaining customers the number is five times higher at 15%. That is, across all economic sectors and consumer industries included in the ACSI data, a consumer who has complained is *five times* as likely to indicate that their next purchase for a good or service within that same category will almost certainly be with a new or different company. Similar results are observed on all of the lowest points on the scale from 1 through 4, with complaining customers four or five times more likely to pick these "disloyalty" options than non-complaining customers.

Yet the results in Fig. 7.2 also show that a customer's complaint behavior is not the sole determinant of loyalty intention. While 48% of non-complainants indicate that they are "very likely" to repurchase from the same firm again, the corresponding rate among complaining customers is 24%. That is, almost one-quarter of the customers that do have a problem significant enough to lead them to lodge a complaint with a company suggest that they will stay loyal to the same company in the future. But, if 15% of complainants are almost certain to defect, why are an even larger proportion—24% of complainants—almost certain to remain loyal? To be sure, brand loyalty, price competitiveness, limitations in alternatives, and similar explanations play some role. But the factor mostly responsible for dividing complaining customers into those who are almost certain to defect and those who are equally certain to remain loyal lies in successful complaint management by firms. This fact is confirmed in Fig. 7.3, which shows average repurchase likelihood among non-complaining customers and complaining customers who say their complaint was handled almost perfectly.

As we see in Fig. 7.3, the analysis of a large cross-sector and over time sample of ACSI data supports the existence of a service recovery paradox. For six of the seven economic sectors included in our sample (all but the manufacturing sector including both durable and nondurable goods and its underlying industries), complaining customers who have their complaint handled perfectly (i.e., rating the complaint handling experience a "10" on a 1–10 scale during surveying) give on average a *higher* repurchase or loyalty intention score than average non-complaining customers. The SRP "gap" is largest for transportation and warehousing (e.g., express parcel delivery) and finance and insurance (e.g., banks, credit unions, and insurance providers). In other words, for all sectors except manufacturing, "perfectly managed complainants" are significantly more likely to remain loyal than non-complaining customers.

In sum, the SRP and the imperative for firms to manage complaints effectively derived from it appears to be real. For most companies—or at least those that rely on customer loyalty to realize profitable growth—finding ways to handle complaints very well is necessary. While based on more complex analysis, however, we can also state definitively that the importance of complaint management to companies varies across industries, with some industries needing to more aggressively manage complaints than others.[8] This can be seen in Fig. 7.3, where complaint handling produces less pay-off in terms of increased loyalty likelihood than others. And because industry differences impact customers' purchasing behaviors following complaint handling, the financial ramifications of firms' complaint management efforts differ as well. Nevertheless, most firms interested in repeat business must seek to turn many complaining, unhappy customers into loyal ones, and must do so via effective complaint management.

7.4 Satisfaction, Loyalty, and Recommendation Are Different!

While we have closed most of the preceding chapters in the book with a discussion of the possible form consumer perceptions in these various areas might take in the near future, to close Chap. 7 we follow a different path. In this case, we discuss the future of the *measurement* of customer loyalty, and in some sense, the future of measurement of the customer experience as a whole. However, this discussion is not tangential to the future of customer loyalty; indeed, it bears directly on its future and that of other consumer perceptions. That is, because how companies measure consumer insights often has a dramatic impact on how they perform and improve (or fail to improve) in providing positive consumer experiences, this discussion is an important one that cannot be ignored. When combined with recent and troubling trends in customer loyalty measurement, the significance of this metric discussion is greater than ever before.

Over the past decade or so, a handful of researchers, other marketing professionals, and even CEOs and related business leaders, have come to question traditional consumer experience and customer satisfaction measurement. The arguments and justifications of those in this group vary. For some, consumer experience and satisfaction measurement systems are valuable, but are simply too costly, complex, and time-consuming to undertake, especially in an era when the prevalence of consumer surveying has grown exponentially, response rates have declined dramatically, and data collection has become more difficult.[9] For others, measurement of different key performance indicators (KPIs) is simply deemed preferable for assorted reasons. A minority of these latter doubters have gone so far as to suggest that customer satisfaction is "worthless" and reject the need for its measurement or management entirely.[10] According to these more extreme contrarians, customer loyalty—and not customer satisfaction—is all that matters, and thus loyalty is all that should be measured. Perhaps the most influential example of this type of thinking comes from advocates of the "Net Promoter Score" (NPS™).

First outlined in-depth in the book *The Ultimate Question*—published in 2006 but actually an expanded version of an earlier, shorter 2003 article published in the Harvard Business Review—NPS supporters argue that measurement of customer satisfaction is an unnecessary waste of resources and that all companies really need to do is measure a proxy for and correlate of customer loyalty: how likely the consumer is to recommend the company/brand to others.[11] Because likelihood to recommend is both strongly associated with the individual's own loyalty intentions and behaviors, along with the ability to promote and attract new customers to the company through recommendation, so the argument goes, it alone is the one number companies need to measure and understand, the "one number they need to grow."

Described briefly, the NPS survey question asks a group of respondents (i.e., a sample of a company's customers) how likely they are to recommend the company to a friend or colleague (on a 0–10 scale). The NPS metric is calculated from the resulting data as the percentage of the sample of respondents that are "promoters" (those that answer 9 or 10 on the scale) minus the percentage of the sample that are "detractors" (those that answer from 0 to 6), with the difference between the two reflecting the "net" promoter score. (Those respondents giving a 7 or 8 on the scale are ignored as "neutral" or "passive" respondents, neither likely to promote nor to detract, and thus assumed to be silent about their experience.) The resulting statistic—which theoretically ranges from −100 (all detractors) to 100 (all promoters)—serves as the NPS for a company or other organization. And to be sure, over the past ten years or so, many companies have come to accept the advantages of NPS and the claims of its advocates. A large number of high-profile Fortune 500 companies have used or are currently using NPS, and anyone working in market research or consulting would have likely come across NPS at some point.

Why has NPS become so popular and been adopted by so many companies? NPS is, at its core, a rejection of traditional market research via consumer surveys and statistical methods that many companies have long struggled with. The NPS metric abandons all of this, conflates word-of-mouth (recommendation) and customer loyalty—two metrics already important to and measured by many companies—in favor of a simplistic, single-question approach. Then, and critically, its advocates claim that companies with strong NPS scores enjoy greater revenue growth and profitability than those with low scores, and that NPS is a better predictor of firm financial growth than any other metric. For these reasons alone, the idea is appealing to many. Indeed, a metric that promises to be a stronger driver of financial performance than any other, but that is also simple to measure, does not require a long survey, does not require substantial data collection efforts, does not require complex statistical methods, and can be understood by non-statisticians within companies sounds too good to be true. The problem is, however, that the promises made by NPS and its supporters *are* too good to be true.

The problems with NPS begin with how the metric is calculated, transforming a 0–10 scaled variable arbitrarily into a three-category variable. Why, for instance, should we assume that respondents answering 9 or 10 are definitely going to promote the company or brand, while those answering an 8 will do absolutely nothing? Are those respondents giving an "8" on the scale really that different than those that give a "9," in terms of their future behaviors, so much so that we should assume the "8s" will stay totally silent while the "9s" become active, frequent, boisterous promoters of the company and its brands? Conversely, are those respondents answering a 0 versus a 6 all really the same, in terms of their likelihood to speak negatively about a company?

Should a company that finds that 50% of its customers give it a "10" while the other 50% give it a "6" really have the same NPS score as one where 50% of its customers give it a "9" and the other 50% a "0," resulting in a dramatically lower mean score on the raw "likelihood to recommend" survey variable? These and many similar oddities used to calculate NPS cause the experienced market researcher to question the validity of the metric out of the gate.

Yet much has already been written about these issues and about the methodological and statistical shortcomings of NPS that result from transforming an 11-point variable (0–10 scale) into a three-category variable.[12] What are the real, practical implications of the imprecision of NPS, in terms of its sensitivity to differences and thus the meaningfulness of insights gleaned from it? To find out, we examined a sample of data from the ACSI from 2017, the same sample examined and described previously covering customers/survey respondents of nearly 400 companies in 48 different economic industries. To get at the usefulness of NPS, we compared ACSI's 0–100 customer satisfaction variable with the NPS variable from the same sample. Using this data, we calculated company-level mean scores, standard errors, and 95% confidence intervals (CIs) for both variables. The results of this analysis are included in Table 7.3 below.

The 95% CI is the most important statistic in Table 7.3. A cornerstone of inferential statistics, a 95% CI is interpreted as the probability of observing the same results 95 times if you were to draw 100 random samples for the same variables, within a margin of error. The CI is that margin of error. These results show that, on average, we can expect an NPS score to vary randomly 9.1 points across samples. In other words, a company that sees its NPS at 32 and 41 across two separate samples may only be seeing random noise instead of a real difference. By comparison, the ACSI satisfaction variable varies only 2.3 points on average. Normalizing these estimates for the different sizes of the scales (−100 to 100 vs. 0–100), the results show that while the ACSI variable should be expected to randomly vary about 2.2% on its scale between samples, the NPS score varies about 4.5%, or more than twice as much variance. This larger random noise exists for NPS when compared to the ACSI variable precisely because of the way in which the metric is calculated and in how respondents are arbitrarily assigned to the underlying NPS categories.

Table 7.3 NPS, ACSI, and statistical precision

Variable	N (companies)	Mean	SD	SE	95% CI	Lower	Upper
ACSI (0–100)	395	76.9	19.2	1.2	2.3	74.6	79.2
NPS (−100 to 100)	395	32.0	75.8	4.6	9.1	22.9	41.1

Source: Authors' creation from American Customer Satisfaction Index data and methods

Likewise, any additional analysis done on the NPS variable—such as any type of correlation or regression analysis—is much more likely to produce unreliable results because of this same random variance.

The source of the much greater random error in NPS—the transformation of the variable from its original 0–10 scale into three arbitrary categories—also complicates any practical efforts for companies working to improve their NPS. That is, assuming firms seek to improve their NPS by maximizing "promoters," the data becomes even more error-prone and even less reliable. Across the same sample of companies analyzed, the "promoter" group shows average normalized variance of 5.7%. Thus, even a very large boost in the proportion of promoters for a company—from 55% to 60%, for example—may represent nothing more than random noise, rather than the effects of any actions taken.

Finally, because the average sample size of completed interviews per company in the analysis is reasonably large (more than 425 respondents per company), it is important to note that at smaller sample sizes the random variance in NPS will increase dramatically, making interpretation of the metric even more difficult. For instance, holding all else constant in the analysis, but changing the company-level sample sizes to a smaller but not at all uncommon 100 interviews per company instead of 425, the 95% CI for NPS increases to 14.8, meaning that an NPS of 46 and one of 32 might not actually be meaningfully different (for sake of comparison, the same sample size change would take the 95% CI for the ACSI variable to only 3.8 from 2.3).

Based on the comparisons, it is unsurprising that NPS' central claim, the argument that first garnered attention and resulted in its adoption by many companies—that the metric is the strongest predictor of firm revenue and profitability growth—has been repeatedly disproven.[13] The NPS metric is not the strongest predictor of growth, and its failure to predict growth is directly related to the random noise created when calculating it. The logic is simple to understand, as we have illustrated in this section. But the statistical and econometrics rationale go much deeper as well. Specifically, as we also stated in Chap. 6, simply measuring customer satisfaction as a function of how likely a customer is to recommend a good or service to another potential customer does not capture the full variance of satisfaction or loyalty, nor its predictive impact, level, and change over time. The noise in the NPS data has serious implications. As a very coarse-grained example, any company leader would be hard pressed to justify the chance that revenue for the year, for example, would be 11% different just by chance (or an 11% drop in stock price). Why would a company then be accepting an absolute data difference 14.8% for NPS versus 3.8% for ACSI? That margin of error is too large.

But even beyond the ability of the NPS metric to predict growth, it must be noted that it is never advisable to disconnect customer satisfaction, customer loyalty, recommendation, or any other outcome variable from the broader context in which these perceptions emerge. Doing so ignores vital information. For example, there is typically a very strong (though neither perfect nor consistent) positive statistical relationship between customer satisfaction and loyalty; as satisfaction increases, so too does loyalty. But the linkage between the two measures varies both across different industries and over time. In practice, this means that satisfaction can matter more or less to loyalty in some industries rather than others, and that this relationship can shift for a single industry or company based on other external factors (such as competition in the market, macroeconomic conditions) over time. Thus, tracking not just the scores but also the relationship between the two metrics at regular intervals is critical.

Moreover, most high-quality and action-oriented market research measures not only customer satisfaction and loyalty, but also the key drivers of satisfaction (i.e., predictive influencing factors) for the company and its products and services, with the goal of better understanding how these can be manipulated and improved to increase satisfaction and loyalty. For example, a bank may certainly want to know its customers' satisfaction, loyalty, and propensity to recommend the bank to others, but it must also measure how things like number of branches or ATMs, quality of customer service personnel, quality of the website, and so forth are viewed by consumers, and how these variables impact both satisfaction and loyalty. Only with this information can the company make efficient improvements in the attributes that matter most to customers and thereby most effectively improve their experiences.

Across Chaps. 3, 4 and 5, we discussed in detail the dynamics of customer satisfaction over the last 25 years. In particular, in those chapters we focused on the fact that satisfaction improvements appear to have been driven almost entirely by improved consumer perceptions of value, while consumer perceptions of quality have been unchanged. Quality, as we said earlier, has more potential power in driving satisfaction but has been limited in doing so because of the flatness of the perceptions of quality of the last 25 years. Based on this data, we concluded that the Information Age has allowed companies to pass efficiency-driven cost savings on to consumers, lessening the need for investments in quality, and that this, therefore, is how companies have gone about providing higher satisfaction to consumers. But could there be another parallel development responsible for this trend, for the lack of improvement in quality and companies relying on price to boost satisfaction? Based on the analysis of NPS, another explanation for lagging consumer perceptions of quality over the last 25 years, and particularly the small decline in quality over the last ten years, should be considered.

Could it be that popular but highly flawed and uninformative metrics like NPS have failed firms, leading them to misunderstand the importance of quality to improved satisfaction—or even *how* to improve quality at all? Are companies wasting time and resources chasing the noise endemic to NPS, time, and resources that would be far better deployed on solid measurement that can help realize real changes that will improve the customer experience? These possibilities must be considered. After all, low-quality metrics often lead to poor decision-making, and are sometimes worse than no metrics at all. Moving forward, companies that want to compete on more than price, that want to improve their customers' experiences in an efficient way that also improves perceptions of quality relative to competitors and drives business their way, are far better served relying on concise, well-designed, and reliable consumer surveys and statistical models in doing so (a one-question NPS survey or a 410-question JD Power survey are not the answers—the NPS for the reasons discussed and the JD Power satisfaction assessment for survey fatigue reasons, where the quality of the data the respondents provide deteriorate to the point of being unreliable and invalid). Absent this, the stagnant quality consumers perceive from the economy may continue, and ultimately lead to weaker satisfaction and economic troubles, both for firms and national economies.

Notes

1. For examples of the business community worrying about the loyalty of these generational cohorts, see: Glasheen, J. "Millennial Brand Loyalty Comes into Question," *RetailWire.com*, November 26, 2018; Sharma, V. "Marketing to Gen Z: Death of Brand Loyalty," February 5, 2019.
2. See: Fry, R. "Millennials Projected to Overtake Baby Boomers as America's Largest Generation," *Pew Research Center*, March 1, 2018. Accessed online at: https://www.pewresearch.org/fact-tank/2018/03/01/millennials-overtake-baby-boomers/
3. See: Gherini, A. "Gen-Z is About to Outnumber Millennials. Here's How That Will Affect the Business World," *INC.com*, August 22, 2018. Accessed online at: https://www.inc.com/anne-gherini/gen-z-is-about-to-outnumber-millennials-heres-how-that-will-affect-business-world.html.
4. For a review of the importance of customer loyalty, see: Anderson, E. W., C. Fornell and D. R. Lehmann (1994). "Customer Satisfaction, Market Share, and Profitability: Findings from Sweden," *Journal of Marketing*, 58(3), 53–66.
5. The ACSI customer retention variable is derived from a 1–10 scaled question asking the consumer their "likelihood to purchase from the same company in

the future." The resulting 1–10 scaled variable is transformed to an estimate of customer retention, with those scoring very low on the scale (1–4) given a "0%" probability of being retained, and most of the rest of the responses divided by 10 to create a probability equal to their response (e.g., 5 = 0.5, 6 = 0.6). As no consumer is certain to remain loyal in the future, those replying with a "10" are given only a 90% probability of being retained.

6. Like almost all studies of its kind, the ACSI only interviews consumers 18 years of age or older.

7. For a recent study on this topic using ACSI data, see: Morgeson, F. V., III, Hult, T., Mithas, S., Keiningham, T., Fornell, C., & Duan, Q. (2020). Customer Loyalty Payoffs from Complaint Management: A Comprehensive Examination, Working Paper, Ann Arbor, MI: American Customer Satisfaction Index.

8. See: Morgeson, F. V., III, Hult, T., Mithas, S., Keiningham, T., Fornell, C., & Duan, Q. (2020). Customer Loyalty Payoffs from Complaint Management: A Comprehensive Examination, Working Paper, Ann Arbor, MI: American Customer Satisfaction Index.

9. For a discussion of this trend, see: Kennedy, C. and H. Hartig. "Response Rates in Surveys Have Resumed Their Decline," *PewResearch.org*, February 27, 2019. Accessed online at: https://www.pewresearch.org/fact-tank/2019/02/27/response-rates-in-telephone-surveys-have-resumed-their-decline/.

10. For this argument, see: Gitomer, J. (1998). *Customer Satisfaction is Worthless, Customer Loyalty is Priceless: How to Make Customers Love You, Keep Them Coming Back and Tell Everyone They Know*, Bard Press: Austin, TX.

11. For the original article, see: Reichheld, F. F. "The One Number You Need to Grow," *Harvard Business Review*, December 2003. For the larger book on the topic, see: Reichheld, F. F. (2006). *The Ultimate Question: Driving Good Profits and True Growth*, Cambridge, MA: Harvard Business School Press.

12. For an excellent review of the many problems of Net Promoter Score, see: Zaki, M., D. Kandeil, A. Neely and J. R. McColl-Kennedy (2016). *The Fallacy of the Net Promoter Score: Customer Loyalty Predictive Model*. University of Cambridge: Cambridge Service Alliance. Accessed online at: https://pdfs.semanticscholar.org/6b43/8d668d66ce8a3bdd569758c4f6368b316d87.pdf

13. See: Keiningham, T. L., B. Cooil, T. W. Andreassen and L. Aksoy (2007). "A Longitudinal Examination of Net Promoter and Firm Revenue Growth," *Journal of Marketing*, 71(3), 39–51.

References and Further Reading

Anderson, E. W., Fornell, C., & Lehmann, D. R. (1994). Customer Satisfaction, Market Share, and Profitability: Findings from Sweden. *Journal of Marketing, 58*(3), 53–66.

DeWitt, T., Nguyen, D. T., & Marshall, R. (2008). Exploring Customer Loyalty Following Service Recovery: The Mediating Effects of Trust and Emotions. *Journal of Service Research, 10*(3), 269–281.

Fornell, C. (2007). *The Satisfied Customer: Winners and Losers in the Battle for Buyer Preference*. New York: Palgrave Macmillan.

Fornell, C., & Bookstein, F. L. (1982). Two Structural Equation Models: LISREL and PLS Applied to Consumer Exit-Voice Theory. *Journal of Marketing Research, 19*(4), 440–452.

Fry, R. (2018, March 1). Millennials Projected to Overtake Baby Boomers as America's Largest Generation. *Pew Research Center*. Retrieved from https://www.pewresearch.org/fact-tank/2018/03/01/millennials-overtake-baby-boomers/

Gherini, A. (2018, August 22). Gen-Z is About to Outnumber Millennials. Here's How That Will Affect the Business World. *INC.com*. Retrieved from https://www.inc.com/anne-gherini/gen-z-is-about-to-outnumber-millennials-heres-how-that-will-affect-business-world.html

Gitomer, J. (1998). *Customer Satisfaction Is Worthless, Customer Loyalty Is Priceless: How to Make Customers Love You, Keep Them Coming Back and Tell Everyone They Know*. Austin, TX: Bard Press.

Glasheen, J. (2018, November 26). Millennial Brand Loyalty Comes into Question. *RetailWire.com*. Retrieved from https://www.retailwire.com/discussion/millennials-brand-loyalty-comes-into-question/

Gupta, S., & Lehmann, D. (2005). *Managing Customers as Investments: The Strategic Value of Customers in the Long Run*. Upper Saddle River, NJ: Pearson Education.

Hart, C. W., Heskett, J. L., & Earl Sasser, W., Jr. (1990). The Profitable Art of Service Recovery. *Harvard Business Review, 68*(4), 148–156.

Hirschman, A. O. (1970). *Exit, Voice, and Loyalty: Responses to Decline in Firms, Organizations, and States*. Cambridge: Harvard University Press.

Hult, G. T. M., Morgeson, F. V., Morgan, N. A., Mithas, S., & Fornell, C. (2017). Do Managers Know What Their Customers Think and Why? *Journal of the Academy of Marketing Science, 45*(1), 37–54.

Keiningham, T. L., Cooil, B., Andreassen, T. W., & Aksoy, L. (2007). A Longitudinal Examination of Net Promoter and Firm Revenue Growth. *Journal of Marketing, 71*(3), 39–51.

Kennedy, C., & Hartig, H. (2019, February 27). Response Rates in Surveys Have Resumed Their Decline. *PewResearch.org*. Retrieved from https://www.pewresearch.org/fact-tank/2019/02/27/response-rates-in-telephone-surveys-have-resumed-their-decline/

Morgan, N. A., & Rego, L. L. (2006). The Value of Different Customer Satisfaction and Loyalty Metrics in Predicting Business Performance. *Marketing Science, 25*(5), 426–439.

Morgeson, F. V., III, Hult, T., Mithas, S., Keiningham, T., Fornell, C., & Duan, Q. (2020). Customer Loyalty Payoffs from Complaint Management: A Comprehensive Examination, Working Paper, Ann Arbor, MI: American Customer Satisfaction Index.

Reichheld, F. F. (2003). The One Number You Need to Grow. *Harvard Business Review, 81*(12), 46–55.

Reichheld, F. F. (2006). *The Ultimate Question: Driving Good Profits and True Growth.* Cambridge, MA: Harvard Business School Press.

Sharma, V. (2019, February 5). Marketing to Gen Z: Death of Brand Loyalty. *MediaPost.com.* Retrieved from https://www.mediapost.com/publications/article/331541/marketing-to-gen-z-death-of-brand-loyalty.html

Zaki, M., Kandeil, D., Neely, A., & McColl-Kennedy, J. R. (2016). The Fallacy of the Net Promoter Score: Customer Loyalty Predictive Model. Cambridge: University of Cambridge. Retrieved from https://pdfs.semanticscholar.org/6b43/8d668d66ce8a3bdd569758c4f6368b316d87.pdf

8

Satisfied Customers: An Asset Driving Financial Performance

Chapter Overview

In this chapter, we seek to answer what is possibly the most important question addressed in the book: Is there a significant relationship between the experiences customers have with a company, measured as customer satisfaction, and a company's financial performance? Can customer satisfaction help predict a company's long-term financial performance? The chapter begins with a brief and non-technical review of the foundations of the relationship between consumer experiences, customer satisfaction, outcomes of satisfaction and subsequent consumer behaviors, and company financial performance. We continue by considering the empirical evidence relating satisfaction (as measured by ACSI) to a variety of important financial performance metrics tracked by most companies and market analysts. The chapter concludes with an in-depth analysis of the relationship between ACSI and stock market performance, arguably the most-watched measure of a company's overall financial success.

Key Conclusions

- The theoretical and practical foundations of the linkages between customer satisfaction and financial performance connect consumer experiences, satisfaction, and the outcomes of satisfaction, which then impact a company's financial performance.

Significant parts of this chapter are based on the authors' article titled, "Stock Returns on Customer Satisfaction Do Beat the Market: Gauging the Effect of a Marketing Intangible." This article was originally published in the *Journal of Marketing* in 2016.

© The Author(s) 2020
C. Fornell et al., *The Reign of the Customer*, https://doi.org/10.1007/978-3-030-13562-1_8

- Customer satisfaction as measured by ACSI has been positively linked to a wide range of a company's financial performance metrics, including revenue growth, market share, earnings, and various metrics of market value.
- Notably, customer satisfaction (ACSI) has consistently been found to be a positive and significant predictor of a company's stock market performance that consistently outperforms the S&P 500.

8.1   Foundations of the Customer Satisfaction-Financial Performance Relationship

In the preceding chapters, we have examined a wealth of data regarding consumer perceptions of their experiences with goods and services, focusing on the evolution of these perceptions over the past 25 years. At the center of the ACSI model, as we described in Chap. 1 (see Fig. 1.1 and the Appendix to Chap. 1), lies customer satisfaction or ACSI, the "hub" of the model sitting between and mediating the relationship between consumer experiences and their future attitudes and behaviors. The ACSI model is a cause-and-effect model with drivers of satisfaction on the left side (customer expectations, perceived quality, and perceived value), customer satisfaction (the so-called ACSI index) in the center, and outcomes of satisfaction on the right side (customer complaints and customer loyalty, including customer retention and price tolerance). These right-hand variables are the ones that then oftentimes are modeled to have an effect on a company's financials—our focus in Chap. 8. Customer satisfaction is the most general and powerful metric included in the ACSI model, as it serves as a proxy for the totality of consumer attitudes toward their experiences with goods and services, simultaneously a consequence of the consumer perceptions and the strongest predictor of future behaviors. These relationships are significant at the individual customer, company, and country levels, as several of the previous chapters have addressed.

For example, in Chap. 5, we provided strong evidence that customer satisfaction does indeed fulfill this multi-purpose, opting to describe the observed relationship between ACSI and important macroeconomic indicators, and thus showing the importance of aggregate customer satisfaction to a national economy. But our earlier discussion left open a critical question: For the individual company, does customer satisfaction really matter, or is it just a "feel good" marketing and public relations tool, as many companies seem to view and use it? In other words, is customer satisfaction predictive of company financial performance, and if so, how does the relationship work? In this chapter, we seek to answer these questions in more concrete detail than we did in Chap. 5. The customer satisfaction to performance link is powerful, and incredibly important for companies and policymakers to understand.

Let us begin by briefly describing the foundations of the theoretical relationship between customer satisfaction and company financial performance. In simplified form, the linkages between customer satisfaction, its drivers and outcomes, and financial performance can be summarized graphically as shown in Fig. 8.1.

The relationship between customer satisfaction and company financial performance begins with the totality of consumer experiences with a company's offerings. This includes some that precede the actual acquisition of the good or service, like experiences with advertising, information about and perceptions of the company's brand, and the customer's expectations about a forthcoming experience. Once the consumer has actually acquired the good or service and thus becomes a customer, he or she experiences the cost of acquiring the good/service via the price paid and directly experiences the quality of the product and/or service by use, consumption, or participation in its delivery. This happens both immediately, as a judgment about its usefulness and value to the individual customer upon first use, and over time regarding its reliability and durability. Common customer experiences may also include problems or failures with the good or service and the company's efforts to resolve these problems quickly and effectively (see more in Chap. 6), along with a variety of more finite and idiosyncratic attributes specific to only certain consumer industries (attributes that we have described throughout Chaps. 2, 3, 4, 5, 6 and 7).

Fig. 8.1 The customer satisfaction-financial performance relationship. (Source: Authors' creation from American Customer Satisfaction Index data and methods)

The aggregate of all of these customer experiences over a period of time eventually leads the consumer to a judgment. The judgment may not result from a defined or "tidy" cognitive process. It may, in fact, only exist subconsciously in the consumer's mind, and/or it may not occur until well after the original purchase and consumption when the consumer begins to consider a new purchase of the same or a similar type of good or service—a determination of customer satisfaction. It is based on this satisfaction determination that the consumer makes a final judgment about pleasure and fulfillment with the consumption experience provided by a particular company. In this moment, the consumer considers the sum total of his or her experiences with the past purchase, use, and consumption, and based on this information, decides about future purchasing behaviors.

It is the satisfaction determination on the part of the customer that drives a number of potential outcomes relating to future customer behaviors, including (but not limited to): a desire by the customer to remain loyal to the company, or alternatively to seek another supplier and defect (loyalty intention and behavior); a decision to speak to others and recommend the company and its goods (recommendation or word-of-mouth); a desire to buy or use the company's goods and services more, buy new or different products from the company, or to buy more expensive alternatives from the company (increased usage, cross-selling, up-selling). Based on too many research studies to outline here (but some that are included in citations in this and other chapters), customer satisfaction has shown to be positively associated with all of these behaviors. In turn, all of these behaviors are considered to be positively related to a company's financial prospects in various ways such as stronger sales and revenue growth, stronger and less variable cash flow growth, and larger market share, claims we provide evidence for below.

Importantly, companies that enjoy stronger loyalty through satisfaction have also been shown to require less advertising, marketing, and price discounting in order to retain current customers or to win new customers, which provides financial benefits to the company via lower customer acquisition or price inducement costs (and thus greater earnings and profitability). Among the many benefits of customer satisfaction, it has also been shown to reduce costs related to warranties and defective goods, complaints and complaint management, and field service costs for companies. Empirical evidence also suggests that customer perceptions of superior quality, which are strongly related to customer satisfaction, are associated with stronger economic returns. Several case-based research studies have also found that customer satisfaction is positively associated with employee loyalty, cost competitiveness, profitable performance, and long-term growth.[1]

Few scholars and businesspeople would dispute, at least in theory, the existence of most of the satisfaction-related relationships considered so far, as they lie at the heart of not only the marketing function, but at the very center of the concept of free market capitalism. In our collective understanding of free markets since the active days of Adam Smith, around the time when the United States Declaration of Independence was adopted in 1776, higher utility-producing companies (i.e., more satisfying companies) are expected to thrive and grow, while companies that do the opposite are expected to shrink and go bankrupt. If we were to find that these conditions did not hold, that more satisfying companies somehow performed the same as any other company financially, we would need to fundamentally rethink our basic understanding of capitalism. Yet while the logic may be simple and convincing, what about real, solid evidence? Innumerable studies have confirmed a link between customer satisfaction and firm financial performance. We review a selection of these studies in Chap. 8, starting with the empirical evidence of the satisfaction-performance link.

8.2   Evidence of the Customer Satisfaction-Financial Performance Relationship

While we have only included content in the book that tells the ACSI story, provide learning, and value, perhaps the most important content we can provide to those who may be skeptical about the impact of customer satisfaction relates to the empirical evidence of the customer satisfaction—financial performance relationship. Companies really do benefit significantly from managing customer satisfaction. Positively, numerous scientific articles have been written showcasing the reliable and valid link between customer satisfaction and a company's financial performance. In this section of the book, we summarize the voluminous literature that finds a positive relationship between customer satisfaction, as measured by ACSI, and the financial performance of companies, focusing only on robust, academic, peer-reviewed studies investigating the types of financial metrics most often used by companies.[2] We proceed in order from the association between ACSI and company sales and revenue growth, through to several other core financial metrics—such as market share, earnings and profitability, and overall firm market value. Given the importance many publicly traded companies place on stock price, we dedicate a separate section, as follows, to provide an in-depth discussion of the customer satisfaction—stock market relationship.

Sales/Revenue Growth. Virtually any financial or accounting performance metric is important in the context of validating the critical nature of customer satisfaction for a company (and a country). Let us begin with revenue and sales growth, measures of financial success that are, in many respects, the most basic and fundamental indicators of company financial performance. That is, among the many diverse objectives of varied businesses, a common goal of virtually all of them is to sell more of their products and services to consumers this year (or quarter) than last year (or quarter). Revenue growth is typically measured by companies as the change in total dollar sales (or the company's home-country currency) from one period to the next but can also be measured as the period-to-period change in unit sales, service usages rates, room occupancy (for hotels), and so forth.

As described earlier, the theoretical basis of the relationship between customer satisfaction and firm sales or revenue growth results from positive customer experiences with a company's products and services, resulting in stronger customer satisfaction, which in turn leads to favorable outcomes like stronger customer loyalty (stabilizing revenue through repeat business), stronger word-of-mouth (helping to bring in new customers and more revenue), and more up- and cross-selling activity and usage (bolstering sales of new or more expensive goods). A variety of academic studies have confirmed these relationships and found statistically significant and sizable relationships between customer satisfaction and revenue/sales growth.

For example, using ACSI satisfaction data, both Keiningham et al. (2007) and Morgan and Rego (2006) find a strong, positive impact of customer satisfaction on both firm revenue and revenue growth. Importantly, both studies also compare the effect of ACSI on revenue and revenue growth to a variety of other marketing metrics—including customer complaint rate, "top-box" customer satisfaction, and Net Promoter Score (NPS)—and find that ACSI is a significantly stronger predictor of revenue than the other satisfaction metrics. Other research teams (Gruca and Rego 2005) have confirmed and helped to explain this evidence by finding a positive relationship between stronger customer satisfaction and stronger, more consistent cash flow for companies. Thus, as anticipated and predicted by theory, firms with stronger satisfaction do in fact experience stronger revenue and revenue growth, confirming the connection between satisfaction and these desirable financial outcomes for companies.[3]

Market Share. In virtually all private sector industries, companies are not alone in seeking to attract customers. With the exception of a few highly regulated industries (e.g., energy utilities and public sector services), competitors almost always exist. Market share as a performance measure gauges the success of a company by understanding how much of the total market of consumers a company controls relative to its competitors. While difficult in some cases to determine definitively, especially in highly differentiated industries with many small competitors, market share metrics are produced by dividing a company's revenue in a particular category by the total revenue generated from all sales in that category (i.e., collective sales by all companies that operate in the category).

The theoretical basis for expecting a positive customer satisfaction-market share relationship is similar to that for revenue growth. In both instances, companies that provide better experiences to their customers, resulting in stronger satisfaction, enjoy stronger loyalty (with satisfaction as a form of "defensive marketing" protecting existing market share), an ability to cost-effectively recruit a larger number of new customers (with satisfaction and word-of-mouth as tools for "offensive marketing" and new customer acquisition), the ability to better market new goods that increase share, and so forth. And here too, a strong association between customer satisfaction and market share has been discovered, though the relationship is not as simple and straightforward as might be expected.

In one study comparing satisfaction (as measured by ACSI) to a variety of other marketing metrics as predictors of a range of business outcomes, Morgan and Rego (2006) find that satisfaction is a positive, significant, and the relatively strongest predictor of market share of the metrics examined. In another study primarily focused on the impact of service failure on satisfaction and market share in the airline industry, researchers (Keiningham et al. 2014) find that customer satisfaction has a positive effect on market share, but that this relationship is mitigated by the existence of both major and minor service failure incidences. Interestingly, also using ACSI data as their measure of satisfaction, Morgan et al. (2013) find a negative association between ACSI and market share, though they attribute this finding mostly to the inability of some companies, once they become very large and dominant in a market, to satisfy more diverse consumer needs as their customers become more heterogenous. That is, while a company's customer satisfaction drives company revenue and market share to grow in tandem for a time, once a company grows very large and gains a large proportion of market share, the greater diversity of customers and customer needs make delivering consistently strong satisfaction more difficult. Thus, these largest market share companies seem to grow less satisfying over time.[4]

Earnings and Profitability. While both revenue growth and market share capture significant aspects of business success, they can at times conceal the means by which a company is increasing its revenue and share. Some companies, and especially younger companies seeking to grow their sales and market share, will often sacrifice earnings and profitability to achieve this market growth, anticipating that profitable growth will come in time. Measures of earnings and profitability, which can be computed simply by dividing revenue by expenses, account for this possibility and thus give a clearer picture of business success. Here too, the satisfaction of a company's customers can help inform how profitable a company is likely to be. And once again, the system of theoretical relationships described above explains the linkage. For example, a satisfying company that is creating loyal customers via high quality consumer experiences is less likely to require costly discounting to lure new customers or to keep old ones, increasing the firm's prospects for profitable growth. Similarly, that same company, because it is maintaining customer loyalty through these positive experiences, is less likely to require as much advertising or other marketing vehicles to attract new customers, again bettering the prospects for profitability.

As with revenue and market share, studies of the relationship between satisfaction and earnings suggest a positive relationship. Fornell et al. (2016) find a positive relationship between ACSI and both earnings per share and earnings surprises, or company earnings reports that exceed/fall short of analysts' forecasts. As we discuss in the next section on ACSI and stock returns, this latter finding is thought to be the mechanism through which customer satisfaction results in better-than-market stock performance for firms. Ngobo et al. (2012) find similar results and conclude that customer satisfaction as measured by ACSI is a powerful yet overlooked tool for analysts (and others) seeking to predict a company's earnings performance.[5]

Market Value. What is the real economic value of a company? While widely used and very important in their own right, the financial metrics reviewed so far focus first and foremost on a company's direct (and in some sense, relatively recent) success in improving the quantity of its exchanges with buyers, along with the profitability of those exchanges. The final category of financial performance examined in this section looks beyond this information and integrates the perceptions of the broader financial and investment community, including what it thinks of a company's past performance and future prospects for success—market value. The theory earlier explains the expected positive relationship between customer satisfaction and market value. In short, a company that enjoys all or many of the positive outcomes of satisfaction—including more loyal customers, customers willing to recommend a product or service, and customers willing to buy new or more expensive products from a company along with the need for less advertising, lower marketing and customer acquisition costs, and so forth—ought to enjoy a greater market value. The reason for this greater market value is the positive financial consequences of customer satisfaction initiatives, like stronger revenue growth, market share, and earnings, all of which are predictive of company performance in the stock market. To the extent that the investment community perceives these stronger company-customer relationships as responsible for the positives financials, they might also perceive greater future potential for the company, investing more than might otherwise be the case.

In its simplest formulation, the market value of a company can be measured as the sum total of everything that has been invested in the company at any given point in time (e.g., the market value of equity). A more complex and telling measure, however, is Tobin's q, which measures a company's overall market value as the ratio of its market value of equity divided by the cost to replace all the company's assets at current value. A Tobin's q greater than 1 (i.e., higher equity market value than replacement cost) indicates that a firm's market value is greater than the value of the sum of the company's assets. This suggests that the market perceives some unmeasured or unrecorded assets of the company and is more optimistic about the company's future prospects than the simple sum of its assets should otherwise warrant. In this context, that unrecorded, intangible strategic company asset is customer satisfaction, viewed from an asset-perspective as the strength of the company's relationships with its customers. On the other hand, a Tobin's q less than 1 indicates that the market value is less than the recorded value of the assets of the company. This suggests that the investment community may be undervaluing the company, or that it is considering other intangible factors (e.g., weak customer relationships and satisfaction) when (under)valuing the company's future prospects.

A large number of studies have found a positive relationship between customer satisfaction and Tobin's q—more, in fact, than need to be discussed here. One such study, by Anderson et al. (2004), examined the satisfaction—Tobin's q relationship both in the aggregate and across a broad range of individual consumer industries, and discovered that in virtually all cases the relationship was strong, positive, and significant. Since this study, there have been at least a dozen additional such studies conducted, all finding similar results.[6] Taken together, these findings suggest that customer satisfaction provides vital information about the value of a company that goes far beyond the sum total of its tangible assets. This intangible value takes the form of customer satisfaction—a strategic company asset—that represents a company's relationship with its customers that creates, or that the investment community believes will create, the conditions for the company to overperform relative to what its "assets on the book" suggests is likely.

In the final section of Chap. 8, we delve more in depth into a customer satisfaction-financial performance relationship that is related to all of the preceding metrics, one that is arguably more important than all of these—the relationship between customer satisfaction and stock returns of publicly traded companies.

8.3   Customer Satisfaction and Stock Returns

To almost anyone reading this book, the following statement will probably seem trivial: A publicly traded company's stock market performance is very important. From the perspective of the firm, the sale of securities provides vital capital to spend on new or increased production capacity, research and development, new or improved product advertising and marketing, and a host of other activities essential to long-term business success. Poor stock market performance can make it difficult for firms to keep or raise this capital, and also to service debt already accumulated. For a company's management team, stock market success or failure is vital as well. A substantial proportion of CEOs have their variable compensation tied to the market returns of their company. These CEOs also often receive share options as a substantial portion of their bonuses, which thus become more or less valuable as a consequence of market performance. Conversely, poor stock market performance can lead to the replacement of a firm's management team, and innumerable CEOs have been replaced due, at least in part, to perceptions that the firm's stock market performance is sub-par (though the wisdom of these moves and their positive impact on equity prices is questionable[7]).

At its core, the stock market value of a publicly traded company reflects the collective perception from the business and investment community about the current performance and both short- and long-term prospects of a company—how it has performed in the past, is performing now, and how well it is likely to perform in the future. For example, stock market pricing is related to, and driven by, all of the financial performance metrics discussed earlier in Chap. 8, along with others. And if, as both the theory and the empirical evidence reviewed suggest, customer satisfaction tends to improve repeat business, usage levels, up- and cross-selling opportunities, positive word-of-mouth, and resultant future revenues, market share, earnings, and market value, it seems logical to expect that these effects will impact company stock prices and changes in those prices. We would expect these effects to be direct, but also mediated through satisfaction's impact on the financial performance measures discussed above. Do these expectations hold? Is customer satisfaction included in this list of predictors of company stock market performance?

The first definitive study on the topic (Fornell et al. 2006) found a strong and positive relationship between a company's customer satisfaction and its stock market performance, after controlling for industry differences and related variables. Since this study, a debate about whether firms with superior customer satisfaction also earn better-than-average stock returns has taken hold in the business and marketing literature. Hoping to end the debate once and for all about the effect of customer satisfaction on stock prices, three authors (Fornell et al. 2016) recently conducted a 15-year analysis using data from the ACSI to represent customer satisfaction and stock market returns from publicly traded companies in the U.S.. The study also replicated the analysis using similar data in the U.K.[8]

For the U.S. analysis, the satisfaction scores for the publicly traded companies were related to actual stock portfolio returns and changes from a fund trading exclusively on customer satisfaction information.[9] In other words, real returns from a real portfolio of strong customer satisfaction companies were purchased over time to test this relationship, and the results were not merely based on "hypothetical" back-testing, which is often open to "researcher manipulation." The findings were nothing short of remarkable.

When examining the cumulative satisfaction portfolio returns, the results show 518% growth over a 15-year period, compared to only a 31% increase for the S&P 500 over the same period (see Fig. 8.2). The consistency of the over performance is uncanny; on an annual basis, the customer satisfaction

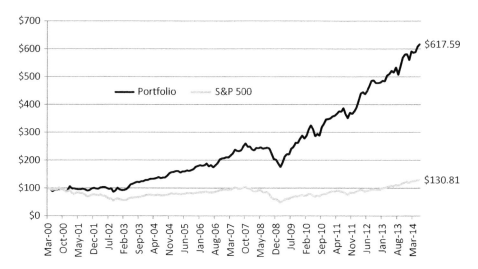

Fig. 8.2 Cumulative returns on $100 invested in the customer satisfaction portfolio versus the S&P 500, April 2000–June 2014. (Source: Authors' creation from American Customer Satisfaction Index data and methods)

portfolio outperformed the S&P 500 in 14 out of the 15 years included in the analysis. But do these results generalize across time and space and over economic contexts? As to the question of whether the results hold in a different stock market, the authors validated their analysis in another country, the U.K., using similar data available in that market, allowing for direct comparisons between the U.S. and U.K. markets. As Fig. 8.3 shows, the results are highly consistent in the U.K. when compared to those in the U.S.

Going a bit deeper into the results from the U.S. data, where there is a longer 15-year period to study, the data show a large, positive, and significant "alpha," which indicates above-market returns outside the realm of random chance. The effect of customer satisfaction on stock price is also found to be, at least to some degree, channeled through earnings surprises, consistent with the findings discussed earlier. In other words, customer satisfaction allows firms to outperform what analysts (and others) believe will be the company's near-term financial performance, with the stock market reacting once this information is made public. As mentioned earlier, customer satisfaction has a significant effect on both earnings as well as earnings surprises.

As suggested by the sheer size of the abnormal stock returns based solely on trading with customer satisfaction information, the reward for having satisfied customers is much greater than is generally known. Customer satisfaction-based trading generates "excess" stock returns of about 10% per year. In short, companies and their management teams, whose fortunes are often closely tied

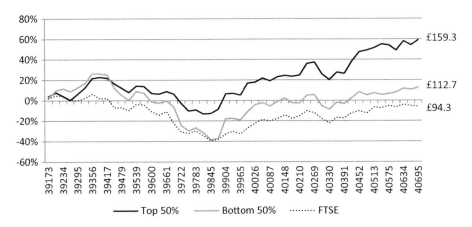

Fig. 8.3 Cumulative returns on £100 invested: High NCSI portfolio, low NCSI portfolio, and the FTSE 100. (Source: Authors' creation from American Customer Satisfaction Index data and methods. Note: The "High NCSI portfolio" consists of the top 50% of measured companies in customer satisfaction; the "Low NCSI portfolio" consists of the bottom 50% of measured companies in customer satisfaction)

to the stock market performance of their companies, ought to be closely tracking and managing their companies' customer satisfaction.

Given this, why are many firms not focusing adequate attention on improving the satisfaction of their customers? That is, if the economic benefits of high customer satisfaction in terms of improved consumer utility and shareholder value are as large as these findings suggest, why do many companies fail to improve customer satisfaction? Without a doubt, many companies ignore the importance of customer relationships. The explanation for this is likely to be found in inadequate customer data collection and/or a general misunderstanding of just how strategically valuable satisfied customers are as assets to a firm. In fact, many companies—even large, high-profile companies—do not even know what their customers think about them and why.[10] Many data collection vehicles exist and even a wealth of satisfaction data exist for companies. Yet, it is safe to say that there has not been corresponding progress in strategically developing and implementing satisfaction initiatives in many companies, as evidenced by the findings discussed in earlier chapters.

In fairness, it should be recognized that customer satisfaction information is not without interpretational challenges, some of which we discussed in Chap. 5. Consequently, it would be unrealistic to expect that equity markets would be frictionless with respect to such information. In addition to the friction associated with arbitrage costs, imperfect information, limitations on investors' cognitive and reasoning skills, and institutional rigidities that impair market efficiency, customer satisfaction is not a part of the analysis models most investors use. But based on these findings, it should be. We appear to be at a point where we should re-evaluate whether it is earnings or customer satisfaction that belongs among the "risk factors" used by investors to price assets. Empirically, they are correlated. One mitigates the effect of the other. But which one should be mitigated? What comes first, earnings or customer satisfaction? The answer is that earnings per se do not cause customer satisfaction, but there is ample evidence pointing in the other direction.

Notes

1. For a selection of articles that make these and related points, see: Anderson, E., C. Fornell and D. R. Lehmann (1994). "Customer Satisfaction, Market Share, and Profitability: Findings from Sweden," *Journal of Marketing*, 58, 53–66; Rust, R., A. Zahorik and T. L. Keiningham (1995). "Return on Quality (ROQ): Making Service Quality Financially Accountable," *Journal of Marketing*, 59(Apr.), 58–70; Heskett, J., W. E. Sasser and L. Schlesinger (1997). *The Service Profit Chain: How Leading Companies Link Profit and*

Growth to Loyalty, Satisfaction, and Value, Cambridge, MA: Harvard University Press; Bolton, R. (2004). "Linking Marketing to Financial Performance and Firm Value," *Journal of Marketing*, 68, 73–75; Gupta, S. and V. Zeithaml (2006). "Customer Metrics and Their Impact on Financial Performance," *Marketing Science*, 25(6), 718–739.

2. Ambler, T., F. Kokkinaki and S. Puntoni (2004). "Assessing Marketing Performance: Reasons for Metrics Selection," *Journal of Marketing Management*, 20, 475–498.

3. Gruca, Thomas S., and L. L. Rego (2005). "Customer Satisfaction, Cash Flow, and Shareholder Value," *Journal of Marketing*, 69(July), 115–130; Keiningham, Timothy L., Bruce Cooil, Tor Wallin Andreassen and Lerzan Aksoy (2007), "A Longitudinal Examination of Net Promoter and Firm Revenue Growth," *Journal of Marketing*, 71(July), 39–51; Morgan, N. A. and L. L. Rego (2006). "The Value of Different Customer Satisfaction and Loyalty Metrics in Predicting Business Performance," *Marketing Science*, 25(5); Anderson, E., C. Fornell and S. Mazvancheryl (2004). "Customer Satisfaction and Shareholder Value," *Journal of Marketing*, 68, 172–185.

4. Keiningham, T. L., F. V. Morgeson III, L. Aksoy and L. Williams (2014). "Service Failure Severity, Customer Satisfaction, and Market Share: An Examination of the Airline Industry," *Journal of Service Research*, 17(4), 415–431; Morgan, N. A. and L. L. Rego (2006). "The Value of Different Customer Satisfaction and Loyalty Metrics in Predicting Business Performance," *Marketing Science*, 25(5); Rego, Lopo L., Neil A. Morgan and Claes Fornell (2013). "Reexamining the Market Share–Customer Satisfaction Relationship," *Journal of Marketing* 77(5), 1–20.

5. Fornell, C., F. V. Morgeson III and T. Hult (2016). "Stock Returns on Customer Satisfaction Do Beat the Market: Gauging the Effect of a Marketing Intangible," *Journal of Marketing*, 80(5), 92–107; Ngobo, Paul-Valentin, Jean-Francois Casta and Olivier Ramond (2012), "Is Customer Satisfaction a Relevant Metric for Financial Analysts?" *Journal of the Academy of Marketing Science*, 40(3), 480–508.

6. For a small selection of the studies examining the ACSI-Tobin's q relationship, see: Luo, X. and C. B. Bhattacharya (2006). "Corporate Social Responsibility, Customer Satisfaction, and Market Value," *Journal of Marketing*, 70, 1–18; Morgan, N. A. and L. L. Rego (2006). "The Value of Different Customer Satisfaction and Loyalty Metrics in Predicting Business Performance," *Marketing Science*, 25(5); Lariviere, B., T. L. Keiningham, L. Aksoy, A. YalCIn, F. V. Morgeson III and S. Mithas (2016). "Modeling Heterogeneity in the Satisfaction, Loyalty Intention, and Shareholder Value Linkage: A Cross-Industry Analysis at the Customer and Firm Levels," *Journal of Marketing Research*, 53(1), 91–109; Fornell, C., S. Mithas, F. V. Morgeson III and M. S. Krishnan (2006). "Customer Satisfaction and Stock Prices: High Returns, Low Risk," *Journal of Marketing* 70(1), 3–14.

7. Studies of CEO turnover, whether forced or voluntary, have been associated with greater volatility and downside risk for company stock market performance. See: Clayton, M. J., J. C. Hartzell and J. V. Rosenberg (2003). "The Impact of CEO Turnover on Equity Volatility," *Staff Reports 166*, Federal Reserve Bank of New York.

8. Fornell, C., S. Mithas, F. V. Morgeson III and M. S. Krishnan (2006). "Customer Satisfaction and Stock Prices: High Returns, Low Risk," *Journal of Marketing*, 70(1), 3–14; Fornell, C., S. Mithas and F. V. Morgeson III (2009). "The Economic and Statistical Significance of Stock Returns on Customer Satisfaction," *Marketing Science*, 28(5), 820–825; Fornell, C., F. V. Morgeson III and T. Hult (2016). "Stock Returns on Customer Satisfaction Do Beat the Market: Gauging the Effect of a Marketing Intangible," *Journal of Marketing*, 80(5), 92–107.

9. This fund has since been established as an exchange-traded fund (ETF) that can be purchased by any investor with the ticker symbol "ACSI." Information about the ETF can be viewed here: http://acsietf.com.

10. For evidence of managers' lack of understanding of their own customers, see: Hult, G. Tomas M., Forrest V. Morgeson III, Neil A. Morgan, Sunil Mithas and Claes Fornell (2017). "Do Managers Know What Their Customers Think and Why?" *Journal of the Academy of Marketing Science*, 45(1), 37–54.

References and Further Reading

Anderson, E., Fornell, C., & Lehmann, D. R. (1994). Customer Satisfaction, Market Share, and Profitability: Findings from Sweden. *Journal of Marketing, 58*, 53–66.

Anderson, E., Fornell, C., & Mazvancheryl, S. (2004). Customer Satisfaction and Shareholder Value. *Journal of Marketing, 68*, 172–185.

Bolton, R. (2004). Linking Marketing to Financial Performance and Firm Value. *Journal of Marketing, 68*, 73–75.

Fornell, C. (1992). A National Customer Satisfaction Barometer: The Swedish Experience. *Journal of Marketing, 55*(Jan.), 1–21.

Fornell, C., Mithas, S., & Morgeson, F. V., III. (2009a). The Statistical Significance of Portfolio Returns. *International Journal of Research in Marketing, 26*(2), 162–163.

Fornell, C., Mithas, S., & Morgeson, F. V., III. (2009b). The Economic and Statistical Significance of Stock Returns on Customer Satisfaction. *Marketing Science, 28*(5), 820–825.

Fornell, C., Mithas, S., Morgeson, F. V., III, & Krishnan, M. S. (2006). Customer Satisfaction and Stock Prices: High Returns, Low Risk. *Journal of Marketing, 70*(1), 3–14.

Fornell, C., Morgeson, F. V., III, & Hult, T. (2016). Stock Returns on Customer Satisfaction Do Beat the Market: Gauging the Effect of a Marketing Intangible. *Journal of Marketing, 80*(5), 92–107.

Gruca, T. S., & Rego, L. L. (2005). Customer Satisfaction, Cash Flow, and Shareholder Value. *Journal of Marketing, 69*(July), 115–130.

Gupta, S., & Zeithaml, V. (2006). Customer Metrics and Their Impact on Financial Performance. *Marketing Science, 25*(6), 718–739.

Heskett, J., Sasser, W. E., & Schlesinger, L. (1997). *The Service Profit Chain: How Leading Companies Link Profit and Growth to Loyalty, Satisfaction, and Value.* Cambridge, MA: Harvard University Press.

Hult, G. T. M., Morgeson, F. V., III, Morgan, N. A., Mithas, S., & Fornell, C. (2017). Do Managers Know What Their Customers Think and Why? *Journal of the Academy of Marketing Science, 45*(1), 37–54.

Keiningham, T. L., Cooil, B., Andreassen, T. W., & Aksoy, L. (2007). A Longitudinal Examination of Net Promoter and Firm Revenue Growth. *Journal of Marketing, 71*(July), 39–51.

Keiningham, T. L., Morgeson, F. V., III, Aksoy, L., & Williams, L. (2014). Service Failure Severity, Customer Satisfaction, and Market Share: An Examination of the Airline Industry. *Journal of Service Research, 17*(4), 415–431.

Kumar, V., & Shah, D. (2009). Expanding the Role of Marketing: From Customer Equity to Market Capitalization. *Journal of Marketing, 73*, 119–136.

Lariviere, B., Keiningham, T. L., Aksoy, L., YalCIn, A., Morgeson Iii, F. V., & Mithas, S. (2016). Modeling Heterogeneity in the Satisfaction, Loyalty Intention, and Shareholder Value Linkage: A Cross-Industry Analysis at the Customer and Firm Levels. *Journal of Marketing Research, 53*(1), 91–109.

Luo, X., & Bhattacharya, C. B. (2006). Corporate Social Responsibility, Customer Satisfaction, and Market Value. *Journal of Marketing, 70*, 1–18.

Morgan, N. A., & Rego, L. L. (2006). The Value of Different Customer Satisfaction and Loyalty Metrics in Predicting Business Performance. *Marketing Science, 25*(5), 426–439.

Ngobo, P.-V., Casta, J.-F., & Ramond, O. (2012). Is Customer Satisfaction a Relevant Metric for Financial Analysts? *Journal of the Academy of Marketing Science, 40*(3), 480–508.

Rego, L. L., Morgan, N. A., & Fornell, C. (2013). Reexamining the Market Share-Customer Satisfaction Relationship. *Journal of Marketing, 77*(5), 1–20.

Rust, R., Zahorik, A., & Keiningham, T. L. (1995). Return on Quality (ROQ): Making Service Quality Financially Accountable. *Journal of Marketing, 59*(Apr.), 58–70.

9

Your Future: Opportunities for Customer Centricity and Satisfaction

Chapter Overview

In this concluding chapter, we begin with a discussion of economic globalization, where goods and services are traded more freely between nations than ever before, and firms seek to spread their operations, goods, and services to all corners of the globe. We outline how this evolving and more complex business world—where companies often market to larger and more diverse populations of consumers—demands better and more exact metrics to measure and understand performance. However, small, medium, and large corporations alike seem to be ignoring this need for more robust metrics, too often turning to fad methods and confusing the availability of "Big Data" or easy-to-get data with data collected correctly and analyzed via valid analytical tools. The chapter closes with a look at the enormous potential value of a "Global Customer Satisfaction Index" based in the ACSI model to aid national economies, multinational corporations, and the worldwide economy as a whole as economic globalization proceeds.

Portions of this chapter are based on two of the authors' earlier articles: Morgeson III, Forrest V., Tomas Hult, and Pratyush Nidhi Sharma (2015). "Cross-National Differences in Consumer Satisfaction: Mobile Services in Emerging and Developed Markets." *Journal of International Marketing, 23*(2), 1–24; Morgeson III, Forrest V., Sunil Mithas, Timothy L. Keiningham, and Lerzan Aksoy (2011). "An Investigation of the Cross-National Determinants of Customer Satisfaction." *Journal of the Academy of Marketing Science, 39*(2), 198–215.

Key Conclusions

- Rapid globalization, especially over the past 20 years, has resulted in a more economically open world, with goods and services crossing national borders and companies internationalizing their operations more than ever before.
- Due to globalization, marketing research is more important than ever (domestic, foreign country-based, and cross-countries), with firms needing to measure the experiences of their customers in multiple, diverse markets simultaneously.
- Yet, global market research has in many ways regressed over the last 20 years, with companies turning to "quick-fix solutions" that have led them astray. Couple this lax research with the exponential increase in trade across country borders and the result is that companies are taking undue risks with their customer assets.
- We conclude the chapter with a call for a "Global Customer Satisfaction Index" and its advantages for multinational companies, national economies, and the global economy as a whole.

9.1   Economic Globalization

According to Pulitzer-prize-winning author Tom Friedman, as discussed in his bestseller *The World Is Flat*, the world became "tiny" with the advent of Globalization 3.0 around the year 2000. And the process of globalization continues. The World Economic Forum recently rolled out the foundational premise for a Globalization 4.0, and Klaus Schwab (Founder and Executive Chair of the World Economic Forum) pointedly said that "Globalization 4.0 has only just begun, but we are already vastly under-prepared for it."[1] Globalization 4.0 represents rapid emergence of ecological constraints, the advent of an increasingly multipolar international order, and rising inequality, but also tremendous customer expectations of increases in trade across country borders, supply chain efficiencies, and quality standards—all issues that directly affect customer satisfaction. Consequently, while the world and its many small, medium, and large corporations have managed customer satisfaction and the customer experience reasonably well in the Globalization 1.0, 2.0, and 3.0 periods summarized by Friedman, Globalization 4.0 presents unique challenges related to diversity, population increases, distinctive customer needs and wants, and global connectedness expectations, among myriad issues that affect how companies leverage their strategic customer assets.

It is no wonder that economic globalization and international trade are at the forefront of the minds of most business executives today. Due to advances in communications technology and commercial transportation, the people, economies, and governments of the world are more interconnected than ever before. The effects on each of these entities from the "shrinking" of the world have been profound. Focusing on the consequences of economic globalization, or the dramatic opening of most of the world's markets to dramatically increased foreign trade and investment, in Chaps. 4 and 5 we discussed some of the benefits (via better prices) being realized by consumers through globalization. Yet these trends deserve fuller attention, as they illustrate both the radical growth in global trade over the past 25 years and highlight their profound impact on consumers and markets worldwide. They also help problematize these globalization developments for firms seeking to satisfy their customers today.

The data are very telling on trade and production, and the implications for customer satisfaction are also profoundly telling. The value of trade across borders has grown faster than the growth in the cumulative production (GDP) of all countries for more than half a century. The value of world trade is forecasted to be about *167 times larger* in 2020 than it was in 1960, and the world economy to be 65 times larger in the same span. These numbers are inarguably astounding, yet may appear strange. Surely, we cannot trade more than we make, and of course we do not. What accounts for this trade growth is the combined trade of raw materials, work-in-process (e.g., component parts), and finished products. When we talk about trade, oftentimes we think only about the latter, just the finished goods that we as end-customer buy and use. But finished products account for less of the total trade value across countries than ever before. Over the years, companies have developed incredibly delicate and globalized value chains. For example, it is not unusual for a car manufactured by General Motors (e.g., Chevrolet) or Porsche (e.g., Cayenne) to have some 30,000 parts from about 80 countries.

At the macro level, Figs. 9.1 and 9.2 illustrate the dynamics that the world has seen in trade, production, population, and regional trade agreements (i.e., agreements involving more than two countries) since 1960. World trade and world production are indexed at 100 in 1960 in the figures. Figure 9.1 has data from 1960 to 2020, and Fig. 9.2 has data from 1960 to 2025, with the last five years forecasted using statistical forecasting techniques. Trade is defined as cross-country border trade, and production is defined as cumulative production for all countries (i.e., GDP for each country added together). Population is captured in millions on the left y-axis, and number of regional trade agreements in force is captured in actual numbers on the right y-axis. As

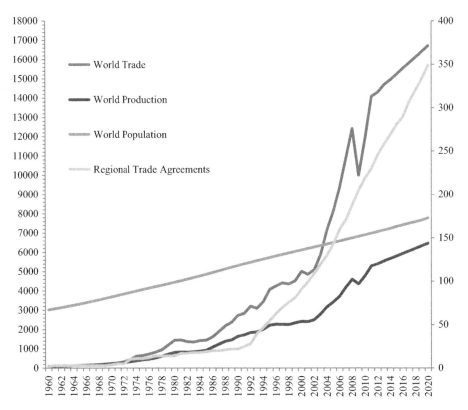

Fig. 9.1 The international marketplace, 1960–2020. (Source: The data are from United Nations, World Bank, and World Trade Organization)

expected, the globe's population has grown at a fairly steady rate from some 3.0 billion people in 1960 to about 7.8 billion people in 2020, with an estimate that global population will peak at some 11 billion people and then level off in about a century. Finally, at a coarse-grained level, global efficiency is defined as the value of total world trade relative to countries' total GDP production. A higher number means the world operates more "globally efficient."

Several reasons exist for why countries and companies realize value based on global efficiencies by engaging in multiple border crossings to make one product (such as, for example, automobiles). Lowering barriers to border transactions (e.g., tariffs) and specialization in production (e.g., component parts) are two of the primary macro-specific reasons. In short, the globe has become structured as a dynamic, always-evolving, and increasingly efficient web of supply chains. We have come to rely on these increased global efficien-

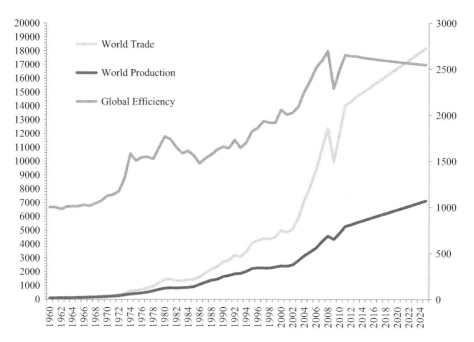

Fig. 9.2 Global efficiency, 1960–2025. (Source: The data are from United Nations, World Bank, and World Trade Organization. Years 2020–2025 are forecasted)

cies in production to progress toward a better world, improve standards of living, and aiding emerging markets to become higher-income nations. Recent trends in anti-globalization and economic nationalism notwithstanding, the efficiencies and benefits realized via economic globalization are likely to push this process forward in the future. Customers expect and demand these global efficiencies to increase, not decrease as we have seen since 2011 (Fig. 9.2).

There is cause for alarm on the globalization front. More customers (an increase from 3.0 to 7.8 billion people on the globe in the least 60 years) mean more diversity and heterogeneity in tastes, needs, and wants. More trading across country borders mean more heterogeneity in market segments and how to target the segments (i.e., a global, standardized approach is unlikely to appeal to Generation Z customers). More nationalistic tendencies—at least for now—mean less global efficiency in global supply chains and production. At the same time, there is no stopping the cross-border flow of raw materials, work-in-process (e.g., component parts), and finished products. Customers demand these trade flows to continue despite potentially higher costs due to lowered global efficiencies.

Let us illustrate the global efficiency dilemma we are facing (based on data in Fig. 9.2). For decades, global supply chains have supported a cumulative win-win for the world. From 1960 until 1972, the ratio between the value of what was traded across country borders to the cumulative production (GDP) for all countries was between 1.00 and 1.17. Basically, we traded about the same value of goods and services as what we produced. From 1973 to 1999, the trade-to-production ratio was between 1.32 and 1.92. But, from 2000 to 2017, we have hovered between annual ratios of 2.00 and 2.60. The troubling part is that for the first time in seven years, we saw the global efficiency ratio go below 2.60 in 2018, be at 2.57 in 2019, and then also expected to stay below 2.60 in 2020 (forecasted at 2.59). What does this mean? Generally, we can say that the efficiencies the world has developed in its global web of supply chains are now threatened with the escalation of tariffs and various forms of trade wars. So, we are faced with a world where costs may be increasing (e.g., tariffs), trade increasing, global efficiencies (slightly) decreasing, and customers who have come to rely on the international marketplace as one market, where they can buy anything that is produced anywhere.

9.2 Globalization and the "Marketing Metrics Problem"

Needless to say, based on the discussion above regarding economic globalization, but firms are increasingly focused on international markets to improve their total sales and profitability. As illustrated in the previous section, these globally active companies operate in a very complex and dynamic international business ecosystem.[2] Customers demand that the companies solve these complexities, and we as customers do not really want to be "in the know," per se, on how companies solve delivering on our needs and wants. It just needs to be done! Clearly, the international opportunities for all types of companies are endless given that the international marketplace has gone from some 3.0 billion people in 1960 to 7.8 billion people in 2020, with purchasing power increasing throughout the world (e.g., the globe has fewer poor people than ever in percentage of the total population). For small, medium, and large corporations alike, expanding into international markets carries the promise of more profitable sales growth. In 2018, for instance, about 43% of the total sales of S&P 500 listed U.S. firms were classified as foreign sales, an impressive percentage yet still well below its peak from prior to the Great Recession.[3] Crossing national boundaries to market goods, however, is not without difficulties. Indeed, moving from a single market where the firm has (typically) become good or excellent at pleasing one group of customers by meeting their wants and needs, to offering goods to many diverse groups of consumers in many markets simultaneously can be very difficult.

Many large, otherwise highly successful companies have experienced the difficulties of internationalization firsthand. Even firms with exceptional track records of success in globalizing their businesses sometimes fail to find success in certain national markets. This list includes high-profile companies like Home Depot (China), Walmart (South Korea, Germany), and even early leader in globalization McDonald's (Iceland, Barbados).[4] A simple search on the web provides numerous examples of companies that have failed for largely cultural reasons to become successful in some part of the world. Fortunately, the days when failure internationally was commonplace for many companies are over. Historically, these companies could continue to rely on their domestic, home-country markets and maintain performance success. Figures 9.1 and 9.2 illustrate that the exponential increase in trade across countries, especially in the last 20 years, will continue, and companies that cannot handle such international competitiveness will fail and they will fail across the board. International competition in foreign markets and international competition in companies' home-country markets will not be kind to the companies that do not nurture the customer experience appropriately, deliver on customer satisfaction, and treat customers as strategic company assets. Simplistically, while failures to globalize businesses almost always have multiple causes, they also almost always involve some level of an inadequate understanding of the firm's existing and new customers (e.g., the needs of existing customers are not static and cannot be treated as such).

The scaling-up of operations from a population of customers of size X to a much larger population of customers is invariably challenging, whether doing so inside a single market or across national markets. To clarify, we do not expect that every company needs to think about the international marketplace as a market that has increased from 3.0 billion people in 1960 to 7.8 billion people in 2020. Many of these people are not customers for all products and services. As always, segmentation of the marketplace needs to be done, but it is also clear that each market segment is much larger now than in 1960. Some of these related customer challenges are simply logistical and operational, of course, and emerge from the challenges inherent in serving a larger number of consumers. But when done internationally, scaling up is typically even more difficult, as not only are logistical challenges larger, but because customers in different national markets often have very different cultures, customs, traditions, expectations, wants, and needs. As such, for the multinational firm that is either considering expansion into a new national market or judging the performance of its operations already in that market, metrics for gauging its success in satisfying customer needs and wants are even more critical. In short, the strength and precision of marketing metrics must advance as the complexity of the environment to which they are being applied increases.

Whether focused on the internationalization of their brand or not, companies seem, in fact, to have at least recognized the increased importance of measuring their performance with customers. Today, companies are doing an enormous amount of market research, more than ever before (but not necessarily as rigorous in terms of reliability and validity as we mentioned earlier). Globally, spending on traditional market research and other emerging data collection and analysis efforts (e.g., AI, machine learning, social media monitoring) grew to more than US$80 billion in 2018.[5] It is not uncommon for large domestic U.S. firms to spend millions of dollars annually on data collection, data analysis, and implementation of learnings from analyzed data toward improving their consumers' experiences. Multinational firms have likewise followed suit. Many large MNCs now conduct cross-national market research programs examining consumer perceptions of their products and services across very diverse national markets simultaneously (e.g., developed and less developed, culturally distinct).[6] In many of these studies, data are collected using standardized survey instruments in multiple languages across a dozen or more countries/markets and the results are then compared across these markets and utilized as the basis for performance incentives, operational decision-making, and process improvement.

This stronger emphasis on market research, and especially as it is being deployed cross-nationally, has been aided by the appearance of "Big Data." Due to the Information Age, the internet, and the rise of computing power, phenomena we have discussed throughout earlier chapters, there is more data available for companies to analyze than ever before. One estimate suggests that the amount of data is growing so fast that more than 90% of the data that exists in the world has been created in just the last two years.[7] This rate of data creation is only accelerating, and Big Data refers to the vastly larger amount of information for companies to analyze—much of it publicly and freely available for analysis by any researcher or company—toward learning more about their customers. This is the age of Big Data but also the era of data overload and data noise. This type of abundance of data emerges from an array of sources, including traditional primary consumer survey data (though collected more easily and efficiently via the internet) but also includes customer loyalty program data, social media data, and internet search query data.

The combination of the three factors mentioned above—globalization, the proliferation of market research (both within and across national markets), and Big Data—is definitive of and essential to the rich information environment confronting companies today. Together, they have made possible and contributed to the rise of one final trend: "Customer Experience Management" (CEX or CXM) tools and applications. In the past, we often talked about Customer Relationship Management in the spirit of CEX, and now we are also moving to the notion of Customer Engagement as a new frontier that has to be managed relative to customer satisfaction. Given these customer-centric phenomena and strategic initiatives, a significant number of new companies, many of them only a decade or so old, have emerged to fulfill the needs of research-hungry companies trying to better understand their customers within and across multiple markets and better utilize the wealth of data available. These companies often focus on different aspects of the research process—such as online data collection, social media monitoring, dashboards for completing simple analysis, and attractively presenting results, among other tasks. Companies with names like Qualtrics, Medallia, Brandwatch, Tableau, Cint, and others lead the way in the CEX tools and applications space.

Given all of the trends considered above, let us now ask a question: Are these trends, which include economic globalization and a heightened emphasis on market research, new sources and types of data and information, the sheer quantity of data available, and CEX tools for more easily managing analysis of this wealth of data, really helping companies? Based on the data and findings presented thus far, we are in a position to answer this question, at least vis-à-vis the U.S. market. The U.S. remains the world's largest and wealthiest single market and the market where, it is fair to proclaim, most large domestic and multinational firms that attempt to enter it work hardest to please consumers and win market share. Thus, if anywhere at all, we would expect to see the fruits of these efforts (if they exist) to appear most clearly in the U.S. Have they appeared?

As we have discussed in earlier chapters, the historical trends in ACSI customer satisfaction data (including the other ACSI model variables—customer expectations, perceived quality, perceived value, complaint behavior, and customer loyalty) do not seem to point to either a longer or nearer-term explosion in consumer pleasure. The national ACSI score has increased significantly over the past 25 years, up 3.4% over the period. Over the past decade, when many of the trends discussed above along with the CEX tools designed to make analysis and presentation of data easier and more efficient really began to grow, the growth in satisfaction is even lower. National customer satisfaction is up only 1.3% over this period. But given the customer heterogeneity in the international business ecosystem, with the increase in population, and the exponential increase in international trade, the flatness of customer satisfaction (i.e., ACSI score) is predictable and understandable. This is the international marketplace that companies will continually face when targeting international consumers. And if companies do not target international consumers at an increasing rate, other companies will do so. So, companies need to understand the dynamics in the international marketplace, have a sophisticated way to assess customer satisfaction metrics that center on customers as a strategic company asset, and compete fiercely with myriad options that customers have to satisfy their needs and wants. Relatively speaking, there are no country borders in the international marketplace, at least that is the mindset of today's customers, and especially the Generation Z individuals.

Furthermore, and as we also outlined in previous chapters, the improvement in customer satisfaction is moderate, and is also being driven mostly by consumer perceptions of value (price) and almost not at all by improvements in quality. Quality is essentially unchanged over the past 25 years and has actually declined −0.1% over the past decade, as was mentioned in Chap. 3. And since market research, data analysis in general, and CEX analytical tools predominantly focus on improving *quality* attributes like customer service, product quality, website quality, call center support staff, and so forth, it is reasonable to conclude that these tools—along with more market research and/or the emergence of Big Data—have had very little positive effect on customer satisfaction.

How can this be? How can firms have more data than ever before, more research and analytics examining this data, and new and "better" tools for completing this analysis, and yet see little or no improvement in consumer perceptions of quality or satisfaction? We hinted at one answer to these questions in Chap. 7. Poor marketing metrics seem to have grown in popularity even as robust and accurate measurement of the consumer experience has become more important. In many ways, ironically enough, the trend toward these kinds of gimmicky metrics—which often emphasize single-question surveys and dubious analytical methods that ignore more than a century of sound statistical practice—is a product of a complex, Big Data world that demands exactly the opposite.

The proliferation of large amounts of data, data collection, and more complex kinds of analysis has proven confusing and cumbersome to marketing managers and other executives. The false promise of methods that are simple and "even better" under such conditions will, naturally, seems appealing to data-weary managers and researchers. Methods like the Net Promoter Score, which we described in detail in Chap. 7, promise to cut through the complexity of the longer and more complex consumer experience surveys used in many firms and replace all that cost and effort with a single question survey anyone can ask and a metric anyone can compute. But as is often the case, things that appear too good to be true usually are. ACSI data shows that they have done little to improve consumer perceptions of their experiences with companies. The answer is not a one-question Net Promoter Score survey, nor a 410-question JD Power survey (the former is not reliable and valid in scientific rigor and the latter creates respondent fatigue which means the quality of the data is problematic). The answer is to manage the quality of the data (e.g., reliability and validity) with a parsimonious survey that can explain levels, changes, and impacts in a predictive sense. Companies need to know that if they implement a certain customer-centric initiative that there is a cause-and-effect outcome that is beneficial for them, the customers, and they achieve profitable customer loyalty.

While one would expect consumer satisfaction to improve as companies gather more data and have access to more information about what their customers want and need, poor metrics are blocking this development. Indeed, learning requires more than just data, and Big Data and tools for presenting this data are not enough. A few key lessons from long-accepted best practices in data collection and analysis for market research deserve renewed attention. Consider the following:

Big Data Versus Little Data. Big Data provides companies with more data on more consumers and aspects of the shopping and consumption process than ever before. In effect, we now have data on every portion of the customer experience and how it relates to customers as strategic company assets. The quality of the data, the quality of the analysis undertaken on the data, and the quality of the interpretations of the practical implications that can be gleaned from the data are still very much debatable. For example, almost no matter how big, Big Data is not exempt from the laws of probability. Accurately measuring samples of customers that are representative of an entire customer population or a sub-segment of customers of greatest interest to the business manager is still essential. History offers a cautionary tale still famous with survey researchers. In the 1936 presidential race, Literary Digest used a sample of 2.5 million respondents—50 times larger than the sample used by George Gallup's startup company—to predict a landslide for Alf Landon. Gallup, with a much smaller sample, projected a landslide for Franklin Roosevelt. "Little Data" used probability sampling of much less data, and predicted the outcome correctly, while Big Data failed. Similarly, if a company has access to millions of data points but a poorly calculated metric, decisions based on this metric will be misleading.

Long Surveys. While many marketing managers have turned to a reliance on short, single-question surveys, the opposite impulse exists as well. Much of the Big Data analyzed today relies on surveys that are much too long. The online data collection environment, where data collection is easier and cheaper, has fed this impulse and allowed for the creation of massive surveys. Yet virtually no human respondent can provide meaningful answers to 300 or more survey questions before succumbing to mental fatigue and providing random responses. The Chevrolet commercial that has been popular on TV for some time in 2019 talks about JD Power using 410 questions in their surveys to assess who is best in class, with Chevrolet the winner in a number of categories. We would argue that such surveys are fraught with survey fatigue. Consequently, problems exist with the quality of the responses to these long surveys.

Data Versus Information. Most consumer data, especially from surveys, is notoriously noisy. Methods for dealing with noise and turning raw data into valuable information exist, but are rarely used in simple CEX tools and applications. In customer experience survey data, for example, just about everything is correlated to everything else. Therefore, it is difficult to determine what causes what. Worse yet, the high correlations make it more important to distinguish between causes and associations. That is, one might target something for improvement that it is highly correlated to but does not truly drive or cause customer satisfaction or customer loyalty. Causal analysis systems for strong analysis of data exist, but they do not exist in most CEX tools due to their complexity. Rarely do we hear about reliability, validity, common method bias, and a variety of other quality issues with data in consumer surveys, but these issues are part of the science of customer satisfaction (which we discussed in the Appendix in Chap. 1). A one-question Net Promoter Score (NPS) survey or a 410-question JD Power survey is seldom the answer to these reliability, validity, and common method bias issues.

Calibration Toward Objectives. Satisfied and loyal customers are a conduit for achieving company financial objectives—customer retention, revenue, profit, market share, stock price, and so forth. We outlined many of the financial performance metrics empirically associated with customer satisfaction in the last chapter. Whatever the customer satisfaction gauge or measure used, it must be calibrated so that its increase will contribute to this objective. In other words, the idea is to optimize customer satisfaction with respect to the desired outcome. There are systems for this, but they are rarely used in the simple CEX tools or single-question surveys popular today. On the contrary and rather inexplicably, many Fortune 500 companies use an NPS metric that, as we described in Chap. 7, is poorly calculated and designed to actually increase noise in the data. In the age of social media, customer recommendations are indeed important, but they are not a substitute for customer satisfaction and loyalty, especially when measured via NPS.

We hope that the wealth of data presented in these pages are useful in their own right, helping business and marketing professionals better understand their consumers and the dynamics of consumer perceptions over time. But perhaps it will also have an additional effect. Perhaps this data will inspire market researchers to again remember the importance of not just a lot of data or simplistic measures promising more than they can deliver, but high-quality metrics produced through data (big or small) as well. In the next section, we outline one venture we argue could be highly beneficial in truly improving the goods and services offered to consumers—not just in any one national market, but globally.

9.3   Global Indices of Customer Satisfaction and Global Competitiveness

Thus far in the book, our focus has been on the purposes of the ACSI project at its inception and over its history, the methods and structures used by the project to measure customer satisfaction, and, most critically, the findings from 25 years of ACSI data collection and analysis. In what follows, our focus shifts to the future importance of national indices of satisfaction in a globalized economic world. Perhaps little known, the American Customer Satisfaction Index has collected data and done work in dozens of countries already. Here we will examine the relevance of these national indices—and more specifically, a substantial number of these indices conducting harmonized measurement using common models and methods across a variety of nations actively engaged in international trade, or a "Global Customer Satisfaction Index"—in understanding the *competitiveness of economies* in an era of increasingly free trade and cross-national economic competition.

As we have described in detail, international trade is a central feature and vital component of the modern globalized economy. Brief political roadblocks and unavoidable economic downturns notwithstanding, international trade will almost certainly grow even more important moving forward into the future. Corresponding with the age of economic globalization, the interconnectedness of national economies through free market trade is greater now than it has ever been, and the proven efficiencies realized therein are likely to inspire more of it rather than less. And while many of the myriad effects of the growth in international trade are beyond the scope of this book, one effect is of particular interest: To succeed in this new global economy, economic policymakers and participants (i.e., national markets and companies alike) must be more concerned about the *competitiveness* of the goods and services produced within their national economies, and thus more attentive to strategies for measuring and tracking that competitiveness over time.

From one perspective, as barriers to international trade have fallen and the flow of goods and services across borders has increased, economic policymakers must worry more than ever about the ability of domestic firms to satisfy consumers with high-quality goods and services. Otherwise, these local companies—which often provide the backbone of local employment and pay the largest share of taxes—are sure to lose market share to foreign suppliers through cross-border trade. In other words, monitoring and tracking the quality delivered by local suppliers of goods and services can provide advance notice (to both the firms themselves and to national policymakers and politicians) that these suppliers are falling behind in the eyes of consumers, and that consumer demand for these (local) suppliers may decline as well. In turn, this could possibly open-up opportunities for foreign suppliers to enter the market and steal market share.

Advance knowledge about declining success in the eyes of consumers could, therefore, provide a degree of insulation—or at very least, point toward the need for innovation—for a national economy against international competitors looking to make inroads. From a macroeconomic perspective, this knowledge might also help shield a national economy from growing trade imbalances and fluctuations in the value of currencies. One need only look at the slow, painful decline of the U.S. auto industry—which went from dominating global auto sales to being supplanted (at least at times) by Japanese automakers for the top spot in even *domestic U.S. sales*—for an example of the potentially detrimental effects of this phenomenon.

From another angle, the ability of local domestic firms to produce competitive, high-quality goods and services speaks, at least in part, to the potential of a national economy to export goods to other markets and find success. An individual company or an entire domestic industry that produces highly satisfying goods and services enjoyed by local consumers should (all other things being equal) be better able to successfully export these goods to foreign markets and compete successfully with existing suppliers. The converse is true as well, with numerous examples of large corporations attempting to enter foreign markets and finding only limited success due to deficiencies in competitiveness the company did not fully understand (see Home Depot, Walmart, and McDonald's above). From this perspective, economic policymakers and firms are certainly better off if they understand how well their goods and services might compete in the global marketplace.

In 1994, Professor Claes Fornell first proposed the idea of a national index of customer satisfaction (first in Sweden, then in the U.S.) as a means for measuring the quality of the output of a national economy, rather than just its quantity. The history of this idea and the underlying purposes of such indices were described in Chap. 1. This idea was from the start linked to measuring quality as a means for determining the competitiveness of some goods and services relative to others, as it was designed and deployed first for a Swedish economy battling new competitors within the European Union. But as the world now finds itself in the midst of Globalization 4.0, where the world has become "tiny" and cross-border trade increasingly important to economies large and small, it is necessary to take this recommendation one step further. The globalized economy needs a Global Customer Satisfaction Index, a system of harmonized national indices of satisfaction based in a common methodology, to measure the quality, rather than just the quantity, of the goods and services produced and distributed across national boundaries.

With these conditions and the challenges of the global marketplace in mind, and this "call to arms" for a global system of customer satisfaction measurement offered, let us now consider just a handful of the ways in which such a system of national indices of satisfaction could help both national economies and the global economy as a whole. We outline five advantages such a system might offer to both companies and economic policymakers looking for an edge in a hyper-competitive world.

Track Performance of (Key) Domestic Firms in (Key) Industries. A basic, inward-looking use for a national customer satisfaction index is to monitor and track the performance of important domestic firms in key economic industries, with a focus on how well these local firms are performing relative to foreign competitors (should these already be competing in the market). Not all industries are built alike for national economies, with some far more important to the future economic success of a nation than others. In markets where little or no foreign competition yet exists, this type of measurement system can be used to reveal how susceptible the industry might be to the entry of foreign competitors. In other words, should domestic companies prove to perform poorly or if quality and satisfaction are degrading, this may signal that this critical industry is at risk of losing market share to foreign competitors, should they exist or arrive.

Identify Industry Performance Leaders and Best Practices. Related to this first objective, tracking the quality and satisfaction produced by companies within key economic industries can help insulate these industries from foreign competition in other ways. By tracking and comparing firms on quality and satisfaction, top performers can be identified—whether these are domestic or foreign companies—that are outperforming others. Understanding who the strongest performers are can provide critical information about best practices for lower-scoring or lagging firms, information that can help the latter improve their own products and services and improve the satisfaction of their consumers. Cross-company benchmarking toward quality and satisfaction improvement can not only aid individual companies compete within their own market, but can help in their quest to increase their customer base through future internationalization.

Conduct Cross-National Performance Benchmarking. From a different, outward-looking perspective, a national index of satisfaction allows for benchmarking performance in quality and satisfaction delivery across industries in multiple countries simultaneously. The goal of this activity is discovering not only potential sources of future competition, but also markets that may be open to the introduction of higher quality goods and services because domestic firms are falling short. Additionally, this type of cross-national benchmarking can help reveal information about best-in-class foreign industries or companies worthy of emulation, as a means to improve the performance of domestic suppliers.

Multinational Firm Performance Tracking. A national customer satisfaction index—or more accurately, the system of such indices we recommend, spanning a variety of national markets—can also allow for monitoring the performance of large multinational companies operating in several markets simultaneously. In turn, this information can help these companies know how they are doing in their oftentimes expansive, disparate operations, and guide them to areas (countries or markets) where they may be underperforming and need to make improvements (and decide how to do so). And as many economies rely disproportionately on the performance of a handful of large multinational companies, knowing how these are doing can be vital to understanding national economic growth writ large.

Monitor National Economic Performance. By producing national-level, economy-wide satisfaction data and scores (like that produced by the ACSI in the U.S. and described in Chap. 5), a national index of satisfaction can offer a means for monitoring overall national performance in delivering quality and satisfaction. That is, data at the aggregate level provides information and insight into the overall, general health of the national economy, and whether that health is improving or declining. The ACSI score, as we discussed in Chap. 5, is predictive of gross domestic product and consumer spending growth, indicators vital to the health of every economy. As such, comparing this data across nations gives information about the comparative health of multiple national economies, and the direction these economies may be heading over both the near and long term.

This list of the benefits of a Global Customer Satisfaction Index is obviously only partial. These are just some of the advantages that such a system of national indices of satisfaction can provide for economies around the globe. And given the realities of the modern economy, it is perhaps not surprising that national indexes of satisfaction are in fact now being conducted in dozens of countries around the world. Research groups in a wide range of countries in North America, South America, Europe, Africa, and Asia have inaugurated national indexes of satisfaction, many emulating or directly partnering with ACSI for this purpose.[8] Yet work remains. As international competition and trade are likely to continue to grow and become more intense, and with the positive role these indices can play in understanding and even predicting this evolution, it is necessary that many more such indexes be developed, a positive for both these economies and the companies and consumers within them. To bookend our book and to stress this macro-micro dynamic (e.g., countries, economic sectors, industries, firms, and customers), we leave you with the quotation we started with in Chap. 1:

> To understand more fully the modern economy, and the firms that compete in it, we must measure the quality of economic output, as well as its quantity. *Claes Fornell, Chair of the Board and Founder, American Customer Satisfaction Index, 1995.*

Notes

1. Schwab, Klaus. "Globalization 4.0—What Does It Mean?" *World Economic Forum*, November 5, 2018, https://www.weforum.org/agenda/2018/11/globalization-4-what-does-it-mean-how-it-will-benefit-everyone
2. The international business ecosystem is defined as the organisms of the business world—including stakeholders, organizations, and countries—involved in exchanges, production, business functions, and cross-border trade through both marketplace competition and cooperation—Hult, G. Tomas M., Maria Alejandra Gonzalez-Perez and Katarina Lagerström (2020). "The Theoretical Evolution and Use of the Uppsala Model of Internationalization in the International Business Ecosystem." *Journal of International Business Studies*, 51(1).

3. Silverblatt, Howard (2019). *S&P 5002018: Global Sales*. Accessed online at: https://us.spindices.com/indexology/djia-and-sp-500/sp-500-global-sales
4. For good analyses of these companies' challenges in internationalizing in certain markets, see: Sang-Hun, Choe. "Wal-Mart Selling Stores and Leaving South Korea," *New York Times*, May 23, 2006. Accessed online at: https://www.nytimes.com/2006/05/23/business/worldbusiness/walmart-selling-stores-and-leaving-south-korea.html; Bhasin, Kim. "Why IKEA Took China By Storm, While Home Depot Failed Miserably," *Business Insider*, September 14, 2012. Accessed online at: https://www.businessinsider.com/ikea-home-depot-china-failed-2012-9
5. Palacio, Xabier. "ESOMAR's Latest Global Market Research Report Values Global Research and Data Industry Market at US $80 billion," *ResearchWorld.com*. Accessed online at: https://www.researchworld.com/esomars-latest-global-market-research-report-values-global-research-and-data-industry-market-at-us-80-billion/
6. Brooke, Zach. "3 Common Pitfalls of International Market Research (and How to Avoid Them)," American Marketing Association, October 1, 2017. Accessed online at: https://www.ama.org/marketing-news/3-common-pitfalls-of-international-market-research-and-how-to-avoid-them/
7. For this and other information on Big Data, see: Baesens, Bart (2014). *Analytics in a Big Data World*, Wiley and SAS Business Series.
8. For more information on these national indexes of satisfaction based on the ACSI model, visit the ACSI website at: https://www.theacsi.org/products-and-services/international/global-csi

References and Further Reading

Baesens, Bart (2014). *Analytics in a Big Data World*. Wiley and SAS Business Series.
Bhasin, K. (2012, September 14). Why IKEA Took China By Storm, While Home Depot Failed Miserably. *Business Insider*. Retrieved from https://www.businessinsider.com/ikea-home-depot-china-failed-2012-9
Brooke, Z. (2017, October 1). 3 Common Pitfalls of International Market Research (and How to Avoid Them). *American Marketing Association*. Retrieved from https://www.ama.org/marketing-news/3-common-pitfalls-of-international-market-research-and-how-to-avoid-them/
Friedman, T. (2005). *The World is Flat: A Brief History of the Twenty-first Century*. New York, NY: Farrar, Straus and Giroux.
Hollister, D., Tadgerson, R., Closs, D. J., & Hult, G. T. M. (2016). *Second Shift: The Inside Story of the Keep GM Movement*. New York: McGraw Hill Professional.

Hult, G. T. M., Closs, D. J., & Frayer, D. (2014). *Global Supply Chain Management: Leveraging Processes, Measurements, and Tools for Strategic Corporate Advantage.* New York: McGraw-Hill Professional.

Morgeson, F. V., III, Hult, T., & Sharma, P. N. (2015). Cross-National Differences in Consumer Satisfaction: Mobile Services in Emerging and Developed Markets. *Journal of International Marketing, 23*(2), 1–24.

Morgeson, F. V., III, Mithas, S., Keiningham, T. L., & Aksoy, L. (2011). An Investigation of the Cross-National Determinants of Customer Satisfaction. *Journal of the Academy of Marketing Science, 39*(2), 198–215.

Palacio, X. ESOMAR's Latest Global Market Research Report Values Global Research and Data Industry Market at US $80 billion. *ResearchWorld.com.* Retrieved from https://www.researchworld.com/esomars-latest-global-market-research-report-values-global-research-and-data-industry-market-at-us-80-billion/

Rosling, H. (2018). *Factfulness: Ten Reasons We're Wrong About the World—And Why Things Are Better Thank We Think.* New York: Flatiron Books.

Sang-Hun, C. (2006, May 23). Wal-Mart Selling Stores and Leaving South Korea. *New York Times.* Retrieved from https://www.nytimes.com/2006/05/23/business/worldbusiness/walmart-selling-stores-and-leaving-south-korea.html

Silverblatt, H. (2019). *S&P 500 2018: Global Sales.* Retrieved from https://us.spindices.com/indexology/djia-and-sp-500/sp-500-global-sales

Appendix A: The Science of Customer Satisfaction (ACSI)

This Appendix briefly presents ACSI's patented science of customer satisfaction and the 14 generic survey questions that are used in the data collection to assess the ACSI model in Fig. 1.1. In the actual data collection, each question is customized to the industry and several customer qualifiers are included to ensure quality data. The instrument also includes additional questions (e.g., demographics), for a variety of reasons, as well as a breakdown of product and service quality assessments, as applicable. A 10-point scale is used with the exception of question 12, with the end points identified for each question in parenthesis.

The American Customer Satisfaction Index uses the customer interviews as input into a multi-equation econometric model developed at the University of Michigan's Ross School of Business. The ACSI model is a cause-and-effect model with indexes for the drivers of satisfaction on the left side (customer expectations, perceived quality, and perceived value), customer satisfaction (the so-called ACSI index) in the center, and outcomes of satisfaction on the right side (customer complaints and customer loyalty, including customer retention and price tolerance). These right-hand variables are the ones that then oftentimes are modeled to have an effect on a company's financials (this link is discussed in Chap. 8).

Given this modeling, very specifically, the ACSI Model can account for *levels* (i.e., a score from 0 to 100 on each variable), *changes* in variables' scores between time periods, and *impacts* of the variables (i.e., represented by the arrows in the model). The ACSI system has two U.S. patents (No. 8666515 and No. 6192319 B1).

The indexes, also referred to as variables or constructs (shown in Fig. 1.1), are multivariable components measured by several questions that are weighted

© The Author(s) 2020
C. Fornell et al., *The Reign of the Customer*, https://doi.org/10.1007/978-3-030-13562-1

within the model. The questions assess customer evaluations of the determinants of each index. These are the indexes that are reported on a 0–100 scale. The survey and modeling methodology quantifies the strength (i.e., impact) of the effect of the index on the left to the one to which the arrow points on the right. These arrows represent "impacts." The ACSI model is self-weighting to maximize the explanation of customer satisfaction (ACSI) on customer loyalty. Looking at the indexes and impacts, users can determine which drivers of satisfaction, if improved, would have the most effect on customer loyalty.

Customer Expectations

Customer expectations is a measure of the customer's anticipation of the quality of a company's products or services. Expectations represent both prior consumption experience, which includes some non-experiential information like advertising and word-of-mouth, and a forecast of the company's ability to deliver quality in the future.

1. How high did you expect the overall quality of the *product/service* to be? (Not very high—Very high)
2. How well did you expect the *product/service* to meet your personal requirements? (Not very well—Very well)
3. How often did you expect things with the *product/service* to go wrong? (Not very often—Very often)

Perceived Quality

Perceived quality is a measure of the customer's evaluation via recent consumption experience of the quality of a company's products or services. Quality is measured in terms of both customization, which is the degree to which a product or service meets the customer's individual needs, and reliability, which is the frequency with which things go wrong with the product or service.

4. How high has the overall quality of the *product/service* actually been? (Not very high—Very high)
5. How well has the *product/service* actually met your personal requirements? (Not very well—Very well)
6. How often have things actually gone wrong with the *product/service*? (Not very often—Very often)

Perceived Value

Perceived value is a measure of quality relative to price paid. Although price (value for money) is often very important to the customer's first purchase, it usually has a somewhat smaller impact on satisfaction for repeat purchases.

7. Given the quality of the *product/service*, how would you rate the price you paid? (Not very good—Very good)
8. Given the price you paid for the *product/service*, how would you rate the quality? (Not very good—Very good)

Customer Satisfaction (ACSI)

The customer satisfaction (ACSI) index score is calculated as a weighted average of three survey questions that measure different facets of satisfaction with a product or service. ACSI researchers use proprietary software technology to estimate the weighting for each question.

9. Considering all of your experiences to date with the company/brand, how satisfied are you? (Very dissatisfied—Very satisfied)
10. Considering all of your expectations, to what extent has the *company/brand* fallen short of or exceeded your expectations? (Fallen short of expectations—Exceeded expectations)
11. Forget the *company/brand* you bought for a moment. Imagine an ideal *product*. How well do you think the *company/brand* you bought compares with that ideal? (Not very close to ideal—Very close to ideal)

Customer Complaints

Customer complaints are measured as a percentage of respondents who indicate they have complained to a company directly about a product or service within a specified time frame. Satisfaction has a negative relationship with customer complaints, as the more satisfied the customers, the less likely they are to complain.

12. Have you complained about your *product/service* to the company within the past six months? (Yes—No)
13. How well was the complaint handled? (Handled very poorly—Handled very well)

Customer Loyalty

Customer loyalty is a combination of the customer's professed likelihood to repurchase from the same supplier in the future, and the likelihood to purchase a company's products or services at various price points (price tolerance). Customer loyalty is the critical component of the model as it stands as a proxy for profitability.

14. The next time you seek to buy a new *product/service*, how likely is it you will buy the same brand again? (Not very likely—Very likely)

Appendix B: All-Time Top-100 Research Publications on Customer Satisfaction

The ranking of the all-time top-100 research publications (articles and books) on customer satisfaction was based on total citations in Google Scholar on January 4, 2020 (see last column labeled GSC for the Google Scholar citations). These top-100 publications are from the more than 2.6 million publications that resulted from the overall customer satisfaction query on Google Scholar. The abbreviated customer-satisfaction-focused descriptions of the publications in this table use quotations as much as possible to stay true to the authors' intent.

The Google Scholar search was limited to the words "customer" and "satisfaction" appearing in the titles of the publications to focus primarily on strategic-oriented satisfaction publications (and no derivatives of customer satisfaction, such as "consumer" satisfaction, or related terms were used). The Google Scholar top-1000 publications that included "customer" and "satisfaction" in the titles were manually evaluated for inclusion in the top 100. Total citations was the sole criteria. The "field" column represents the main category of the publication (although many publications span multiple fields).

The top-100 publications collectively have 170,332 total citations. The average number is 1703 citations per publication. On January 4, 2020—when the Google Scholar data were compiled and analyzed—it took 606 citations to be in the all-time top-100 research publications on customer satisfaction. Any customer satisfaction publication included in Google Scholar, with the search parameters used, could be included. Effectively, publications from 1965 to 2015 made the top-100 ranking for total impact via citations.

© The Author(s) 2020
C. Fornell et al., *The Reign of the Customer*, https://doi.org/10.1007/978-3-030-13562-1

It took 1143 citations to be in the top 50, and it took 8053 citations to be in the top 3. The top-three articles on customer satisfaction involve one of the coauthors of this book (Fornell, Hult), and these three articles have 26,714 total cites (or 15.7% of the 170,332 total citations for the top 100). Claes Fornell has published 10 of the top-100 articles on customer satisfaction, the most of any author in the top 100.

#	Reference	Field	Customer satisfaction focus	GSC
1	Anderson, Eugene W., Claes Fornell, and Donald R. Lehmann (1994), "Customer Satisfaction, Market Share, and Profitability: Findings from Sweden," *Journal of Marketing*, 58 (3), 53–66.	Marketing	The authors investigate the nature and strength of the link between customer satisfaction and economic returns.	9359
2	Fornell, Claes (1992), "A National Customer Satisfaction Barometer: The Swedish Experience," *Journal of Marketing*, 56 (1), 6–21.	Marketing	The author reports the results of a large-scale Swedish effort to measure quality of total consumption as customer satisfaction.	9302
3	Cronin, J. Joseph, Jr., Michael K. Brady, and G. Tomas M. Hult (1999), "Assessing the Effects of Quality, Value, and Customer Satisfaction on Consumer Behavioral Intentions in Service Environments," *Journal of Retailing*, 76 (2), 193–218.	Retailing	The authors synthesize competing modeling efforts to conceptualize the holistic effects of quality, customer satisfaction, and value on consumers' behavioral intentions.	8053
4	Anderson, Eugene W., and Mary W. Sullivan (1993), "The Antecedents and Consequences of Customer Satisfaction for Firms," *Marketing Science*, 12 (2), 125–143.	Marketing	The authors develop a model to link the antecedents and consequences of satisfaction in a utility-oriented framework.	7346
5	Fornell, Claes, Michael D. Johnson, Eugene W. Anderson, Jaesung Cha, and Barbara Everitt Bryant (1996), "The American Customer Satisfaction Index: Nature, Purpose, and Findings," *Journal of Marketing*, 60 (4), 7–18.	Marketing	The authors discuss the American Customer Satisfaction Index (ACSI) as a performance measure for firms, industries, economic sectors, and national economies.	6341
6	Churchill, Jr., Gilbert A., and Carol Surprenant (1982), "An Investigation into the Determinants of Customer Satisfaction," *Journal of Marketing Research*, 19 (4), 491–504.	Marketing	The authors investigate if it is necessary to include disconfirmation as an intervening variable affecting customer satisfaction.	5979

(continued)

(continued)

#	Reference	Field	Customer satisfaction focus	GSC
7	Meuter, Matthew L., Amy L. Ostrom, Robert I. Roundtree, and Mary Jo Bitner (2000). "Self-Service Technologies: Understanding Customer Satisfaction with Technology-Based Service Encounters," *Journal of Marketing*, 64 (3), 50–64.	Services	The authors describe the results of a critical incident study based on more than 800 incidents involving self-service technologies (SSTs), and categorize the sources of satisfaction and dissatisfaction with SSTs.	3272
8	Szymanski, David M., and David H. Henard (2001), "Customer Satisfaction: A Meta-Analysis of the Empirical Evidence," *Journal of the Academy of Marketing Science*, 29 (1), 16–35.	Marketing	The authors conduct a meta-analysis on customer satisfaction; and find strong influence from equity and disconfirmation.	3158
9	Luo, Xueming, and C.B. Bhattacharya (2006), "Corporate Social Responsibility, Customer Satisfaction, and Market Value," *Journal of Marketing*, 70 (4), 1–18.	Marketing	The authors examine that customer satisfaction mediates relationships between CSR and firm value, corporate abilities moderate financial returns to CSR, and these relationships are mediated by satisfaction.	3142
10	Rust, Roland T., and Anthony J. Zahorik (1993), "Customer Satisfaction, Customer Retention, and Market Share," *Journal of Retailing*, 69 (2), 193–215.	Retailing	The authors provide a mathematical framework for assessing the value of customer satisfaction.	3119
11	Smith, Amy K., Ruth N. Bolton, and Janet Wagner (1999), "A Model of Customer Satisfaction with Service Encounters Involving Failure and Recovery," *Journal of Marketing Research*, 36 (3), 356–372.	Services	The authors develop a model of customer satisfaction with service failure/recovery encounters based on an exchange framework that integrates concepts from social justice.	3082
12	Mittal, Vikas, and Wagner A. Kamakura (2001), "Satisfaction, Repurchase Intent, and Repurchase Behavior: Investigating the Moderating Effect of Customer Characteristics," *Journal of Marketing Research*, 38 (1), 131–142.	Marketing	The authors develop a model that is based on the premise that ratings in customer satisfaction surveys are error-prone measures of the customer's true satisfaction, and they may vary based on consumer characteristics.	2947

13	Taylor, Steven A., and Thomas L. Baker (1994), "An Assessment of the Relationship Between Service Quality and Customer Satisfaction in the Formation of Consumers' Purchase Intentions," *Journal of Retailing*, 70 (2), 163–178.	Retailing	The authors assess the nature of the relationship between service quality and consumer satisfaction in the formation of consumers' purchase intentions across four unique service industries.	2901
14	Anderson, Eugene W. (1998), "Customer Satisfaction and Word of Mouth," *Journal of Service Research*, 1 (1), 5–17.	Services	The author develops a utility-based model of the relationship between customer satisfaction and word-of-mouth.	2856
15	Hallowell, Roger (1996), "The Relationships of Customer Satisfaction, Customer Loyalty, and Profitability: An Empirical Study," *International Journal of Service Industry Management*, 7 (4), 27–42.	Services	The author examines relationships among customer satisfaction, loyalty, and profitability using multiple measures of satisfaction, loyalty, and profitability.	2856
16	McDougall, Gordon H. G., and Terrence Levesque (2000), "Customer Satisfaction with Services: Putting Perceived Value Into the Equation," *Journal of Services Marketing*, 14 (5), 392–410.	Services	The author examines relationships among core service quality, relational service quality, value, satisfaction, and intentions.	2535
17	Caruana, Albert (2002), "Service Loyalty: The Effects of Service Quality and the Mediating Role of Customer Satisfaction," *European Journal of Marketing*, 346 (7/8), 811–828.	Services	The author distinguishes between service quality and customer satisfaction, and proposes a model that links service quality to loyalty via customer satisfaction.	2494
18	Cardozo, Richard N. (1965), "An Experimental Study of Customer Effort, Expectation, and Satisfaction," *Journal of Marketing Research*, 2 (3), 244–249.	Marketing	The author finds that customer satisfaction with a product is influenced by expectations and effort expended to acquire the product.	2478

(continued)

(continued)

#	Reference	Field	Customer satisfaction focus	GSC
19	McKinney, Vicki, Kanghyun Yoon, and Fatemeh "Mariam" Zahedi (2002), "The Measurement of Web-Customer Satisfaction: An Expectation and Disconfirmation Approach," *Information Systems Research*, 13 (3), 296–315.	Information Systems	By synthesizing the expectation-disconfirmation paradigm, the authors separate Website quality into information quality (IQ) and system quality (SQ), and propose nine key constructs for Web-customer satisfaction.	2366
20	Yang, Zhilin, and Robin T. Peterson (2004), "Customer Perceived Value, Satisfaction, and Loyalty: The Role of Switching Costs," *Psychology & Marketing*, 21(10), 799–822.	Psychology/Marketing	The authors develop a conceptual foundation for investigating the customer retention process, with the use of the concepts of customer satisfaction and relationship quality.	2317
21	Lam, Shun Yin, Venkatesh Shankar, M. Krishna Erramilli, and Bvsan Murthy (2004), "Customer Value, Satisfaction, Loyalty, and Switching Costs: An Illustration From a Business-to-Business Service Context," *Journal of the Academy of Marketing Science*, 32 (3), 293–311.	Marketing	The authors extend prior research by developing a conceptual framework linking customer satisfaction, value, loyalty, and switching costs in a business-to-business (B2B) service setting.	2276
22	Ittner, Christopher D., and David F. Larcker (1998), "Are Nonfinancial Measures Leading Indicators of Financial Performance? An Analysis of Customer Satisfaction," *Journal of Accounting Research*, 36 (Supplement), 1–35.	Accounting	The authors examine: (1) does customer satisfaction (CS) effect accounting performance, (2) is economic value of CS reflected in accounting book values, and (3) does the public release of CS measures provide information to the stock market?	2223
23	Shankar, Venkatesh, Amy K. Smith, and Arvind Rangaswamy (2003), "Customer Satisfaction and Loyalty in Online and Offline Environments," *International Journal of Research in Marketing*, 20 (2), 153–175.	Marketing	The authors propose a conceptual framework and test hypotheses about the effects of the online medium on customer satisfaction and loyalty and on the relationships between satisfaction and loyalty.	2016

#	Citation	Field	Description	
24	Anderson, Eugene W., Claes Fornell, and Roland T. Rust (1997). "Customer Satisfaction, Productivity, and Profitability: Differences Between Goods and Services," *Marketing Science*, 16 (2), 129–145.	Marketing	The findings indicate that the association between changes in customer satisfaction and changes in productivity is positive for goods, but negative for services.	2012
25	Gustafsson, Anders, Michael D. Johnson, and Inger Roos (2005), "The Effects of Customer Satisfaction, Relationship Commitment Dimensions, and Triggers on Customer Retention," *Journal of Marketing*, 69 (4), 210–218.	Marketing	In a study of telecommunications services, the authors examine the effects of customer satisfaction, affective commitment, and calculative commitment on retention.	1975
26	Woodside, Arch G., Lisa L. Frey, and Robert Timothy Daly (1989), "Linking Service Quality, Customer Satisfaction, and Behavioral Intention," *Journal of Health Care Marketing*, 9 (4), 5–17.	Health Care	The authors use the service quality and script theory literature and propose a framework of relationships among service quality, customer satisfaction, and behavioral intentions.	1966
27	Hennig-Thurau, Thorsten, and Alexander Klee (1998), "The Impact of Customer Satisfaction and Relationship Quality on Customer Retention: A Critical Reassessment and Model Development," *Psychology & Marketing*, 14 (8), 737–764.	Psychology/ Marketing	The authors develop a conceptual foundation for examining the customer retention process, with the use of customer satisfaction and relationship quality.	1963
28	Anderson, Eugene W., Claes Fornell, and Sanal K. Mazvancheryl (2004), "Customer Satisfaction and Shareholder Value," *Journal of Marketing*, 68 (4), 172–185.	Marketing	The authors specify how customer satisfaction affects future behavior and level, timing, and risk of cash flows.	1720
29	Bowen, John T., and Shiang-Lih Chen (2001), "The Relationship Between Customer Loyalty and Customer Satisfaction," *International Journal of Contemporary Hospitality Management*, 13 (5), 213–217.	Hospitality	The authors develop a method for hotels to identify attributes that will drive customer loyalty via customer satisfaction.	1716

(continued)

(continued)

#	Reference	Field	Customer satisfaction focus	GSC
30	Eggert, Andreas, and Wolfgang Ulaga (2002), "Customer Perceived Value: A Substitute for Satisfaction in Business Markets?" *Journal of Business & Industrial Marketing*, 17 (2/3), 107–118.	Marketing	The authors investigate whether customer value and customer satisfaction represent two distinct concepts, and address value is a better predictor of outcomes in the B2B context.	1710
31	Homburg, Christian, and Annette Giering (2000), "Personal Characteristics as Moderators of the Relationship Between Customer Satisfaction and Loyalty—An Empirical Analysis," *Psychology & Marketing*, 18 (1), 43–66.	Psychology/ Marketing	The authors analyze the moderating effect of selected personal characteristics on the customer satisfaction–loyalty link; strength of the relationship is strongly influenced by characteristics of the customer.	1521
32	Homburg, Christian, Nicole Koschate, and Wayne D. Hoyer (2005), "Do Satisfied Customers Really Pay More? A Study of the Relationship between Customer Satisfaction and Willingness to Pay," *Journal of Marketing*, 69 (2), 84–96.	Marketing	Two studies reveal the existence of a positive impact of customer satisfaction on willingness to pay, and they support a nonlinear structure (i.e., an inverse S-shaped form).	1500
33	Oh, Haemoon (1999), "Service Quality, Customer Satisfaction, and Customer Value: A Holistic Perspective," *International Journal of Hospitality Management*, 18 (1), 67–82.	Hospitality	The author tests (with a luxury hotel sample) a model of service quality, customer value, and customer satisfaction.	1494
34	Kandampully, Jay, and Dwi Suhartanto (2000), "Customer Loyalty in the Hotel Industry: The Role of Customer Satisfaction and Image," *International Journal of Contemporary Hospitality Management*, 12 (6), 346–351.	Hospitality	The authors study relationships between customer loyalty, customer satisfaction, and image in hospitality management.	1491
35	Bergman, Bo, and Bengt Klefsjö (2004), *Quality from Customer Needs to Customer Satisfaction*, Stockholm, Sweden: Studentlitteratur AB.	Economics/Industrial Organization	The authors include a discussion of satisfaction of external and internal customers and what the concepts mean.	1454

36	Johnson, Michael D., Anders Gustafsson, Tor Wallin Andreassen, Line Lervik, and Jaesung Chaa (2001), "The Evolution and Future of National Customer Satisfaction Index Models," *Journal of Economic Psychology*, 22 (2), 217–245.	Psychology/ Economics	The authors' primary goal was to propose and test a number of modifications and improvements to the national customer satisfaction index models.	1439
37	Johnson, Michael D., and Claes Fornell (1991), "A Framework for Comparing Customer Satisfaction Across Individuals and Product Categories," *Journal of Economic Psychology*, 12 (2), 267–286.	Psychology/ Economics	The authors present a conceptualization that integrates economic and psychological perspectives to compare customer satisfaction across individuals and product categories.	1347
38	Kim, Moon-Koo, Myeong-Cheol Park, and Dong-Heon Jeonga (2004), "The Effects of Customer Satisfaction and Switching Barrier on Customer Loyalty in Korean Mobile Telecommunication Services," *Telecommunications Policy*, 28 (2), 145–159.	Telecommunications	The authors argue that the telecommunications industry is shifting its focus from attracting new customers to retaining customers; they investigate how customer satisfaction and the switching barrier influence customer loyalty.	1331
39	Matzler, Kurt, and Hans H. Hinterhuber (1998), "How to Make Product Development Projects More Successful by Integrating Kano's Model of Customer Satisfaction into Quality Function Deployment," *Technovation*, 18 (1), 25–38.	Quality Management	The authors propose a methodology for customers' stated needs and unstated desires and to resolve them into categories which have different impacts on customer satisfaction.	1325
40	Fornell, Claes Sunil Mithas, Forrest V. Morgeson, III, and M. S. Krishnan (2006), "Customer Satisfaction and Stock Prices: High Returns, Low Risk," *Journal of Marketing*, 70 (1), 3–14.	Marketing	The authors present evidence that customer satisfaction leads to excess returns and that satisfied customers are economic assets with high returns/low risk.	1302

(continued)

(continued)

#	Reference	Field	Customer satisfaction focus	GSC
41	Lee, Jonathan, Janghyuk Lee, and Lawrence Feick (2001), "The Impact of Switching Costs on the Customer Satisfaction-Loyalty Link: Mobile Phone Service in France," *Journal of Services Marketing*, 15 (1), 35–48.	Services	The authors examine the moderating role of switching costs in the customer satisfaction-loyalty link, identify customer segments, and then analyze heterogeneity in the satisfaction-loyalty link among the different segments.	1259
42	Sivadas, Eugene, and Jamie L. Baker-Prewitt (2000), "An Examination of the Relationship Between Service Quality, Customer Satisfaction, and Store Loyalty," *International Journal of Retail & Distribution Management*, 28 (2), 73–82.	Retailing	The authors examine the relationships between service quality, customer satisfaction, and store loyalty within the retail department store context; they analyze two complementary models that examine this interrelationship.	1242
43	Kuoa, Ying-Feng, Chi-Ming Wu, and Wei-Jaw Deng (2009), "The Relationships Among Service Quality, Perceived Value, Customer Satisfaction, and Post-Purchase Intention in Mobile Value-Added Services," *Computers in Human Behavior*, 25 (4), 887–896.	Telecommunications	The authors construct an instrument to evaluate service quality of mobile value-added services and examine the relationships among service quality, perceived value, customer satisfaction, and post-purchase intention.	1236
44	Sureshchandar, G. S., Chandrasekharan Rajendran, and R. N. Anantharaman (2002), "The Relationship Between Service Quality and Customer Satisfaction—A Factor Specific Approach," *Journal of Services Marketing*, 16 (4), 363–379.	Services	The authors argue that customer satisfaction should be operationalized along the same factors on which service quality is operationalized.	1231
45	Levesque, Terrence, and Gordon H. G. McDougall (1996), "Determinarts of Customer Satisfaction in Retail Banking," *International Journal of Bank Marketing*, 14 (7), 12–20.	Services/Banking	The authors point out that customer satisfaction and retention are critical for retail banks, and investigate determinants of satisfaction and future intentions in banking.	1210

#	Reference	Category	Description	
46	McCollough, Michael A., Leonard L. Berry, and Manjit S. Yadav (2000), "An Empirical Investigation of Customer Satisfaction after Service Failure and Recovery," *Journal of Service Research*, 3 (2), 121–137.	Services	The authors study the impact of failure expectations, recovery expectations, recovery performance, and justice on customers' post-recovery customer satisfaction.	1192
47	Denga, Zhaohua, Yaobin Lua, Kwok Kee Wei, and Jinlong Zhanga (2010), "Understanding Customer Satisfaction and Loyalty: An Empirical Study of Mobile Instant Messages in China," *International Journal of Information Management*, 30 (4), 289–300.	Telecommunications	The authors examine the determinants of customer satisfaction and loyalty related to mobile instant message in the telecommunications industry.	1176
48	Patterson, Paul G., Lester W. Johnson, and Richard A. Spreng (1996), "Modeling the Determinants of Customer Satisfaction for Business-to-Business Professional Services," *Journal of the Academy of Marketing Science*, 25 (1), 4–17.	Services	The authors research determinants of customer satisfaction or dissatisfaction (CS/D) in professional services. The simultaneous effect of key CS/D constructs, firm variables, and individual-level variables are examined.	1175
49	Nishii, Lisa H., David P. Lepak, and Benjamin Schneider (2008), "Employee Attributions of the 'Why' of HR Practices: Their Effect on Employee Attitudes and Behaviors, and Customer Satisfaction," *Personnel Psychology*, 61 (3), 503–545.	Psychology/ Organization	The authors introduce the construct of "human resource attributions" and the five attributions are differentially associated with job commitment and customer satisfaction.	1153
50	Gruca, Thomas S., and Lopo L. Rego (2005), "Customer Satisfaction, Cash Flow, and Shareholder Value," *Journal of Marketing*, 69 (3), 115–130.	Marketing	The authors strengthen the effects that link customer satisfaction to shareholder value via the link between satisfaction and cash flows.	1143
51	Peterson, Robert A., and William R. Wilson (1992), "Measuring Customer Satisfaction: Fact and Artifact," *Journal of the Academy of Marketing Science*, 20 (10), 61–71.	Marketing	The authors examine the customer satisfaction literature and find that measurements exhibit tendencies of confounding and methodological contamination and reflect numerous artifacts.	1119

(continued)

(continued)

#	Reference	Field	Customer satisfaction focus	GSC
52	Ahearne, Michael, John Mathieu, and Adam Rapp (2005), "To Empower or Not to Empower Your Sales Force? An Empirical Examination of the Influence of Leadership Empowerment Behavior on Customer Satisfaction and Performance," *Journal of Applied Psychology*, 90 (5), 945–955.	Psychology/ Organization	The authors focus on the impact of leadership empowerment behavior on customer service satisfaction and sales performance, as mediated by salespeople's self-efficacy and adaptability.	1012
53	Gerpott, Torsten J., Wolfgang Rams, and Andreas Schindler (2001), "Customer Retention, Loyalty, and Satisfaction in the German Mobile Cellular Telecommunications Market," *Telecommunications Policy*, 25 (4), 249–269.	Telecommunications	The authors argue that customer retention, customer loyalty, and customer satisfaction are important goals for telecommunication network operators to achieve economic success in the liberalized German market.	1008
54	Yuksel, Atila, Fisun Yuksela, and Yasin Bilim (2010), "Destination Attachment: Effects on Customer Satisfaction and Cognitive, Affective and Conative Loyalty," *Tourism Management*, 31 (2), 274–284.	Tourism	The authors examine the role of attachment in predicting customer satisfaction in holiday experiences as well as the outcome of destination loyalty.	984
55	Athanassopoulos, Antreas D. (2000), "Customer Satisfaction Cues To Support Market Segmentation and Explain Switching Behavior," *Journal of Business Research*, 47 (3), 191–207.	Marketing	The author proposes an instrument of customer satisfaction that yielded four distinct facets for business customers and five for individual customers.	972
56	Hess, Jr., Ronald L., Shankar Ganesan, and Noreen M. Klein (2003), "Service Failure and Recovery: The Impact of Relationship Factors on Customer Satisfaction," *Journal of the Academy of Marketing Science*, 31 (2), 127–145.	Marketing	The authors investigate how customers' relationships with a service organization affect their reactions to service failure, recovery, and customer satisfaction.	939
57	Gronholdt, Lars, Anne Martensen, and Kai Kristensen (2000), "The Relationship Between Customer Satisfaction and Loyalty: Cross-Industry Differences," *Total Quality Management*, 11 (4–6), 509–514.	Quality Management	What is the relationship between customer satisfaction and loyalty? The purpose of this paper is to answer this question and to investigate across industries.	936

#	Reference	Category	Description	
58	Jamal, Ahmad, and Kamal Naser (2002), "Customer Satisfaction and Retail Banking: An Assessment of Some of the Key Antecedents of Customer Satisfaction in Retail Banking," *International Journal of Bank Marketing*, 20 (4), 146–160.	Services/Banking	The authors looked into the impact of service quality dimensions and customer expertise on satisfaction in the retail banking industry.	918
59	Vavra, Terry G. (1997), *Improving Your Measurement of Customer Satisfaction: A Guide to Creating, Conducting, Analyzing, and Reporting Customer Satisfaction Measurement Programs*, Milwaukee, WI: ASQ Press.	Quality Management	The author provides rationale, identifies opportunities, and suggests specific programs to improve the measurement of customer satisfaction within the context of customer value management.	918
60	Mithas, Sunil, M.S. Krishnan, and Claes Fornell (2005), "Why Do Customer Relationship Management Applications Affect Customer Satisfaction?" *Journal of Marketing*, 69 (4), 201–209.	Marketing	The authors research the effect of customer relationship management (CRM) on customer knowledge and customer satisfaction.	916
61	Ryu, Kisang, Hye-Rin Lee, and Woo Gon Kim (2012), "The Influence of the Quality of the Physical Environment, Food, and Service on Restaurant Image, Customer Perceived Value, Customer Satisfaction, and Behavioral Intentions," *International Journal of Contemporary Hospitality Management*, 24 (2), 200–223.	Hospitality	The purpose of this study is to propose an integrated model that examines the impact of three elements of foodservice quality dimensions (physical environment, food, and service) on restaurant image, customer perceived value, customer satisfaction, and behavioral intentions.	891
62	Ranaweera, Chatura, and Jaideep Prabhu (2003), "The Influence of Satisfaction, Trust and Switching Barriers on Customer Retention in a Continuous Purchasing Setting," *International Journal of Service Industry Management*, 14 (4), 374–395.	Services	The authors adopt a holistic approach that examines the combined effects of satisfaction, trust, and switching barriers on customer retention in a continuous purchasing setting.	887

(continued)

(continued)

#	Reference	Field	Customer satisfaction focus	GSC
63	Pizam, Abraham, and Taylor Ellis (1999), "Customer Satisfaction and Its Measurement in Hospitality Enterprises," *International Journal of Contemporary Hospitality Management*, 11 (7), 326–339.	Hospitality	The authors review customer satisfaction and its application to the hospitality and tourism industries, list satisfaction measurements, and review global issues that affect satisfaction.	886
64	Johnson, Michael D., Eugene W. Anderson, and Claes Fornell (1995), "Rational and Adaptive Performance Expectations in a Customer Satisfaction Framework," *Journal of Consumer Research*, 21 (4), 695–707.	Marketing	The authors develop and examine alternative models of market-level expectations, perceived product performance, and customer satisfaction.	870
65	Baia, Billy, Rob Law, and Ivan Wen (2008), "The Impact of Website Quality on Customer Satisfaction and Purchase Intentions: Evidence From Chinese Online Visitors," *International Journal of Hospitality Management*, 27 (3), 391–402.	Hospitality	The authors develop and empirically test a conceptual model of the impact of website quality on customer satisfaction and purchase intentions.	862
66	Matzler, Kurt, Franz Bailom, Hans H. Hinterhuber, Birgit Renzl, and Johann Pichler (2004), "The Asymmetric Relationship Between Attribute-Level Performance and Overall Customer Satisfaction: A Reconsideration of the Importance–Performance Analysis," *Industrial Marketing Management*, 33 (4), 271–277.	Marketing	The authors undertook a study on customer satisfaction with a supplier in the automotive industry that was using importance-performance analysis (IPA) to yield prescriptions for the management of customer satisfaction.	834
67	Anderson, Eugene, W., and Claes Fornell (2010), "Foundations of the American Customer Satisfaction Index," *Total Quality Management*, 11 (7), 869–882.	Quality Management	The authors describe the methodology for ACSI, which is a system for evaluating and comparing customer satisfaction across firms, industries, and nations.	822

#	Reference	Field		Description
68	Hennig-Thurau, Thorsten (2004), "Customer Orientation of Service Employees: Its Impact on Customer Satisfaction, Commitment, and Retention," *International Journal of Service Industry Management*, 15 (5), 460–478.	Hospitality	806	Impact of customer orientation (employees' technical skills, social skills, motivation, and decision-making power) on customer satisfaction, and other constructs is examined.
69	Andaleeb, Syed Saad, and Carolyn Conway (2006), "Customer Satisfaction in the Restaurant Industry: An Examination of the Transaction-Specific Model," *Journal of Services Marketing*, 20 (1), 3–11.	Services	789	The authors conduct this study to determine the factors that explain customer satisfaction in the full-service restaurant industry.
70	Jones, Michael A., and Jaebeom Suh (2000), "Transaction-specific Satisfaction and Overall Satisfaction: An Empirical Analysis," *Journal of Services Marketing*, 14 (2), 147–159.	Services	783	The authors investigate transaction-specific customer satisfaction, overall satisfaction, and repurchase intentions, and find that the two types of satisfaction can be distinguished from one another.
71	Olorunniwo, Festus, Maxwell K. Hsu, and Godwin J. Udo (2006), "Service Quality, Customer Satisfaction, and Behavioral Intentions in the Service Factory," *Journal of Services Marketing*, 20 (1), 59–72.	Services	782	The authors investigate whether the typology to which a service belongs explains service quality and its relationship to customer satisfaction and behavioral intentions.
72	Ryu, Kisang, Heesup Han, and Tae-Hee Kimc (2008), "The Relationships Among Overall Quick-Casual Restaurant Image, Perceived Value, Customer Satisfaction, and Behavioral Intentions," *International Journal of Hospitality Management*, 27 (3), 459–469.	Hospitality	763	The authors explain the relationships among overall quick-casual restaurant image, perceived value, customer satisfaction, and behavioral intentions in the quick-casual restaurant industry.

(continued)

(continued)

#	Reference	Field	Customer satisfaction focus	GSC
73	Cooil, Bruce, Timothy L. Keiningham, Lerzan Aksoy, and Michael Hsu (2007), "A Longitudinal Analysis of Customer Satisfaction and Share of Wallet: Investigating the Moderating Effect of Customer Characteristics," *Journal of Marketing*, 71 (1), 67–83.	Marketing	The authors' research provides an examination of customer satisfaction on share of wallet and determines the moderating effects of customer age, income, education, expertise, and length of relationship.	759
74	Yi, Youjae, and Suna La (2004), "What Influences the Relationship Between Customer Satisfaction and Repurchase Intention? Investigating the Effects of Adjusted Expectations and Customer Loyalty," *Psychology & Marketing*, 21 (5), 351–373.	Psychology/ Marketing	The authors examine how loyalty influences the relationship between customer satisfaction and repurchase intention, and consider the effect of time in the relationship.	758
75	Hayes, Bob E. (2008), *Measuring Customer Satisfaction and Loyalty: Survey Design, Use, and Statistical Analysis Methods*, Milwaukee, WI: ASQ Quality Press.	Psychology/ Organization	The author talks about survey design, use, and statistical analysis methods as they relate to customer satisfaction.	743
76	Choi, Thomas Y., and Karen Eboch (1998), "The TQM Paradox: Relations Among TQM Practices, Plant Performance, and Customer Satisfaction," *Journal of Operations Management*, 17 (1), 59–75.	Operations Management	The authors examine a model of TQM, in which TQM practices have a direct impact on customer satisfaction and an indirect impact mediated through plant performance.	727
77	Hu, Hsin-Hui (Sunny), Jay Kandampully, and Thanika Devi Juwaheer (2009), "Relationships and Impacts of Service Quality, Perceived Value, Customer Satisfaction, and Image: An Empirical Study," *The Service Industries Journal*, 29 (2), 111–125.	Services	The authors seek to understand the relationships that exist between service quality and perceived value and how they impact customer satisfaction, corporate image, and behavioral intentions.	725

#	Reference	Category		Description
78	Namkung, Young, and SooCheong Jang (2007), "Does Food Quality Really Matter in Restaurants? Its Impact On Customer Satisfaction and Behavioral Intentions," *Journal of Hospitality & Tourism Research*, 31 (3), 387–409.	Hospitality	712	The authors investigate how food quality is perceived in relation to customer satisfaction and behavioral intentions, and the attributes among food that are critical to improving customer satisfaction and future visits.
79	Heikkilä, Jussi (2002), "From Supply to Demand Chain Management: Efficiency and Customer Satisfaction," *Journal of Operations Management*, 20 (6), 747–767.	Operations	710	The author argues that understanding the customer's situation and need together with the right offering contributes to cooperation in the demand chain, which leads to demand chain efficiency and customer satisfaction.
80	Mägi, Anne W. (2003), "Share of Wallet in Retailing: The Effects of Customer Satisfaction, Loyalty Cards and Shopper Characteristics," *Journal of Retailing*, 79 (2), 97–106.	Retailing	709	The authors examine the effects of customer satisfaction and loyalty cards as well as consumer characteristics on customer share spent on the primary grocery store.
81	Athanassopoulos, Antreas, Spiros Gounaris, and Vlassis Stathakopoulos (2001), "Behavioural Responses to Customer Satisfaction: An Empirical Study," *European Journal of Marketing*, 35 (5/6), 687–707.	Services	703	The authors examine impact of customer satisfaction on customers' behavioral responses (decision to stay with the existing service provider, engagement in word-of-mouth, and intentions to switch providers).

(continued)

(continued)

#	Reference	Field	Customer satisfaction focus	GSC
82	Kassim, Norizan, and Nor Asiah Abdullah (2010), "The Effect of Perceived Service Quality Dimensions on Customer Satisfaction, Trust, and Loyalty in E-Commerce Settings: A Cross Cultural Analysis," *Asia Pacific Journal of Marketing and Logistics*, 22 (3), 351–371.	Marketing	The authors investigate the relationship between perceived service quality, customer satisfaction, trust, and loyalty in e-commerce settings in two cultures—Malaysian and Qatari—at the level of construct dimensions.	701
83	Han, Heesup, and Kisang Ryu (2009), "The Roles of the Physical Environment, Price Perception, and Customer Satisfaction in Determining Customer Loyalty in the Restaurant Industry," *Journal of Hospitality & Tourism Research*, 33 (4), 487–510.	Hospitality	The authors examine the relationships among the physical environment (décor and artifacts, spatial layout, and ambient conditions), price perception, customer satisfaction, and customer loyalty in the restaurant industry.	700
84	Tam, Jackie L. M. (2004), "Customer Satisfaction, Service Quality and Perceived Value: An Integrative Model," *Journal of Marketing Management*, 20 (7–8), 897–917.	Marketing	The author examines the relationships among customer satisfaction, service quality, perceived value, and post-purchase behavior.	691
85	Zhanga, Qingyu, Mark A Vonderembse, and Jeen-Su Lim (2003), "Manufacturing Flexibility: Defining and Analyzing Relationships Among Competence, Capability, and Customer Satisfaction," *Journal of Operations Management*, 21 (2), 173–191.	Operations Management	The authors describe the relationships among flexible competence (machine, labor, material handling, routing flexibilities), flexible capability (volume flexibility, mix flexibility), and customer satisfaction.	691
86	Saeidi, Sayedeh Parastoo, Saudah Sofiana, Parvaneh Saeidia, Sayyedeh Parisa Saeidi, and Seyyed Alireza Saaeidi (2015), "How Does Corporate Social Responsibility Contribute to Firm Financial Performance? The Mediating Role of Competitive Advantage, Reputation, and Customer Satisfaction," *Journal of Business Research*, 68 (2), 341–350.	Management	The authors consider sustainable competitive advantage, reputation, and customer satisfaction as three probable mediators in the relationship between corporate social responsibility (CSR) and firm performance.	686

87	Söderlund, Magnus (1998), "Customer Satisfaction and Its Consequences on Customer Behaviour Revisited: The Impact of Different Levels of Satisfaction on Word-Of-Mouth, Feedback to the Supplier and Loyalty," *International Journal of Service Industry Management*, 9 (2), 169–188.	Services	The author explores the extent to which the form of the relationship between customer satisfaction and customer behavior is different under conditions of "low" satisfaction and "high" satisfaction.	676
88	Ugboro, Isaiah O., and Kofi Obeng (2000), "Top Management Leadership, Employee Empowerment, Job Satisfaction, and Customer Satisfaction in TQM Organizations: An Empirical Study," *Journal of Quality Management*, 5 (2), 247–272.	Quality Management	The authors surveyed organizations that have adopted TQM to determine the relationship between top management leadership, employees' empowerment, job satisfaction, and customers' satisfaction.	667
89	Yang, Zhilin, and Xiang Fang (2004), "Online Service Quality Dimensions and Their Relationships with Satisfaction: A Content Analysis of Customer Reviews of Securities Brokerage Services," *International Journal of Service Industry Management*, 15 (3), 302–326.	Services	The authors extend our understanding of service quality and customer satisfaction within the setting of online securities brokerage services.	662
90	Liao, Chechen, Jain-Liang Chen, and David C. Yen (2007), "Theory of Planning Behavior (TPB) and Customer Satisfaction in the Continued Use of E-Service: An Integrated Model," *Computers in Human Behavior*, 23 (6), 2804–2822.	eCommerce	The authors show that a customer's behavioral intention toward e-service continuance is mainly determined by customer satisfaction and additionally affected by perceived usefulness and subjective norm.	660

(continued)

(continued)

#	Reference	Field	Customer satisfaction focus	GSC
91	Chi, Christina G., and Dogan Gursoy (2009), "Employee Satisfaction, Customer Satisfaction, and Financial Performance: An Empirical Examination," *International Journal of Hospitality Management*, 28 (2), 245–253.	Hospitality	The authors examine the relationship between employee satisfaction and customer satisfaction, and the impact of both on a hospitality company's financial performance.	657
92	Naser, Kamal, Ahmad Jamal, and Khalid Al-Khatib (1999), "Islamic Banking: A Study of Customer Satisfaction and Preferences in Jordan," *International Journal of Bank Marketing*, 17 (3), 135–151.	Services/Banking	The authors argue that the Islamic banking system is gaining momentum. This research attempts to assess customer awareness and satisfaction toward an Islamic bank in Jordan.	649
93	Akbar, Mohammad Muzahid, and Noorjahan Parvez (2009), "Impact of Service Quality, Trust, and Customer Satisfaction on Customers' Loyalty," *ABAC Journal*, 29 (1), 24–38.	Telecommunications	The authors investigate the effects of customers' perceived service quality, trust, and customer satisfaction and customer loyalty for a telecommunications company.	639
94	Johnson, Jeff W. (1996), "Linking Employee Perceptions of Service Climate to Customer Satisfaction," *Personnel Psychology*, 49 (4), 831–851.	Psychology/Organization	The author evaluates the effectiveness of a climate for service via relationships between service climate and customer satisfaction.	635
95	Ranaweera, Chatura, and Jaideep Prabhu (2003), "On the Relative Importance of Customer Satisfaction and Trust as Determinants of Customer Retention and Positive Word of Mouth," *Journal of Targeting, Measurement and Analysis for Marketing*, 12 (1), 82–90.	Marketing	The authors examine the combined effects of customer satisfaction and trust on customer retention and positive word-of-mouth (WOM) using data from telephone users in the UK.	627

#	Citation	Category	Description	
96	Barsky, Jonathan D., and Richard Labagh (1992), "A Strategy for Customer Satisfaction," *Cornell Hotel and Restaurant Quarterly*, 33 (5), 32–40.	Hospitality	A hotel's customer-satisfaction strategy is critical to its being competitive. The authors introduce a tool that uses guest information to support strategic decision-making.	616
97	Shemwell, Donald J., Ugur Yavas, and Zeynep Bilgin (1998), "Customer-Service Provider Relationships: An Empirical Test of a Model Of Service Quality, Satisfaction and Relationship-Oriented Outcomes," *International Journal of Service Industry Management*, 9 (2), 155–168.	Services	The authors test a model of relationships among service quality, customer satisfaction, and behavioral outcomes. Attention was paid to delineating the cognitive aspects of the service provider-consumer relationship from the affective, emotive factors.	611
98	Luo, Xueming, and Christian Homburg (2007), "Neglected Outcomes of Customer Satisfaction," *Journal of Marketing*, 71 (2), 133–149.	Marketing	The authors find that customer satisfaction boosts the efficiency of future advertising and promotion investments.	608
99	Wu, Cedric Hsi-Jui, and Rong-Da Liang (2009), "Effect of Experiential Value on Customer Satisfaction with Service Encounters in Luxury-Hotel Restaurants," *International Journal of Hospitality Management*, 28 (4), 586–593.	Hospitality	The authors show restaurant factors and interactions with employees and consumers influence consumer experiential value; only interactive relationships with service employees affect consumer satisfaction.	606
100	Johnson, Matthew D., and Anders Gustafsson (2006), *Improving Customer Satisfaction, Loyalty, and Profit: An Integrated Measurement and Management System*, Hoboken, NJ: Wiley.	Marketing	The authors address how a company can ensure that its customers enjoy a consistently satisfying experience.	606

Source: Authors' creation

Index[1]

---

[1] Note: Page numbers followed by 'n' refer to notes.

© The Author(s) 2020
C. Fornell et al., *The Reign of the Customer*, https://doi.org/10.1007/978-3-030-13562-1

Printed by Printforce, the Netherlands